# 100 SCIENCE LESSONS

# YEAR 5

Scottish Primary 6

Published by Scholastic Ltd,
Villiers House,
Clarendon Avenue,
Leamington Spa,
Warwickshire CV32 5PR

© **Scholastic Ltd 2001**
**Text © 2001 Peter Riley** (Introduction,
Unit 1), **Ian Mitchell** (Units 2–3),
**David Glover** (Unit 4),
**Louise Petheram** (Units 5–8)

1 2 3 4 5 6 7 8 9 0   1 2 3 4 5 6 7 8 9 0

**Series Consultant**
Peter Riley

**Authors**
Peter Riley (Introduction, Unit 1),
Ian Mitchell (Units 2–3),
David Glover (Unit 4),
Louise Petheram (Units 5–8)

**Editor**
Joel Lane

**Assistant Editor**
David Sandford

**Series Designers**
David Hurley
Joy Monkhouse

**Designer**
Paul Cheshire

**Cover photography**
Martyn Chillmaid

**Illustrations**
Robin Lawrie

**British Library Cataloguing-in-Publication Data**
A catalogue record for this book is available from the British
Library.

**ISBN 0-439-01806-4**

The right of Peter Riley (Introduction, Unit 1), Ian Mitchell
(Units 2–3), David Glover (Unit 4), and Louise Petheram (Units
5–8) to be identified as the Authors of this work has been
asserted by them in accordance with the Copyright, Designs
and Patents Act 1988.

Teachers should consult their own school policies and
guidelines concerning practical work and participation of
children in scientific experiments. You should only select
activities which you feel can be carried out safely and
confidently in the classroom.

**Acknowledgements**
The National Curriculum for England 2000
© The Queen's Printer and Controller of HMSO. Reproduced
under the terms of HMSO Guidance Note 8.
The National Curriculum for Wales 2000
© The Queen's Printer and Controller of HMSO. Reproduced
under the terms of HMSO Guidance Note 10.

# Contents

# Introduction

**100 Science Lessons** is a series of year-specific teachers' resource books that provide a wealth of lesson plans and photocopiable resources for delivering a whole year of science teaching, including differentiation and assessment.

The series follows the QCA *Science Scheme of Work* in the sequencing of topics. However, instead of having six or seven units, as in the QCA scheme, the book for each year contains eight units. These units are the familiar topics: 1. Ourselves, 2. Animals & plants, 3. The environment, 4. Materials, 5. Electricity, 6. Forces & motion, 7. Light & sound, 8. Earth & beyond. They appear in the same order in every book, but have sub-titles which describe the emphasis of the work in that year. For example, in this book Unit 4 is Materials: Gases, solids and liquids.

By having eight units, this resource builds on the QCA scheme to accommodate the demands of the curricula for Wales, Scotland and Northern Ireland. It also creates opportunities to visit each topic in every year: after visiting a topic in synchrony with the QCA scheme, you can make a further visit the following year for extension or consolidation of the previous year's work. A grid showing how the topics map from one book in the series to the next is given on page 208.

Each unit is divided into a number of lessons, ending with an assessment lesson. The organisation chart at the start of each unit shows the objectives and outcomes of each lesson, and gives a quick overview of the lesson content (Main activity, Group activities, Plenary). The statements of the national curricula for England, Wales, Scotland and Northern Ireland (given in the grids on pages 198–207) provide the basis for the lesson objectives used throughout the book.

## ORGANISATION (15 LESSONS)

| | OBJECTIVES | MAIN ACTIVITY | GROUP ACTIVITIES | PLENARY | OUTCOMES |
|---|---|---|---|---|---|
| LESSON 1 | ● To know that some foods are needed for activity and others for growth.<br>● To use a table to record and interpret data. | Discuss how foods are graded on the nutrients they contain. Use scales to compare the relative weights of nutrients in food samples. | Interpret a table of the nutritional values of different foods. Analyse the contents of packaged food according to given criteria. | Compare judgements on the nutrient content of foods. | ● Can recognise and name some foods for activity (carbohydrates).<br>● Can recognise and name some foods for growth (proteins).<br>● Can group foods according to their relative nutritional content.<br>● Can interpret data in a table. |
| LESSON 2 | ● To be able to plan healthy meals. | Plan healthy meals from information about food groups. Identify foods for growth and activity in pictures of prepared meals. | | Assess the healthiness of the planned meals. Consider extreme versions. | ● Can plan a healthy meal.<br>● Can display the components of a meal clearly and know their value to health.<br>● Can distinguish between a healthy meal and an unhealthy meal. |

## LESSON PLANS

Each lesson plan is divided into four parts: Introduction, Main activity, Group activities and Plenary. In many of the lessons, the introduction is supported by background information and a vocabulary list that will help in delivering the lesson and support assessment of the work. The lesson introduction sets the context for the work. The Main teaching activity features direct whole-class or group teaching, and may include instructions on how to perform a demonstration or an experiment in order to stimulate the children's interest and increase their motivation. There is then usually a choice of two activities to engage groups of children. (In those lessons where a whole-class investigation takes place, there may be a single group activity related to this, and occasionally a 'circus' of group work is suggested.) Advice on differentiation and formative assessment linked to this work is provided. Finally, there are details of a plenary session.

About 60% of the lesson plans in this book, including those for the assessment lessons, are presented in full detail. Many of these are followed by outlines for closely related lessons on the same topics or concepts, using the same background information. To avoid repetition and allow you to focus on the essentials of the lesson, these plans are presented as grids for you to develop. They contain the major features of the detailed lesson plans, allowing you to plan for progression and assessment.

## Detailed lesson plans

The lessons in this book have been designed to reflect the children's developing maturity and interest in the world around them. The investigations suggested assume increasing independence, with greater emphasis on the children deciding what to explore and how to approach the investigation, guided by their teacher. Units 2, 3 and 6, in particular, encourage a broader approach to enquiry; with Unit 6 focusing on design and improvement, for example. The content of these units may be appropriate for teachers in England looking to address QCA Unit 5/6H in Year 5.

Wider issues concerning the impact of science are also introduced, for example reflecting the environmental focus throughout the UK curricula: both environmental sustainability and local environmental studies. For example, Units 2 and 3 consider human impact in some detail, while Units 5 and 6, for example, refer to more environmentally friendly sources of power.

### Objectives

The objectives of the lessons are derived from the statements in all the UK science curriculum documents. They are stated in a way that helps to focus each lesson plan and give a unique theme to each unit. At least one objective for each lesson is derived from the statements related to content knowledge. In addition, there may be one or more objectives relating to scientific enquiry; but you may choose to replace these with others to meet your needs and the skills you wish the children to develop. The relationship of the curriculum statements to the coverage of each unit's lessons is given in the grids on pages 198–207.

Wherever relevant, the focus and content of each unit coincides with that of the matching unit in the QCA *Science Scheme of Work*. However, we have not distinguished in the lesson objectives which content is specific to any one curriculum, and have left it to your professional judgement to identify those activities that are best suited to the age and ability of your class and to the minimum requirements spelled out in your local curriculum guidance. If you wish to check whether a particular activity cross-references directly to your curriculum, please refer to the curriculum grids on pages 198–207.

### Resources and Preparation

The Resources section provides a list of everything you will need to deliver the lesson, including any of the photocopiables presented in this book. Preparation describes anything that needs to be done in advance of the lesson, such as collecting environmental data. As part of the preparation for all practical work, you should consult your school's policies concerning the use of plants and animals in the classroom, so that you can select activities for which you are confident to take responsibility. The ASE publication *Be Safe!* gives useful guidance on what things are safe to use in the classroom.

### Background

The Background section provides relevant facts and explanations of concepts to support the lesson. In some cases, the information provided may go beyond what the children need to learn at Year 5/Primary 6; but you may value this further knowledge in order to avoid reinforcing any misconceptions the children may have.

### Vocabulary

Each fully detailed lesson plan has an associated vocabulary list, containing words that should be used by the children in discussing and presenting their work, and in their writing. The words relate both to scientific enquiry and to knowledge and understanding.

It is important that children develop their science vocabulary in order to describe their findings and observations and to explain their ideas. Whenever a specialist word is used, it should be accompanied by a definition, as some children in the class may take time to understand and differentiate the meanings of words such as 'loud' and 'high pitched'.

### Introduction

The lesson introductions contain ideas to get each lesson started and to 'set the scene'. You may also wish to draw on the background information or make links with other lessons in your scheme of work.

### Main teaching activity

This section presents a direct, whole-class (or occasionally group) teaching session to follow the introduction. This will help you to deliver the content knowledge outlined in the lesson objectives to the children before they start their group work. It may include guidance on discussion, or on performing one or more demonstrations or class investigations to help the children understand the work ahead.

The relative proportions of the lesson given to the Introduction, Main teaching activity and Group activities vary. If you are reminding the children of their previous work and getting them on to their own investigations, the group work may dominate the lesson time; if you are introducing a new topic or concept, you might wish to spend all or most of the lesson engaged in whole-class teaching.

## Group activities

The Group activities are very flexible. Some may be best suited to individual work, while others may be suitable for work in pairs or larger groupings. In the detailed lesson plans, there are usually two Group activities provided for each lesson. You may wish to use one after the other; use both together, to reduce demand on resources and your attention; or, where one is a practical activity, use the other for children who complete their practical work successfully and quickly, or even as a follow-up homework task. Some of the Group activities are supported by a photocopiable sheet.

The Group activities may include some writing. These activities are also aimed at strengthening the children's science literacy, and supporting their English literacy skills. They may involve writing labels and captions, developing scientific vocabulary, writing about or recording investigations, presenting data, explaining what they have observed, or using appropriate secondary sources. The children's mathematical skills are also developed through number and data-handling work in the context of science investigations.

## Differentiation

For each of the lessons, where appropriate, there are suggestions for differentiated work for the more able and less able children in the class. Differentiated group activities are designed so that all the children who perform these tasks can make a contribution to the plenary session.

## Assessment

Each lesson includes advice on how to assess the children's success in the activities against the lesson objectives. This may include questions to ask or observations to make to help you build up a picture of the children's developing ideas and plan future lessons. A separate summative assessment lesson is provided at the end of each unit of work.

## Plenary

This is a very important part of the lesson. It is important not to let it get squeezed out by mistiming other activities in the lesson. Suggestions are given for drawing the various strands of the lesson together in this session. If an investigation has been tried, the work of different groups can be compared and evaluated. The scene may be set for another lesson, or the lesson objectives and outcomes may be reviewed and key learning points highlighted.

## Homework

On occasions, tasks may be suggested for the children to do at home. Tasks, such as collecting things to add to a class display or observing the Moon cannot easily be done in school time, while other lessons may offer opportunities for follow-up work, for example using the photocopiables provided at home, or to research a broader knowledge of the topic under discussion.

## Outcomes

These are statements related to the objectives; they describe what the children should have achieved through the lesson.

## Links to other units or lessons

The lesson may be linked to other lessons in the same unit to provide progression or reinforce the work done, or it may be linked to other units or lessons elsewhere in the book. You may like to consider these links in planning your scheme of work – for example, linking work on Water and the environment in Unit 3 with the occurrence of ice, water and water vapour as the three states of matter in Unit 4: Materials.

## Links to other curriculum areas

These are included where appropriate. They may include links to subjects closely related to science, such as technology or maths, or to content and skills in subjects such as art, history or geography.

## Lesson plan grids

These short lesson plans, in the form of a grid, offer further activity ideas to broaden the topic coverage. As the example below shows, they have the same basic structure as the detailed lesson plans. They lack the Introduction, Background and Vocabulary sections, but these are supported by the previous and related detailed lesson plans. Notes suggesting a Main activity with ideas for Group activities are provided for you to develop. Generally, there are no photocopiables linked to these lesson plans.

## LESSON 3

| Objective | ● To identify foods for activity and for growth in prepared dishes. |
|---|---|
| Resources | Pictures of well-known dishes such as vegetable curry, chilli con carne or spaghetti bolognese; access to cookery books, paper, pencils. |
| Main activity | The children work in groups to look at pictures of dishes, write down the names of the main food items, identify foods for growth and foods for activity, and record these in a table. Provide cookery books for the children to find out how to make similar dishes, if it is not clear from the pictures or their experience. |
| Differentiation | Less able children can label pictures of dishes with the names and food groups of the main items. More able children can examine dishes more critically, looking for a limited content of meat, eggs or dairy products and a higher content of cereals, fruit or vegetables. *Does the dish seem to have lots of sugar or fat in it?* They can go on to consider the sources of the ingredients. |
| Assessment | Note how quickly and easily the children can identify foods for activity (sugars and starches) and for growth (proteins) in each prepared dish. Are they confident about which foods are in each group? |
| Plenary | Assess together each group's identification of the foods in each dish and their nutritional composition. |
| Outcomes | ● Can identify foods for energy and for growth (in prepared dishes). |

## RESOURCES

### Photocopiable sheets

These are an integral part of many of the lessons and are found at the end of the relevant unit, marked with the 'photocopiable' symbol: . They may provide resources, quizzes, instructions for practical work, information or written assignments, and so on.

### Classroom equipment and space

A wide range of resources are needed for the lessons in this book. However, every attempt has been made to restrict the list to resources that will be readily available to primary schools. You may wish to borrow some items (such as a retort stand, boss and clamp, data-logger or microscopes) from the science department of your local secondary school, though these would be very useful permanent additions to your science resources.

Each lesson plan includes a resources list. When you have planned which lessons you wish to use, you could make up your own resources list for the term's or year's work. Encourage your colleagues to do the same for other years, so that you can compare lists, identify times when there may be a high demand for particular resources and make adjustments as necessary.

### ICT

Many of the lessons in this book can be enhanced by the use of ICT. As new products are entering the market all the time, few are specified in this book. However you may like to consider opportunities for ICT work under these headings:

### Information retrieval

Throughout this book, the children are encouraged to research further information from secondary sources, including CD-ROMs and the Internet. Where this is the case, it is important that the children have a focus for their enquiries and that the materials offered are at an appropriate level. By Year 5/Primary 6 children should be encouraged to carry out more complex searches, for example using the logical operators AND/OR, and to be critical of the appropriacy and accuracy of the information they obtain. It is important to guard against children simply retrieving pages of information in answer to a question without using skills in

comprehension or analysis. For example, a question such as 'What can you find out about the Solar System?' may produce a booklet of colourful pictures of the planets and text straight from a source which has demanded little intellectual activity. Prior to an information retrieval exercise, examine the CD-ROM or selected website and set questions to test comprehension and analysis so that the children must interact with the material in some way as they prepare their answers.

### Data-logging

Data-logging equipment should be introduced in Year 5/Primary 6 – if it has not been demonstrated before – to record the change of temperature, light or sound over a given length of time, providing an instant record of the changes and a graphical representation. More able children should be encouraged to use this equipment themselves with support, but with less able children the data-logger can provide a clear, visual record of an environmental change without introducing anomalies due to the children's lower level of recording and graphing skills.

### Presentations

Children should be taught to use a wide variety of methods to present their results and conclusions. As well as displays and written records that may be produced using desktop publishing software, this may include personal presentations or them beginning to use multimedia applications. Digital photographs or video recordings can be stored on your computer for use in presentations or as evidence of achievement. Visual records should be annotated to provide a complete record, not just a picture of the children's experiences.

## Assessment

The assessments in this book indicate the likely progress of children in Year 5/Primary 6. The statements relate specifically to work in this book, and are arranged in groups to reflect different levels. In this year's work, it is expected that most children will be approaching or working at NC Level 4/Scottish Level C/D, but some may not progress so well and achieve only Level 3/Scottish Level C, while others may progress further in some aspects to achieve Level 5/ Scottish Level D.

You may find it useful to determine what the children already know before embarking on each unit. If appropriate, look at the previous book in the series, find the corresponding unit and check with your colleagues what work has been covered. Talk to the children about what they know, and use the results to plan differentiated activities and provide materials as you teach the unit.

The last lesson in every unit focuses on summative assessment. This assessment samples the content of the unit, focusing on its key theme(s); its results should be used in conjunction with other assessments you have made during the teaching of the unit. The lesson comprises two assessment activities which may take the form of photocopiable sheets to work on or practical activities with suggested assessment questions for you to use while you are observing the children. Any end of unit tests are set out to reflect the English National Curriculum Key Stage 2 SAT paper for science. These activities may include a mark scheme, but this will not be related directly to curriculum levels of attainment. These tasks are intended to provide you with a guide to assessing the children's performance.

The pupil's work from the assessment lessons could be kept in their portfolios to support your teacher assessment judgments.

## SUPPORT FOR PLANNING

### Developing your scheme of work

This book is planned to support the QCA *Science Scheme of Work* and the statements of the UK national curricula. In planning your school scheme of work, you may wish to look at the units in this book or throughout the series along with those of the QCA scheme. You may also wish to relate the objectives in your planning more directly to those of the curriculum. The grids on pages 198–207 show how the statements of the national curricula for knowledge and understanding and science enquiry for England, Wales, Scotland and Northern Ireland provide the basis for the lesson objectives used in the eight units in this book. In the organisation grids, each statement is cross-referenced to one or more lessons to help with curriculum planning.

## Planning progression

The Series topic map on page 208 shows the focus of each of the units in the books in this series, to help you work out your plan of progression. By looking at the charts of curriculum coverage on pages 198–207 and the organisation chart for each unit, you can plan for progression through the year and from one year to the next, covering the whole of the work needed for Reception and Years 1–6/ Primary 1–7.

You may choose to use all or most of the lessons from the units in this book in their entirety, or make a selection to provide a 'backbone' for your own curriculum planning and supplement it with lessons you have already found successful from other sources. The pages in this book are perforated and hole-punched, so you can separate them and put them in a planning file with other favourite activities and worksheets.

## TEACHING SCIENCE IN YEAR 5/PRIMARY 6

The units in this book broaden some of the concepts that have been introduced in previous years (lower KS2/P4–5) and provide a firm base for Year 6/Primary 7 and, in England, the Key Stage 2 SAT in science. It is expected that most children will attain NC Level 4/Scottish Level C/D in Year 5/ Primary 6.

An underlying theme of this book is the application of science knowledge to our everyday world. As the children are maturing, this approach allows them to consider issues in which the consequences of using science can alter our everyday life. This should help them see that it is important to know about science (to become scientifically literate) in order to form opinions which in future can help in the sensible development of their world. This notion is only introduced here, but it should help prepare the children for work in later years on this topic.

A brief description of the unit contents follows, to show more specifically how the themes are developed:

● **Unit 1: Ourselves** focuses on 'Growing up healthy', featuring the effects of diet and exercise, the changes associated with puberty, and how harmful substances can change the body.

● **Unit 2: Animals & plants** looks at 'Life cycles', concentrating on the flowering plant. A key theme of this unit is the interdependence of life cycles, giving the content a strong environmental bias and offering material for teachers in England looking to resource QCA unit 5/ 6H in Year 5.

● **Unit 3: The environment** focuses on the importance of water for living things and how humans use and misuse water resources, including the effects of fishing and farming. The environmental surveying in this unit could support QCA units 5/6H.

● **Unit 4: Materials** builds on the children's previous knowledge of matter to look at another major feature of the environment – gases in the atmosphere – and considers how gases, liquids and solids undergo change.

● **Unit 5: Electricity** focuses on 'Making and using electricity'. This unit brings electricity and magnetism together. As the children may have studied electricity in several previous years, this unit provides an opportunity to look in a little more depth at electrical devices and revisit work on magnetism to develop a concept of electromagnetism and look at some of its applications. In considering how electricity is generated, it is suggested that the children should consider environmental impact and alternatives available.

● **Unit 6: Forces & motion** links the concept of a force with the concept of energy. This unit takes a design approach to the content, making it a useful source of ideas for teachers in England looking to resource QCA unit 5/6H.

● **Unit 7: Light & sound** focuses on 'Bending light and changing sound' and considers what happens when light and sound pass through a range of materials.

● **Unit 8: Earth & beyond** consolidates the children's knowledge of the motions of the Sun, Moon and Earth. For schools following the QCA scheme, this is the unit where this knowledge must be secured before the end of Key Stage SAT (although it may be briefly revised in Year 6 when the Solar system is considered).

# Growing up healthy

## ORGANISATION (15 LESSONS)

| | OBJECTIVES | MAIN ACTIVITY | GROUP ACTIVITIES | PLENARY | OUTCOMES |
|---|---|---|---|---|---|
| **LESSON 1** | ● To know that some foods are needed for activity and others for growth.<br>● To use a table to record and interpret data. | Discuss how foods are graded on the nutrients they contain. Use scales to compare the relative weights of nutrients in food samples. | Interpret a table of the nutritional values of different foods. Analyse the contents of packaged food according to given criteria. | Compare judgements on the nutrient content of foods. | ● Can recognise and name some foods for activity (carbohydrates).<br>● Can recognise and name some foods for growth (proteins).<br>● Can group foods according to their relative nutritional content.<br>● Can interpret data in a table. |
| **LESSON 2** | ● To be able to plan healthy meals. | Plan healthy meals from information about food groups. | | Assess the healthiness of the planned meals. Consider extreme versions. | ● Can plan a healthy meal.<br>● Can display the components of a meal clearly and know their value to health.<br>● Can distinguish between a healthy meal and an unhealthy meal. |
| **LESSON 3** | ● To identify foods for activity and for growth in prepared dishes. | Identify foods for growth and activity in pictures of prepared meals. | | Assess each group's work as a class. | ● Can identify foods for energy and growth (in prepared dishes). |
| **LESSON 4** | ● To know that food is digested by a number of organs, together called the digestive system. | Identify parts of the digestive system and place them on a body outline. | Identify parts of the digestive system and place them within a body outline. Match captions to parts of a diagram of the digestive system. Use a stethoscope to listen to chewing, swallowing and stomach digestion. | Trace the path of a sandwich through the digestive system. | ● Can recognise the parts of the digestive system and have some understanding of what each part does. |
| **LESSON 5** | ● To know the basic structure of the respiratory system.<br>● To know that exercise increases the breathing rate.<br>● To make comparisons and identify simple patterns.<br>● To make predictions. | Measure breathing rates at rest and after light exercise. | Investigate how activity affects breathing rate. Answer questions on the breathing mechanism. | Groups report on their results. Compare findings and look for overall conclusions. | ● Can describe how the body draws in and expels air.<br>● Can measure the breathing rate at rest and after exercise.<br>● Can plan an investigation to answer a given question.<br>● Can make predictions.<br>● Can recognise patterns in the results, and suggest explanations. |
| **LESSON 6** | ● To know about the structure and function of the heart and the circulatory system. | Use a balloon pump and diagrams to consider the form and function of the heart. | Use diagrams to look at the mechanism of the heart. Use a diagram to consider the circulation of the blood. | Describe the path of the blood around the body. | ● Can describe the action of the heart.<br>● Can describe the path of the blood through the circulatory system. |
| **LESSON 7** | ● To know that the pulse is produced by the heartbeat.<br>● To plan and carry out an investigation: make a prediction, make observations and measurements, check them by repeating, compare results with the prediction and draw conclusions.<br>● To use tables and bar graphs to communicate data (perhaps using ICT). | Measure pulse rates at rest and after varying amounts of exercise. Explain the results. | | Collate results to identify and explain the overall pattern. | ● Can find the pulse and measure its rate.<br>● Can plan and carry out an investigation: make a prediction, carry out observations and measurements, check by repeating them, record results in an appropriate and systematic manner, compare results with prediction and draw conclusions.<br>● Can use tables and bar graphs to communicate data (perhaps using ICT). |

## ORGANISATION (15 LESSONS)

| | OBJECTIVES | MAIN ACTIVITY | GROUP ACTIVITIES | PLENARY | OUTCOMES |
|---|---|---|---|---|---|
| **LESSON 8** | ● To plan and carry out an investigation. ● To use tables and bar graphs to communicate data (perhaps using ICT). | Use pulse rates to investigate 'fitness'. | | Discuss the effects of lifestyle on fitness. | ● Can plan and carry out an investigation. ● Can use tables and bar graphs to communicate data (perhaps using ICT). |
| **LESSON 9** | ● To be aware that human bodies vary and that this is natural. ● To know that humans have a period of rapid growth called the 'growth spurt'. ● To know that the body parts change in proportion from birth to adulthood. | Investigate the distribution of heights in the class. | Plot and interpret graphs showing changes in height with time. Consider the changes in body proportions with time. | Use collected data to support the idea of natural variation. Introduce the idea of the 'growth spurt'. | ● Is aware that human bodies vary and that this is natural. ● Can identify the time of the 'growth spurt'. ● Can describe how some parts of the body change in proportion from birth to adulthood. |
| **LESSON 10** | ● To know about the changes that take place in the body at puberty. | Discuss the changes in boys and girls at puberty. | Match captions to diagrams showing the changes at puberty. Answer questions on the changes at puberty. | The children try to define words related to puberty and reproduction. Introduce a 'question box' for problems. | ● Recognise the changes that take place at puberty. ● Understand that these changes take place at different times in different people. ● Can name some parts of the reproductive system. |
| **LESSON 11** | ● To know that some drugs can help the body recover from illness. ● To know that people can persuade others to take harmful drugs. | Discuss how medicines and drugs can make people who are ill feel better and aid recovery. | Categorise medicines and drugs according to the parts of the body they help. Use role-play to explore the effects of peer pressure. | Assess the children's posters. Repeat the role-play once with an imbalance of numbers. | ● Recognise some medicines and helpful drugs and know how they assist recovery from illness. ● Recognise how peer pressure can introduce young people to harmful drugs. |
| **LESSON 12** | ● To know how tobacco affects the body. | Use a 'smoking machine' to demonstrate how smoking affects the lungs. | | Discuss why people start smoking and why they should stop. | ● Can explain why smoking is harmful. |
| **LESSON 13** | ● To know how alcohol affects the body. | Use secondary sources to find out about the dangers of alcohol and the treatment of alcoholism. | | Display posters. Some children report back on how alcoholic drinks are made. | ● Can describe the effects of alcohol on the body. ● Can explain why drinking alcohol can be harmful. |
| **LESSON 14** | ● To know how solvents affect the body. ● To know how illegal drugs affect the body. | Use secondary sources (or a visit from a health professional) to find out about the dangers of solvent abuse and illegal drugs. | | Display posters. Repeat the role-play as in Lesson 12. | ● Can explain how solvents affect the body. ● Can explain the dangers of using illegal drugs. |

| | OBJECTIVES | | ACTIVITY 1 | ACTIVITY 2 |
|---|---|---|---|---|
| **ASSESSMENT 15** | ● To assess the children's knowledge of the foods needed for growth and activity. ● To assess the children's knowledge of the position and action of the heart. ● To assess the children's ability to make a prediction and plan a fair test. | | Answer questions on nutrition, the heart and the pulse rate. | Plan an investigation into pulse rates. Predict findings. |

# LESSON 1

## OBJECTIVES

- To know that some foods are needed for activity and others for growth.
- To use a table to record and interpret data.

### RESOURCES

**Main teaching activity:** Some cheese (such as Edam) that cuts without crumbling, rice, weighing scales (capable of weighing out 100g), an A3-sized copy of photocopiable page 29, a flip chart and marker pen.
**Group activities: 1.** Photocopiable page 29. **2.** Empty packets of cereals, soups, crisps and biscuits, showing tables of nutritional values; pens or pencils. (For less able children: pictures of the foods featured on page 29, star stickers in three different colours.)

### PREPARATION

Display an enlarged copy of page 29 where the children can easily see it. You may prefer to sit them closer to you around the flip chart at the start of the lesson.

### BACKGROUND

Our bodies require a range of substances from the food we eat to grow and remain healthy. These food substances are called nutrients. They are divided into five groups: carbohydrates (starches and sugars), lipids (fats and oils), proteins, vitamins and minerals. Carbohydrates provide energy that is ready for use; fats provide energy that is stored and used more slowly; proteins provide materials for growth; vitamins and minerals have a wide range of uses that keep the body healthy. The body also needs water to replace water lost, and needs indigestible carbohydrates in the form of fibre to help the muscles of the gut push the food along.

No one food provides all the requirements for the body (milk for an infant is an exception; although cow's milk provides a wide range of nutrients, it does not provide fibre), so we have to eat a combination of different foods. If the combination of foods provides all the requirements, the diet is healthy and balanced. If one or more nutrients are missing, or too much of some nutrients (such as fats) are eaten, the diet is not balanced and ill-health can result.

To help provide people with information to choose a healthy diet, all packaged foods are analysed and the amounts of different nutrients in a 100g sample displayed on the label. In this lesson, the information is simplified to a star rating so the children can easily see that there are different quantities of nutrients in different foods. This may help them to select healthy snacks, or to choose foods for a meal when there is no parental supervision.

### INTRODUCTION

Start by saying that the biggest changes to our bodies occur in the school years of life (about 10–16), when we are growing and changing into adults. Food affects the way we grow, so in these three lessons we are going to look at food in some detail. Ask the class: *What are your favourite foods? What foods would you eat all the time if you could (or take to a desert island with you)?* Develop the idea that it may not be a good thing just to live on a few foods (such as a diet of chips). Discuss why not (see Background). The children should realise that they need a variety of foods for good health. Build on this by explaining that foods can be divided into foods for growth and foods for energy. Foods for energy can be split into two groups: fats and oils, and sugars and starches (you may introduce the term 'carbohydrate' if you wish, for foods needed for energy, and 'protein' for foods needed for growth).

### MAIN TEACHING ACTIVITY

Tell the children that the amounts of nutrients in foods can be worked out; and that to display this simply in the lesson, a star rating has been used. Show them the enlarged copy of page 29. The star rating is based on the contents of 100g of the food. One star represents up to 10g of the substance present, two stars represents 11–20g, three stars 21–30g, four stars 31–40g, and five stars above 41g (write this on the board so it can be used in Group activity 2).

Ask some of the children to help you in the following weighing activities. Weigh 100g of cheese and cut it into two pieces, one slightly larger than the other. Say that although the food substances are mixed throughout the cheese, if you could separate the fat and protein they would form two pieces as shown. In this case, both parts are over 41g, so the cheese has a five-star rating for both fat and protein. Weigh out 100g of rice; remove a small pinch (about 1g) to represent fat and a larger pinch (about 6g) to represent protein. The remaining rice represents starch – so the rice has a one-star rating for fat and for protein, but a five-star rating for starch.

**Vocabulary**

fats, oils, sugar starch, translucent, protein, carbohydrate, nutrient

## GROUP ACTIVITIES

**1.** Give each child a copy of page 29 and let them work through it. The answers are: 1. jam, spaghetti, rice; 2. butter, peanuts, cheese; 3. cheese, peanuts, chicken, lentils; 4. milk. 5. A = fish; B = butter, peanuts; C = jam, potato, rice, lentils. (Peanuts and lentils could also be included in A.)
**2.** Refer the children to the star rating system you have written on the board. Ask them to use this to give star ratings to packaged foods by reading their ingredients lists, and then to record their findings in a table.

## DIFFERENTIATION

**1.** Give less able children a collection of pictures of food that match to page 29 and some star stickers in three colours. Ask them to use one colour for each food group, and to stick the correct number of stars on each picture. More able children who finish page 29 early and correctly, showing at the end of question 5 that in their judgement some foods could be allocated to more than one group, could be asked to arrange all the foods in the table into groups and justify their decisions.
**2.** Less able children could examine a few product labels to find those which have a five-star rating and a one-star rating. Let more able children use secondary sources to find out how a packaged food is produced.

## ASSESSMENT

Can the children generalise about the foods needed for growth and activity? Ask them, for example: *What nutrients do you think beef, cod and carrot contain?*

## PLENARY

In summing up, draw the children's attention to the judgements that are made when allocating a food to a group. Refer to Group activity 1 to support this. You may like to ask them to think about what foods they would recommend to someone who needed more food for activity (such as an athlete training). Check the children's star ratings for packaged foods with the class.

## OUTCOMES

- Can recognise and name some foods for activity (carbohydrates).
- Can recognise and name some foods for growth (proteins).
- Can group foods according to their relative nutritional content.
- Can interpret data in a table.

## LESSON 2

| | |
|---|---|
| **Objective** | • To be able to plan healthy meals. |
| **Resources** | A large selection of catalogues and magazines containing pictures of food; paper plates or sheets of paper to which pictures can be stuck, plain paper, coloured pencils or crayons, scissors, adhesive. |
| **Main activity** | Food can be divided into five groups: 1. meat and eggs, 2. dairy products, 3. cereals, 4. fruit and vegetables, 5. sweets and cakes. Many health authorities recommend that each day, we eat one 'serving' (or 'helping') of each of groups 1 and 2, and three 'servings' of each of groups 3 and 4. Group 5 should only be an occasional treat. With this information, let groups plan and display one or more meals. They should draw and label their own pictures of foods, or cut out pictures and stick them onto paper plates or plate outlines. |
| **Differentiation** | Less able children could use pictures and paste them on to sheets of paper or paper plates. More able children could cross-reference these food groups to those considered in Lesson 1. |
| **Assessment** | Examine the meals planned and displayed by the children. Do they follow the recommendations given? |
| **Plenary** | Each group should display their work and have it assessed for healthiness by other groups. Consider possible meals for 'healthy' and 'unhealthy' weeks. |
| **Outcomes** | • Can plan a healthy meal.<br>• Can display the components of a meal clearly and know their value to health.<br>• Can distinguish between a healthy meal and an unhealthy meal. |

# LESSON 3

| Objective | • To identify foods for activity and for growth in prepared dishes. |
|---|---|
| Resources | Pictures of well-known dishes such as vegetable curry, chilli con carne or spaghetti bolognese; access to cookery books, paper, pencils. |
| Main activity | The children work in groups to look at pictures of dishes, write down the names of the main food items, identify foods for growth and foods for activity, and record these in a table. Provide cookery books for the children to find out how to make similar dishes, if it is not clear from the pictures or their experience. |
| Differentiation | Less able children can label pictures of dishes with the names and food groups of the main items. More able children can examine dishes more critically, looking for a limited content of meat, eggs or dairy products and a higher content of cereals, fruit or vegetables. *Does the dish seem to have lots of sugar or fat in it?* They can go on to consider the sources of the ingredients. |
| Assessment | Note how quickly and easily the children can identify foods for activity (sugars and starches) and for growth (proteins) in each prepared dish. Are they confident about which foods are in each group? |
| Plenary | Assess together each group's identification of the foods in each dish and their nutritional composition. |
| Outcome | • Can identify foods for energy and for growth (in prepared dishes). |

# LESSON 4

## OBJECTIVE
• To know that food is digested by a number of organs, together called the digestive system.

## RESOURCES

**Main teaching activity:** A large piece of paper (such as plain wallpaper) on which to draw the outline of a child; a thick cord or rope about 5–6m long, adhesive tape, a piece of carpet or PE mat (if you do not have a carpeted area in the classroom), cardboard for shapes, large labels on cards ('mouth', 'gullet', 'stomach', 'small intestine', 'large intestine', 'rectum', 'liver', 'pancreas'), Blu-tack, photocopiable page 30. (Alternatively, a tunic or tabard with major body organs attached by Velcro could be purchased from an educational supplier.)
**Group activities: 1.** Photocopiable pages 31 and 32, coloured pencils, scissors, adhesive.
**2.** Pencils, small pieces of food (such as squares of bread), a stethoscope. Make sure that the pieces of food are prepared hygienically. If bread is used, check that none of the children are coeliacs. If other foods are used, be aware of possible food allergies.

## PREPARATION

Make two sets of large cardboard shapes of the mouth, gullet, stomach, liver, pancreas and large intestine (including the rectum), using the illustration overleaf as a guide. Do not make shapes for the small intestine: the coiled rope will give a better effect. Make large labels for the various parts. Make a cardboard sandwich shape for the Plenary. Rehearse how you will place the organs and labels on the sheet during the lesson.

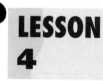

*Vocabulary*

gullet (or oesophagus), stomach, liver, pancreas, small intestine, large intestine (or colon), rectum anus, enzyme, stethoscope

## BACKGROUND

The body can only take in nutrients that are dissolved in water, so that they can be carried round the body in the blood (which itself is mostly water) and supplied to the parts where they are needed. In many foods, the nutrients are insoluble in water and so must be broken down into soluble forms by the process of digestion. The 'digestive system' is also called the alimentary canal or gut. Digestion is a two-stage process. In the first stage, the food is physically broken down by the action of the teeth; in the second stage, it is chemically broken down by the action of enzymes. You may like to invite the children to examine their teeth in the introduction to this lesson, consolidating their work in Year 3/Primary 4.

On photocopiable page 30, the idea of dissolving the nutrients is greatly simplified. The following is for your information, but may be useful if the children are researching from secondary sources and come across more detailed descriptions than they need at this level. Digestive chemicals called enzymes are produced by various parts of the digestive system. Each enzyme breaks down a specific part of the food. For example, the salivary glands secrete an enzyme which breaks down starch (which is insoluble) to sugar (which is soluble). The stomach produces an enzyme which begins the digestion of protein, and the pancreas produces three

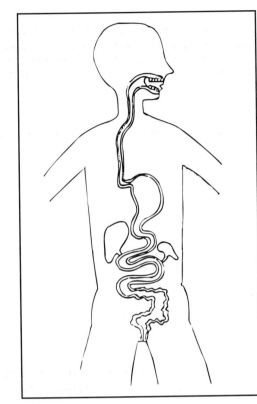

enzymes – one each for the digestion of protein, fat and carbohydrate. The liver produces bile, which makes fat droplets in food very small so that the enzyme can work on them more effectively (smaller fat droplets offer a larger total surface area). When the nutrients are soluble, they are absorbed through the wall of the small intestine into the blood.

Food does not move on its own through the digestive system: it is pushed by muscles in the walls of the gullet, stomach and intestine. Fibre does not dissolve, but forms a solid mass on which the gut muscles can push. The digestive system of an adult is a tube about 7m long, through which a meal passes in about 18 hours.

The answers to page 30 are: 1. The sight and smell of the cooking burger; 2. In the salivary glands; 3. Incisors bit into it, premolars and molars chewed it up; 4. The gullet; 5. It was churned up; 6. They helped the food dissolve; 7. In the small intestine; 8. It went into the blood and around the body; 9. Undigested food.

## INTRODUCTION

Start by saying that we have studied the healthiness of the food we eat – and now we are going to find out where it goes when it enters our bodies. As the food passes through the body, it is digested. This means that it is made into substances which the body can use for energy, growth and keeping healthy.

## MAIN TEACHING ACTIVITY

Divide the class into two and set one half to work individually on copies of page 30. Take the other half of the class, lay down a piece of carpet, place a large piece of paper on top of it and ask a girl to lie on the paper while two of her friends draw around her outline. Arrange the cord on the outline to represent the digestive tract (see diagram) and stick each end to the paper with adhesive tape. Say that the cord represents a tube – 7m long in adults – in which the food is digested. Present each cardboard organ and ask the children where it goes. Steer their responses towards the correct one, then let a child stick the organ in place on the cord. Repeat until all the organs are in place. Now say that although we cannot see what is happening to food inside our body, we can listen to what is happening with a stethoscope. Show the children how to listen to chewing (place the stethoscope next to the jaw), swallowing (place it on the throat) and churning (place it on the stomach). Say that the children will be able to try this for themselves later in the lesson.

Now let the second half of the class construct a digestive system while the first half work on page 30. When constructing the second digestive system, select a boy to be drawn around. (You can use these two body outlines when discussing puberty in Lesson 10, but you do not need to mention that now.)

## GROUP ACTIVITIES

1. Give the children a copy each of pages 31 and 32 and let them complete it.
2. Working in pairs, with adult help, taking turns to eat a little food and listen to their partner's jaw, throat and stomach with a stethoscope.

## DIFFERENTIATION

**Main teaching activity:** Less able children can work with more able children in groups to answer the questions on page 30. More able children could use secondary sources to find out how milk teeth are replaced by adult teeth.

**Group activities: 1.** Less able children could be presented with the names of the organs jumbled up and asked to put them into the correct spellings. More able children could look at pictures or a model torso and see how the digestive system fits among the other major organs of the body. They could use secondary sources to find out how food moves along the digestive system. **2.** Less able children could place the 'action boxes' with help from a more able partner or an adult.

## ASSESSMENT

During the group work, note those children who can position the organs correctly and label the picture accurately. Can they tell you the correct sequence of events in the passage of food through the digestive system?

## PLENARY

Put a cardboard sandwich shape on the mouth of an outline figure and ask the class what will happen to it there. Move the sandwich through the different parts of the digestive system, asking the class what happens to it at each place.

## OUTCOME

● Can recognise the parts of the digestive system and have some understanding of what each part does.

## LINKS

Unit 2, Lesson 10: life cycle of a butterfly.

# LESSON 5

## OBJECTIVES

● To know the basic structure of the respiratory system.
● To know that exercise increases the breathing rate.
● To make comparisons and identify simple patterns.
● To make predictions.

pen barrel
clay
balloon
plastic bottle
adhesive tape
balloon skin

**Vocabulary**

nostril, nasal cavity,
voice box (larynx),
windpipe (trachea)
lung, rib,
diaphragm, inhale
exhale, oxygen,
carbon dioxide

## RESOURCES

**Main teaching activity:** A 2-litre clear plastic bottle, the barrel of a ballpoint pen, a small balloon, a larger balloon, Plasticine, adhesive tape, modelling clay, string, scissors, a stopclock, paper, pencils.
**Group activities: 1.** Stopclocks, paper, pencils. **2.** Photocopiable page 33, pencils.

## PREPARATION

Cut the bottom off the plastic bottle. This represents the chest. Attach the small balloon to one end of the pen barrel with adhesive tape. This represents the windpipe and a lung. Secure the pen barrel in the neck of the bottle with modelling clay. Cut open the large balloon and stretch it over the bottom of the bottle. Fasten it in place with adhesive tape. This piece of balloon represents the diaphragm. Nip the balloon skin (diaphragm) between the finger and thumb, then push it in and pull it out gently so that the small balloon (lung) inflates and deflates.

## BACKGROUND

The respiratory system consists of the windpipe, lungs, chest wall and diaphragm. This system draws air into the body, extracts some oxygen from it, releases carbon dioxide into it and then releases it to the outside – a process commonly known as breathing. The actual movement of air into and out of the lungs is technically called 'ventilation'. At a chemical level, the process of respiration (which is described in the next paragraph) occurs in all living cells, not just in the respiratory system.

All life processes, including those that make our bodies grow and change, require energy. This enters the body in a chemical form, stored within food. Starch is an example of a nutrient that has a high energy content. In digestion, it is broken down into a simple, soluble chemical called glucose, which is a type of sugar. Glucose is the main energy source for the body's activities. In order for the energy to be released from the glucose, oxygen has to be taken into the body and combined with glucose in a chemical reaction called respiration, which causes energy to be released. This reaction produces carbon dioxide, a poison that must be removed from the body.

A common misconception is that oxygen alone is drawn into the lungs, and that carbon dioxide alone is released. In reality, the respiratory system draws in air (which is about 20% oxygen) and removes about 4% of the oxygen from it. The amount of carbon dioxide in inhaled air is about 0.04%; in exhaled air, it is 4%. Most of the air (78%) is nitrogen. While the children do not need to know about these values, they should understand that the exchange of gases affects only a small proportion of the air we breathe.

In exercise, the muscles use more oxygen and more carbon dioxide is produced. This stimulates the brain to make the muscles in the chest and diaphragm work faster, so increasing the frequency and depth of breathing. In the circulatory system, the heart is stimulated to pump more quickly. These changes increase the amount of oxygen entering the blood and the amount of carbon dioxide leaving the body.

The movement of air in and out of the lungs is actually due to changes in air pressure; the children do not need to know this, but they may understand the movement of air as being due to the lungs being squashed or having extra space. If you wish to talk about air pressure, the following information may be useful. Air is a mixture of gases that forms a layer 100km thick around the Earth. Air pushes on everything. The push of the air over an area is called 'air pressure'. Air moves from a region of high pressure to one of lower pressure. When we breathe in, the chest wall rises and the diaphragm drops. This increases the volume of the lungs, and the air pressure inside them becomes lower than the air pressure outside the body. This difference in pressure forces air into the lungs. When we breathe out, the chest wall drops, the diaphragm rises and the volume of the lungs decreases. This makes the air pressure in the lungs greater than the air pressure outside, and so the air is pushed out of the lungs.

## INTRODUCTION

Remind the children that food provides the body with energy. Explain that the body also needs oxygen from the air to release energy from food. When energy is released using oxygen, carbon dioxide is produced. The body contains a group of organs called the respiratory system which take in oxygen from the air and release carbon dioxide into it.

Show the children your bottle model of the chest. Use it to explain how we work. When the diaphragm is pushed in (the larger balloon is pushed up and in), the air in the chest (the bottle) is squashed and the air in our lungs (the small balloon) is pushed out. When the diaphragm is pulled down, there is more space for the air in the chest and air is pulled into the lungs.

Ask the children to hold their rib cage and breathe in and out, looking for signs of change in the rib cage. They should feel the ribs go upwards and outwards when breathing in, and downwards and inwards when breathing out. Ask them to put a hand on their body just below their ribs and breathe in and out. They should feel the body pushing outwards when breathing out, due to the diaphragm pushing down, and feel the body drawn inwards when the diaphragm relaxes and the muscles in the lower body push the body contents back up (see illustration).

## MAIN TEACHING ACTIVITY

Once the children understand how the body takes in and releases air, ask them: *How could we measure how often we breathe?* The children should suggest that the number of breaths in a certain time could be measured. There may be some discussion about how long the time should be; help them to decide on a minute. Let the children sit quietly for a minute and count their breaths. You may wish them to work in pairs. Tell them to relax and breathe naturally, and not force their breathing to reach a high score or hold their breath to reach a low one. After they have counted their breaths for a minute, put their results on the board. Note the variation, and state that such variation is natural.

Ask the children how they think their breathing rate would change if they walked about for two minutes. Write down their predictions on the board and write a simple plan for the investigation together. Let the children walk about for two minutes and then record their breaths for a minute as before. Collect their results and discuss what they have found. Remind the children about the structure and action of the respiratory system, and the way they planned the investigation.

## GROUP ACTIVITIES

**1.** Ask the children to develop the class plan into an investigation of how activity affects breathing rate. They should investigate activities such as resting (lying down), walking and running. The time for breathing should be measured with a stopclock. Remind them of the need to keep the tests fair. They should predict the results before carrying out the tests they have planned. Several children in each group should take part, to reduce the effect of individual variations. They should look for patterns in their results.
**2.** Give the children a copy each of page 33 and let them work through it. The answers are:
1. a rib; 2. upwards and outwards; 3. downwards and inwards; 4. diaphragm; 5. downwards;
6. upwards; 7. nostril, nasal cavity, voice box, windpipe, bronchus, lung.

## DIFFERENTIATION

**1.** Less able children may need guiding through the planning stage and help with counting the number of breaths in a certain time. More able children can plan their investigation and carry it out after it has been checked. They may like to investigate how the breathing rate changes with time after stopping exercise. This will involve counting the breaths for a one-minute period several times.
**2.** Less able children could examine the bottle model when they reach question 4 on the sheet, relate the model to the diagram on the sheet and see how they are different. More able children could follow the completion of the sheet by writing an account of 'What happens when I breathe'.

## ASSESSMENT

**1.** Look for logical structure in the investigation plans, and for reasons for children's predictions. For example: 'The breathing rate will increase more for faster exercise, because more energy is needed for the movement.' Look for the use of 'per minute' in the results, not just numbers without units. Look for patterns being described in results obtained from different people. Look for a mention of 'variation' to explain why everyone does not have the same breathing rate.
**2.** At an appropriate time in the lesson, ask each child to describe the movements made as they breathe; look for confident use of the correct vocabulary in a description.

## PLENARY

Ask each group to report on the results of their investigation. Look for similarities and differences in the results from different groups. Ask the class what they can conclude from all the results they have seen.

## OUTCOMES

- Can describe how the body draws in and expels air.
- Can measure the breathing rate at rest and after exercise.
- Can plan an investigation to answer a given question.
- Can make predictions.
- Can recognise patterns in the results, and suggest explanations.

## LINKS

PSHE: keeping healthy.

## LESSON 6

### OBJECTIVE

- To know about the structure and function of the heart and the circulatory system.

### RESOURCES

**Main teaching activity:** Three 2-litre bottles of water (coloured red for dramatic effect if you wish), lumps of Plasticine, wallpaper, a marker pen, a poster showing the position and structure of the heart, a balloon and balloon pump, an empty plastic bottle, a piece of paper.
**Group activities: 1.** Photocopiable page 34, pencils, scissors, adhesive, a CD-ROM showing heart action (if available). **2.** Photocopiable page 35, pencils, a CD-ROM showing blood circulation (if available).

**Vocabulary**

heart, lungs, blood vessel, valve, artery, pulse, vein, oxygen

### BACKGROUND

The children will have studied the skeleton and muscles in Year 4/Primary 5, and may have studied exercise. They may have been introduced to the pulse and its dependence on the heart. Children often have difficulty with the structure of the heart because of the way it is represented in books: the convention is to show the heart as it would appear in a person facing you, so that the left side of the heart appears on your right. The children should be made aware of this straight away. The structure and function of the heart are explained below.

### INTRODUCTION

Remind the children that nutrients are taken into the blood from the small intestine and that oxygen enters the body from the lungs, which have a rich blood supply. Nutrients and oxygen are transported around the body so that they can release energy for activity and for growth and change in the body. There are six litres of blood in the body (show the class the three bottles of water), and it does not move on its own. It is moved by a pump, the heart, through a set of pipes called blood vessels. The pumping action of the heart can be felt as a regular throbbing or pulse in some blood vessels (called arteries). Let the children find their pulses; then say that the pulse will be investigated in the next lesson.

### MAIN TEACHING ACTIVITY

Ask a child to lie on a piece of wallpaper while one or two friends draw around them. Put the outline drawing on the wall. Ask the first child to clench his or her fist, and ask another friend to mould a piece of Plasticine about the same size as the fist. Say: *Your heart is about the same size*

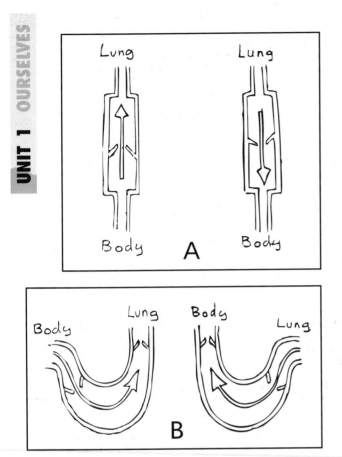

as your clenched fist. Give the first child the Plasticine 'heart'; ask him or her to hold it in the correct place within the body outline, then mark the spot with a cross or draw around the heart. Ask other class members if they can place it more accurately. Finally, compare their efforts with a poster showing the position of the heart and ask them to assess their accuracy.

Show the class a balloon pump and demonstrate how it works. Point out that the air does not leave the balloon when the pump is pulled back, because a valve in the pump stops the air from escaping. Demonstrate how a valve stops the flow of air by holding a piece of paper close to the open neck of an empty plastic bottle: when you press in the sides of the bottle, the paper is blown outwards; when you let the bottle expand again, the paper settles over the open neck and stops air flowing in.

Say that in the heart there are two pumps, each with two valves. One pumps blood from all parts of the body to the lungs, and the other pumps it back from the lungs to the rest of the body. Copy diagram A (see diagram) onto the board. *Do you think your heart might look like this: two balloon pumps?* Draw diagram B on the board to show how the pumps are more 'bent round' in reality, then show the children a picture of a real heart with the two pumps joined together. Explain that the muscles in the walls of the heart squeeze the blood, and the valves open and close to make the blood move in one direction only.

If appropriate, say that blood leaving the heart is pushed very strongly into tubes called arteries that have thick, stretchy walls. Blood returning to the heart from the lungs or the rest of the body is pushed less strongly, and travels in thin-walled tubes called veins. Ask the children to look at the veins in their wrists or on the underside of their lower arm.

## GROUP ACTIVITIES

**1.** If you have a CD-ROM that shows the heart beating, let the children watch it before they work individually to complete photocopiable page 34.
**2.** If you have a CD-ROM that shows how blood flows around the body, let the children watch it before they work individually to complete photocopiable page 35. The answers are: 1. Arrows along A to the lungs; 2. Arrows along B to the heart; 3. Arrows along D to the body; 4. Arrows along C to the heart; 5. Could include brain, muscles, gut, kidneys, liver; 6. A artery, B vein, C vein, D artery.

## DIFFERENTIATION

**1.** Less able children may need more help in recognising the arrangement of the two pumps in the heart, and may need to be shown again how the two pumps are 'bent'. More able children could use secondary sources to label the blood vessels connected to the heart.
**2.** Less able children could try just questions 1–4. More able children could write an account of what they think it would be like to travel round the body in the blood. They could use secondary sources to check their ideas.

## ASSESSMENT

At an appropriate time in the lesson, ask each child to explain how the heart moves blood around the body. In the Plenary session, ask the class to describe the path taken by the blood in the body.

## PLENARY

Enlarge the diagram on page 35. First ask the least able children to describe the path of the blood around the body. Then let more able children identify the arteries and veins and read parts of their accounts.

## OUTCOMES

● Can describe the action of the heart.
● Can describe the path of the blood through the circulatory system.

# LESSON 7

| | |
|---|---|
| **Objectives** | ● To know that the pulse is produced by the heartbeat.<br>● To plan and carry out an investigation: make a prediction, make observations and measurements, check them by repeating, compare results with the prediction and draw conclusions.<br>● To use tables and bar graphs to communicate data (perhaps using ICT). |
| **Resources** | Stopclocks, paper, pencils, a computer with data-handling software (optional). |
| **Main activity** | Show the children how to take their pulse at the wrist, throat or temple. They should count the beats for a minute. Ask them to predict how the pulse rate may vary with exercise, and then to plan an investigation. They should take the pulse when lying down, sitting, standing, after walking and after running, taking each reading several times and recording the results in a table they have prepared themselves. They should produce a bar graph of their results (perhaps using a computer) and compare their prediction with their data. From their data they should see that the pulse rate is least when lying down and greatest when exercising vigorously. Remind them about the blood carrying food and oxygen which the muscles use to release energy, and ask them how this fact could be used to explain their results. They should state that the heart beats faster to provide more food and oxygen for energy as the muscles become more active. They should also note that there is variation in pulse rate between children. |
| **Differentiation** | Less able children could take counts for 15 seconds and (with help) multiply by 4, or double and double again, to find the number of beats per minute. They could take one measurement for each activity. More able children could try to explain the different pulse rates under different conditions (excitement, muscles used to hold body up, blood moving horizontally when lying down, and so on). |
| **Assessment** | Note whether the children can find a pulse and measure the pulse rate. Examine their investigation plan for logical sequence and a level of detail appropriate to ability. Look for tables of results. Examine the graphs for accuracy. |
| **Plenary** | Evaluate the children's investigation plans. Collate the group data and try plotting a class graph for each physical activity. Ask the class to make a statement about heart activity based on these results. Treat the interpretation of the results with care and sensitivity. |
| **Outcomes** | ● Can find the pulse and measure its rate.<br>● Can plan and carry out an investigation: make a prediction, carry out observations and measurements, check by repeating them, record results in an appropriate and systematic manner, compare results with the prediction and draw conclusions.<br>● Can use tables and bar graphs to communicate data (perhaps using ICT). |

# LESSON 8

| | |
|---|---|
| **Objectives** | ● To plan and carry out an investigation.<br>● To use tables and bar graphs to communicate data (perhaps using ICT). |
| **Resources** | Stopclocks, paper, pencils, a computer and data-handling software (optional). |
| **Main activity** | In a fit person with a healthy heart, the heart returns quickly to a 'resting' rate after activity. Challenge the children to use this fact to plan an investigation to check how fit they are. They may need some guidance (including an explanation of what 'fit' means in this context). The essential features of the investigation are taking the pulse when resting, immediately after a short period of exercise and at short (30-second or one-minute) intervals after the exercise has ceased until the 'resting' pulse rate returns. |
| **Differentiation** | Less able children could take the pulse before exercise, immediately after and one or two minutes later. More able children could repeat the whole investigation and compare the results. |
| **Assessment** | Look for clear recording in tables and accurately constructed graphs. |
| **Plenary** | Review the results and say that the heart becomes more healthy if a person takes regular exercise. Ask the children to speculate on how people's hearts might be affected if they take little or no exercise and spend all their free time watching television or playing on computers. They might like to review their own lifestyle. This discussion needs to be handled with care and sensitivity. |
| **Outcomes** | ● Can plan and carry out an investigation.<br>● Can use tables and bar graphs to communicate data, perhaps using ICT. |

# LESSON 9

## OBJECTIVES
- To be aware that human bodies vary and that this is natural.
- To know that humans have a period of rapid growth called the 'growth spurt'.
- To know that the body parts change in proportion from birth to adulthood.

## RESOURCES

**Main teaching activity:** Metre and half-metre rulers, Plasticine, paper, pencils, graph paper.
**Group activities: 1 and 2.** Photocopiable page 36, paper, pencils, graph paper.

*Vocabulary*

height, growth, average, proportions

## BACKGROUND

You may wish to approach the sensitive topic of puberty through PSHE. This unit approaches growth and development from the scientific perspective, looking at the mechanisms of these changes and introducing the structure of the reproductive organs (it is assumed this will be dealt with in more detail in Year 6/Primary 7). This lesson starts by linking the concept of change to the human life cycle. You may like to integrate the work on life cycles in Unit 2 (see page 41) also.

There are a large number of facts in this topic and the content will generate a great deal of interest! It is important that the children build up their factual knowledge sequentially as a basis for later work on reproduction; thus there are two full lesson plans for this topic. In this lesson the notion of variation as being natural is reinforced, to reassure the children that they may not all change at the same time, at the same rate, or to the same extent. This is developed into a projection of the growth of 9–15 year olds, based on the measurements of a large number of people. Once the children are comfortable with the idea of a 'growth spurt', they can consider briefly how the proportions of the body change. This activity involves the children using data about their heights. If this is a particularly sensitive issue with your class, use a group of plants of equal age (such as broad bean seedlings). By introducing general change due to growth from a scientific perspective, this lesson prepares pupils for more specific work on puberty in Lesson 10.

## INTRODUCTION

Tell the children that they are going to look at growth. When we look at any group of living things which are the same age, such as a litter of puppies or a trayful of seedlings, we can see that there is some variation in size. This is also true of the class. Explain that when scientists study the size of individuals in a group, they measure them, divide the measurements into size groups and make a graph.

## MAIN TEACHING ACTIVITY

In pairs, let the children measure and record each other's height. Bring the class together and find the heights of the tallest and shortest children. Divide the range into five or six size groups. (For example, if the range is 126–146cm, use groups of 126–130cm, 131–135cm, 136–140cm, 141–145cm and 146–150cm. Ask the children to rearrange the class data into these groups and draw a bar graph of them. The children should see that there are a few individuals at the edges of the range, but most are in the middle. Say that as they grow, some individuals will move from the edges of the range towards the middle or vice versa. Introduce the Group activities: looking at how people grow between the ages of 9 and 15, and how body shape changes with age.

## GROUP ACTIVITIES

**1.** The children should use the data on page 36 to plot a graph of the heights of girls and boys aged 9–15; age on the x-axis, height on the y-axis. Select a graph scale appropriate to the children's ability. The height scale may be 0–180cm or 130–180cm; using the smaller scale will show the height differences more clearly. The children should comment that the girls grow faster than the boys from 11 to 13, then the boys grow faster than the girls from 14 to 15.
**2.** The children should describe the changes in the sequence of pictures at the bottom of page 36. The answers are: the head becomes proportionally smaller, the face becomes proportionally larger, the body becomes proportionally smaller, the legs and arms become proportionally longer.

## DIFFERENTIATION

**1.** Less able children could have a graph specially prepared and photocopied for them, with a few points plotted and lines drawn in. With support, they could then plot the remaining data and complete the graph. More able children could return to the class height data and divide it into girls' heights and boys' heights. Alternatively, they could measure the heights of different bean plants and calculate the average height and/or graph the heights as they did for the class. Do plants show a similar distribution of heights?

**2.** Less able children could try to make Plasticine models of the four bodies to compare. More able children could speculate on how they would look if they still had the proportions of a baby.

## ASSESSMENT

Look for accurately plotted points on the graph and clear lines connecting them. Look for clear descriptions of the changes in the proportions of the body.

## PLENARY

Discuss how the proportions of our bodies change as we grow. Stress that there is variation in any group of people, and that this is natural. Describe the period of rapid growth that the children are entering as the 'growth spurt'. Highlight that although there is variation, certain changes happen to everyone as they grow into an adult; and these are dealt with in the next lesson.

## OUTCOMES

- Is aware that human bodies vary and that this is natural.
- Can identify the time of the 'growth spurt'.
- Can describe how some parts of the body change in proportion from birth to adulthood. ]

# LESSON 10

## OBJECTIVE

- To know about the changes that take place in the body at puberty.

## RESOURCES

**Main teaching activities:** Pictures of an adult male and female (possibly in swimwear), to show differences in body shape. You may also wish to use the body outlines from Lesson 2.
**Group activities: 1.** Photocopiable page 37, pencils. **2.** Photocopiable page 38, pencils.

*Vocabulary*

development, waist, puberty, breast, nipple, pubic hair, testicles, penis scrotum, vulva, ovary, womb, genitals

## BACKGROUND

The activities in this lesson should be done by all the children at the same time. This lesson builds on Lesson 9, looking at further changes in the external appearance of the body due to puberty, briefly considering the changes inside the body related to reproduction, and considering the changes in attitudes that develop. It is assumed that in Year 6/Primary 7, the structure of the male and female reproductive organs will be taught, and sexual intercourse, ante-natal development and birth will be described. The children should be made aware that they are about to enter 'puberty'; a time of many developmental changes – both external and internal.

## INTRODUCTION

Tell the children that 'growth' (physical enlargement) occurs in humans from birth until they are about 20 years old. After that, a person's body may well stay about the same size until old age, unless too little or too much food is eaten. In old age, a person's body may become slightly smaller. Between the ages of 8 and 17 in girls and 10 and 18 in boys, there are also particular changes or developments to the body in order to prepare it for reproduction (the ability to create new people). These changes affect the body shape, the condition of the hair and skin, and the development of the reproductive organs. This period of change is called 'puberty'.

## MAIN TEACHING ACTIVITY 1

Remind the children of the changes in body shape they studied in Lesson 9. Say that during puberty there are further changes, and that these are different for boys and for girls. Show the pictures of a man and a woman. Point out that the man's shoulders are broader, while the hips are broader in the woman. Highlight the woman's breast development and relate this to feeding a baby. You may add that the female reproductive organs that produce a baby are hidden inside the woman's body. Her external genitals are hidden between her legs and are called the vulva. The male's reproductive organs are partly visible on the outside of the body. The external male genitals are the penis and the scrotum, which contains two testicles. During puberty, the size of the male genitals increases.

At puberty, both boys and girls grow hair under their arms and between their legs. The hair between the legs is called pubic hair. In boys, the hair on the face also starts to grow longer and thicker; the boy may have to shave to remove it. Both boys' and girls' skin produces more oil and this may lead to spots developing. Also when boys go through puberty, their voice-box grows and makes deeper sounds. In the early part of this process, the voice may produce both squeaky and deep sounds and is said to be 'breaking'. This can be embarrassing if the boy needs to speak.

## GROUP ACTIVITY 1

Give the children a copy each of page 37 and let them work through it. The answers are: girl only – breasts and nipples grow, hips grow wider than shoulders, waist develops; boy only – hair grows on face, shoulders grow wider than hips, testicles and penis grow; both – skin and hair become more oily, skin may become spotty, hair grows under armpits, hair grows between legs.

## MAIN TEACHING ACTIVITY 2

Remind the children about some boys being embarrassed when their voices break. Broaden this idea to many children being embarrassed or concerned as their bodies start changing. Say that a common fear is to worry whether you are developing normally, and that this is natural.

People also have to cope with changes taking place inside the body. In boys, the testicles start to produce sperms. These are essential for reproduction. The sperms may be released (in a liquid called semen) through the penis at night when the boy is asleep. When this happens, the boy is said to have had a 'wet dream'.

A girl's body contains two ovaries which produce eggs for reproduction. During puberty, the ovaries start to release eggs. When an egg is released, another part of the girl's reproductive system called the womb develops a thick wall of blood, ready to help a baby develop. If there is no baby, the wall then breaks down and the blood passes out of the reproductive system. When this occurs, the girl is said to be 'having a period'. This can be quite uncomfortable. The releasing of the egg and the development and breaking-up of the womb wall occurs every month, so the girl will experience a monthly period. At this time, she wears a sanitary towel to absorb the blood. These may be available in the girls' toilets or from the school nurse.

The testicles and ovaries also make chemicals known as hormones, which flow around the body in the blood. They cause the body to develop the features of men and women. They can also affect the way that people behave. Boys, for example, commonly become more interested in girls, and vice versa. Girls' hormones can also affect their mood, and may make the girl feel upset or bad-tempered just before the monthly period.

## GROUP ACTIVITY 2

Give each child a copy of page 38 to work through. The answers are: 1. testicles, asleep, semen, wet dream; 2. puberty, eggs, womb, sanitary, period; 3. To make them able to reproduce.

## DIFFERENTIATION

**1.** Less able children could have label lines drawn for them, with an initial word to help them place each label. More able children could use secondary sources to find out about skincare for young people.
**2.** Less able children could work with support, testing each word in the list against each gap in the text as a game. More able children could be 'agony aunts' and write a reply to a young person's question: 'My mum says I've reached puberty. What is this?'

## ASSESSMENT

Look for accuracy in the children's answers. Discuss the work in the Group activities and assess how fluently the children use the new vocabulary.

## PLENARY

Share a 'question and answer' session in which you say some words related to puberty and reproduction and the children give you definitions. Start a question box where the children can put questions about puberty-related problems, written anonymously, to the school 'agony aunt' (a teacher or school nurse). Later, invite the nurse or teacher to read out some of the questions and give their replies.

## OUTCOMES

- Recognise the changes that take place at puberty.
- Understand that these changes take place at different times in different people.
- Can name some parts of the reproductive system.

# LESSON 11

## OBJECTIVES
● To know that some drugs can help the body recover from illness.
● To know that people can persuade others to take harmful drugs.

### RESOURCES
A collection of advertisements (see Preparation), a tumbler, water.

### PREPARATION
Look through a selection of magazines and make a collection of advertisements relating to medicines and other chemicals that we apply to our bodies: foot powders, spot treatments, mouthwash and so on.

### BACKGROUND

*Vocabulary*

medicine, drug, solvent, addict, nicotine, cigarette, alcohol

This lesson and the three that follow it deal with drugs. This issue can be a sensitive one, and care must be taken to take into account the health and domestic circumstances of the children. This lesson presents drugs in a medicinal context, while introducing the idea of harmful drugs. Lesson 12 deals with tobacco, Lesson 13 with alcohol, and Lesson 14 with solvents and illegal drugs. At the end of the four lessons, the children should be able to appreciate the term 'drug' in a broad sense and compare the effects of helpful and harmful drugs on the body. In dealing with questions about why people take harmful drugs, keep the discussion general and steer away from references to specific people. The following ideas may be useful:
● Harmful drugs are poisons that have pleasant short-term effects.
● Children may be introduced to harmful drugs through peer pressure, or through simple curiosity about drugs that are available at home or outside.
● When a person begins to use certain drugs, the body becomes more tolerant and the person cannot feel the same effects unless more of the drug is taken.
● The body gets used to the drug, and a change may take place in the body that makes the person feel unwell unless he or she takes the drug regularly. The person has become dependent on the drug – that is, addicted to it.
● While young people may become addicted through peer pressure, they may become addicted due to unhappiness, feelings of loneliness, or feeling unable to cope with life.
● As addiction can be due to some underlying problem causing unhappiness; if the problem is tackled there is a chance the addiction can be controlled.

It is assumed that these issues will be discussed again in later years. Opportunities and activites are offered, for example, in *100 Science Lessons: Year 6/Primary 7*.

#### Tobacco
Nicotine is the addictive drug in tobacco, but there are a thousand other chemicals in cigarette smoke. Some of these are harmful to the body. The lining of the windpipe has microscopic hairs that move inhaled dust up and out of the respiratory system. Harmful chemicals in smoke stop the action of the hairs, so the dust accumulates in the lungs and has to be removed by continual coughing. The smoke can also cause inflammation of the air passages (bronchitis) and cause cancers to develop. Smoking also affects the heart and circulatory system, increasing the chances of heart disease and lost limbs in later life.

#### Alcohol
Alcohol drunk in moderation is believed to help keep the circulatory system of an adult healthy. You may wish to tell the children this to allay their fears that parents drinking socially are at great risk. The effect of alcohol on the nervous system of the body is related to body size. A large person can drink more alcohol than a small person before the nervous system is affected. The serious danger of alcohol for children is related to their small body size: they may become quickly intoxicated if they drink adult measures of an alcoholic drink. At the very least, intoxication leads to impaired judgement and a later 'hangover' with headaches and nausea. The major danger to young people from drinking alcohol in excess is becoming unconscious and choking on their own vomit. Addiction in adults increases the chances of developing heart disease, hepatitis and cirrhosis of the liver. Heavy drinking can also cause violent and irrational behaviour.

#### Solvents and illegal 'recreational' drugs
Children of this age may be more at risk of coming in to contact with dangerous solvents than illegal drugs. Some everyday substances such as glues and correcting fluids are made with chemical solvents that evaporate readily. If these are sniffed, they produce an effect similar to drunkenness.

# Ben's burger

Read what happened to Ben's burger, then answer the questions.

Ben watched the burger sizzling on the griddle. He sniffed the air and smelled the burger cooking. The sight and smell of the burger cooking made his mouth water. The water in his mouth is called saliva. It is made by salivary glands in his cheeks and under his tongue.

When the burger was ready, Ben could hardly wait to eat it. He bit into it with his chisel-shaped front teeth. They are called his incisors. His fang-like canine teeth tore at the bread. When Ben started chewing, he used his premolar and molar teeth at the back of his mouth.

Ben rolled the chewed food to the back of his mouth with his tongue. He swallowed it, and it moved down a tube called the gullet. At the end of the gullet, the food entered Ben's stomach. There the food mixed with a liquid in the stomach, and muscles in the stomach wall churned up the mixture. Some of the burger broke into smaller pieces. After Ben had eaten his burger, his stomach kept churning it up for some time.

The churned-up burger looked more like soup, and the stomach squirted it into a tube that led to the small intestine. As the food moved along, liquids from the pancreas and liver mixed with it. They helped to dissolve the solid parts of the burger. Some parts of the burger could not dissolve. They were made of fibre, and passed along the small intestine. Other substances in the burger that would provide energy or materials for growth did dissolve. They were taken from the small intestine into the blood, and passed around the body.

Undigested food, including the fibre, eventually passed into Ben's large intestine and then into the rectum. Later, the undigested food would pass through the anus when Ben went to the toilet.

1. What two things made Ben's mouth water? _____

2. Where is the water in the mouth made? _____

3. Which teeth bit into the burger and which teeth chewed it up? _____

_____

4. Where did the food go after it left the mouth? _____

5. What happened to the food in the stomach? _____

6. What did the liquids from the pancreas and liver do? _____

7. Where did the dissolved food leave the digestive system? _____

8. Where did the dissolved food go after it had left the digestive system?

_____

9. What went into the large intestine? _____

# Parts of the digestive system

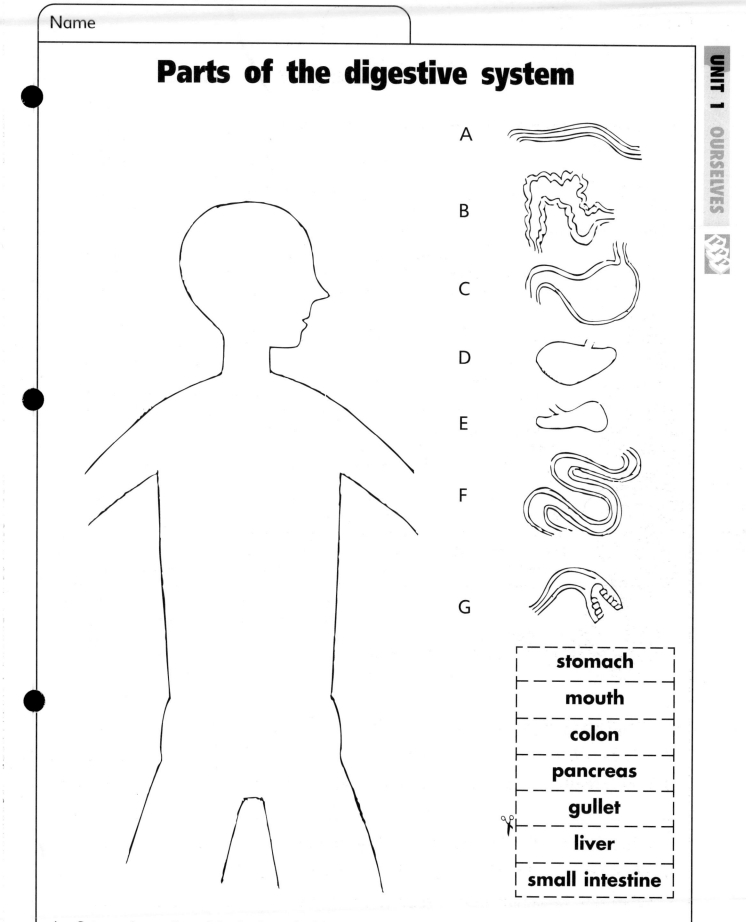

A

B

C

D

E

F

G

| stomach |
| mouth |
| colon |
| pancreas |
| gullet |
| liver |
| small intestine |

1.  Cut out the outline of the body and stick it in the middle of an A4 sheet of paper.
2.  Colour in parts A, C, F and G pink. Colour in part B purple, part D brown and part E red.
3.  Cut out the body parts. Look at the display in the classroom, then put the parts in the correct places inside the body outline. Check your work with your teacher before you stick the parts in place.
4.  Cut out the labels, stick them on the sheet and draw a line from each label to the correct part of the digestive system.

# Action in the digestive system

Read below about the action of each part of the digestive system.

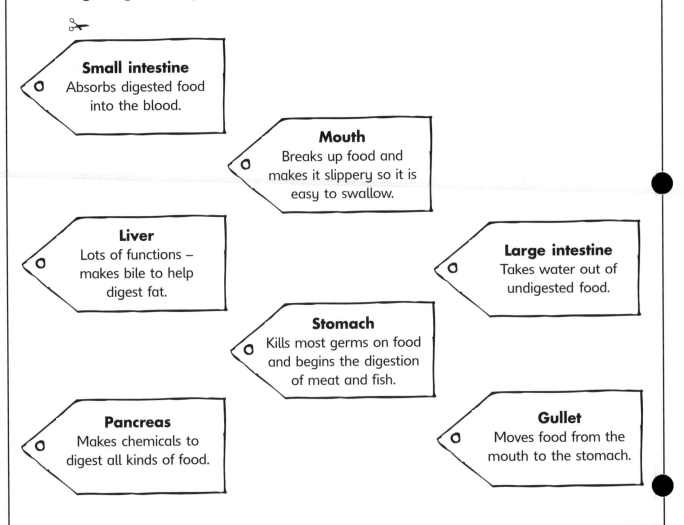

The bile from the liver and the chemicals from the pancreas mix with the food just after it has left the stomach. From here, the mixture goes into the small intestine. When undigested food has passed through the large intestine, it enters the rectum where it is stored. Later, the undigested food passes out of the body through the anus.

Cut out the 'action box' for each part and stick it next to the correct part of the body on your diagram of the digestive system.

**Small intestine**
Absorbs digested food into the blood.

**Mouth**
Breaks up food and makes it slippery so it is easy to swallow.

**Liver**
Lots of functions – makes bile to help digest fat.

**Large intestine**
Takes water out of undigested food.

**Stomach**
Kills most germs on food and begins the digestion of meat and fish.

**Pancreas**
Makes chemicals to digest all kinds of food.

**Gullet**
Moves food from the mouth to the stomach.

# Breathing in and out

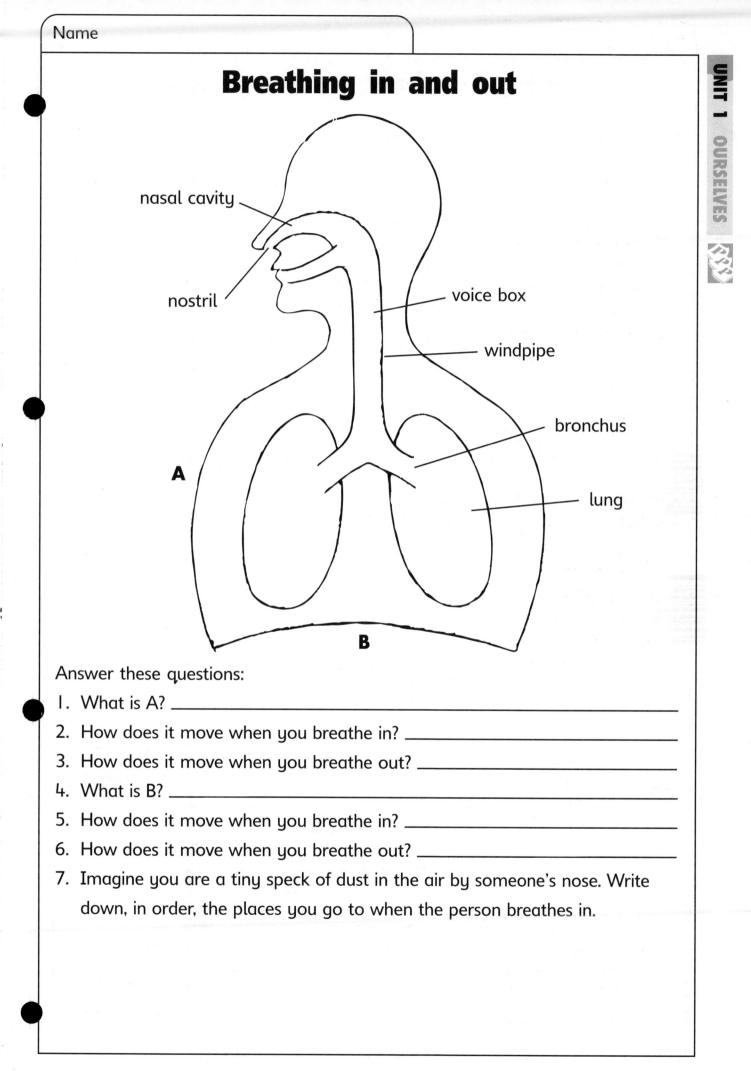

Diagram labels: nasal cavity, nostril, voice box, windpipe, bronchus, lung, A, B

Answer these questions:

1. What is A? _____

2. How does it move when you breathe in? _____

3. How does it move when you breathe out? _____

4. What is B? _____

5. How does it move when you breathe in? _____

6. How does it move when you breathe out? _____

7. Imagine you are a tiny speck of dust in the air by someone's nose. Write down, in order, the places you go to when the person breathes in.

# The beating heart

The heartbeat is made by the sounds of the heart valves closing. The valves close to stop the blood flowing the wrong way when the heart muscle pushes on it. There are two heart sounds. The louder 'lub' sound is made when the larger valves close. The quieter 'dup' sound is made when the smaller valves close. The large valves close first, followed by the smaller valves, so the heartbeat sound is 'lub-dup'.

1. Look at the top two heart pictures and label one as making the 'lub' sound and the other as making the 'dup' sound.
2. Draw arrows showing the path of blood through the open valves.
3. Cut out all of these hearts and stick them in the top right-hand corner of 36 pages of your science book. Write 'lub' or 'dup' next to each one and flick your book to see the heart beat.

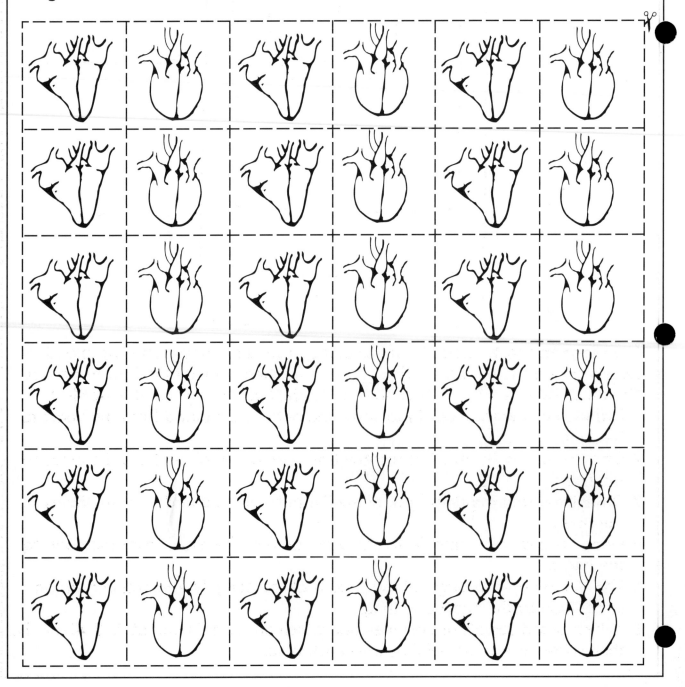

# The path of the blood

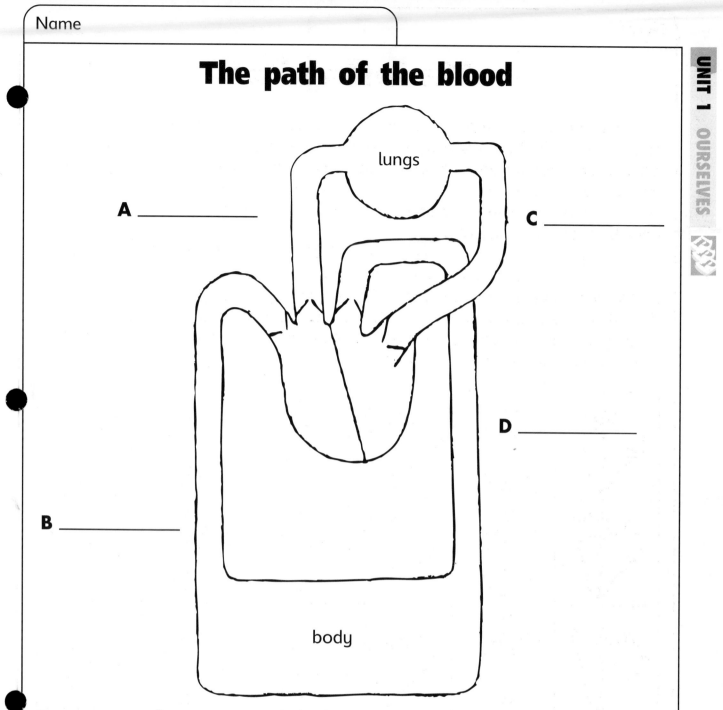

This diagram shows the path of the blood around the body. The two blood vessels close together above the centre of the heart carry blood away from it. The other two blood vessels connected to the heart carry blood towards it.

1. Draw an arrow (marked 1) to show the path of the blood from the heart to the lungs.
2. Draw an arrow (marked 2) to show the path of the blood from the lungs to the heart.
3. Draw an arrow (marked 3) to show the path of the blood from the heart to the body.
4. Draw an arrow (marked 4) to show the path of the blood from the body to the heart.
5. The blood flows through all the organs of the body. Name any two organs in addition to the heart and lungs.
6. Which blood vessels are arteries and which are veins? Look at A, B, C and D, then write 'artery' or 'vein' next to each letter.

# Growth chart

The height of a large number of people aged between 9 and 15 were measured. From this, a typical height for girls and a typical height for boys were found for each year group. The results are shown in this table:

| Age | Height of girls (cm) | Height of boys (cm) |
|-----|----------------------|---------------------|
| 9   | 133                  | 136                 |
| 10  | 139                  | 140                 |
| 11  | 145                  | 144                 |
| 12  | 152                  | 150                 |
| 13  | 158                  | 153                 |
| 14  | 160                  | 163                 |
| 15  | 161                  | 168                 |

On graph paper, draw one line graph showing both these sets of results. Draw the girls' line in red and the boys' line in blue.

Who grows faster, girls or boys? Why do you think that happens?

The diagram below shows the human body at four different ages. All the bodies have been made the same size, so that you can see how the proportions of the body (the amount of the total that any part takes up) have changed. Describe the changes in proportion you can see here as a person grows.

# Changes in the body (1)

These pictures show the bodies of a boy and girl who are about to start puberty. The statements at the bottom of this sheet describe the changes that will happen when one or both go through puberty. Cut out the statements and use them to label the pictures.

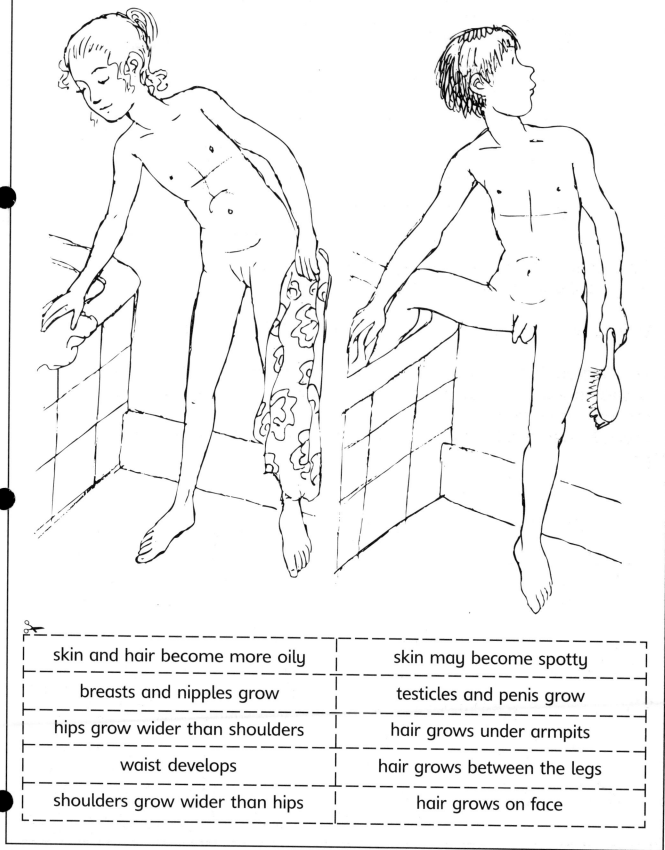

| skin and hair become more oily | skin may become spotty |
| breasts and nipples grow | testicles and penis grow |
| hips grow wider than shoulders | hair grows under armpits |
| waist develops | hair grows between the legs |
| shoulders grow wider than hips | hair grows on face |

# Changes in the body (2)

1. Fill in the missing words in this paragraph. Select the words from the list below. Not all the words in the list are used.

When a boy goes through puberty, his _____ begin to produce sperms. They can pass out of his penis when he is _____. The sperms are in a liquid called _____. When a boy releases semen in his sleep, he is said to have had a _____.

**semen     awake     asleep     testicles     sperms**

**egg     period     nightmare     wet dream**

2. Fill in the missing words in this paragraph. Select the words from the list below. Not all the words in the list are used.

When a girl goes through _____, her ovaries start releasing _____. Every month, the wall of her _____ swells with blood and then breaks down. The blood passes out of the girl's body and is collected by a _____ towel. When the blood leaves her body, the girl is said to be having a _____.

**sperms     eggs     puberty     penis     womb     bath**

**sanitary     kitchen     wet dream     period**

3. Why do you think the bodies of boys and girls change at puberty?

# Growing up healthy

1. Identify two foods for growth in this diagram and colour them in red.
2. Identify two foods that provide energy for activity and colour them in blue.
3. Write a label naming each food you have coloured in.

4. On this diagram of the body, draw the heart in the correct position.

5. Where would you find your pulse? _____

6. What makes the throbbing of the pulse? _____

7. What is the pulse rate? _____

8. How does your pulse rate change as you start to exercise? _____

9. Why does your pulse rate change? _____

_____

_____

# Growing up healthy

Paul has four friends: Abigail, Alex, Dean and Laura. He wants to see whether their hearts all beat at the same rate.

**What could he do to find out?**

**Predict what you think Paul will find out.**

_____

_____

**Why do you think that will happen?**

_____

_____

# Life cycles

## ORGANISATION (15 LESSONS)

| | OBJECTIVES | MAIN ACTIVITY | GROUP ACTIVITIES | PLENARY | OUTCOMES |
|---|---|---|---|---|---|
| **LESSON 1** | ● To know that flowers produce fruits and that fruits contain seeds. ● To revise the vocabulary of the main stages of development of a plant. ● To revise and extend knowledge of plants that humans use as food. ● To know that flowering plants have life cycles. | Revise the main parts of a plant. Establish that fruits develop from flowers and that the fruit contains seeds. | Answer questions on the parts of different plants that we eat. Make a detailed drawing of a section of a fruit. | Reinforce knowledge of plant parts and the plant life cycle. | ● Know that flowers produce fruits and that fruits contain seeds. ● Recognise the parts of some plants that humans use as foods. ● Know the main stages in the life cycle of a flowering plant. |
| **LESSON 2** | ● To know that flowering plants have life cycles. ● To revise and extend knowledge of plants that humans use in processed foods. | Identify the plant ingredients in processed foods as plant parts. | | Test knowledge of the plant life cycle. | ● Develop the concept of a life cycle in relation to a flowering plant. ● Know the parts of some plants that are used in processed foods. |
| **LESSON 3** | ● To know that seeds must be dispersed to help new plants grow. | Use an interactive visual aid to explore seed dispersal. | Design a model windblown seed. Comprehension work on the seed dispersal of British trees. | Evaluate the designs for a model windblown seed. | ● Know the reasons for and the basic methods of seed dispersal. |
| **LESSON 4** | ● To know the factors that affect the germination of seeds. ● To practise and develop investigative skills. | Discuss how to set up experiments on growing seeds in different conditions. | Devise an experiment. Set up the experiment. | Discuss different approaches to similar experiments. | ● Know the factors that affect the germination of seeds. ● Have practised and developed their investigative skills. |
| **LESSON 5** | ● To develop observational and recording skills. | Observe and measure the germinated plants. Record results. | | Make predictions based on the observed results so far. | ● Understand the purpose of accurate observation. ● Understand the need for careful recording. |
| **LESSON 6** | ● To use evidence to identify a link between environmental conditions and seed germination. ● To identify patterns in their observations and draw simple appropriate conclusions. | Observe and measure the final results. Record findings. | | Look for patterns in the class experiments. | ● Can identify patterns from their observations. ● Can determine whether a test is fair. |
| **LESSON 7** | ● To know that insects are attracted to flowers. ● To know the main parts of an insect-pollinated flower. | Read a 'radio play' about a worker bee visiting a flower for the first time. | Label a flower picture and answer questions on bees. Write additional text for the play. | Listen to the children's further speeches for the play. | ● Can name the main parts of an insect-pollinated flower. ● Knows about the activities of a worker bee. |
| **LESSON 8** | ● To observe the structure of an insect-pollinated flower. ● To recognise flowers that attract insects. ● To observe the role of insects in pollination. | Discuss and plan a trip to collect pollen and observe flowers. | Find some insect-pollinated flowers, watch insects, make observational drawings of flowers and collect pollen. | Look at and describe the pollen samples collected. | ● Have observed the structure of an insect-pollinated flower. ● Know some flowers that attract insects. ● Have observed the role of insects in the pollination process. |

## ORGANISATION (15 LESSONS)

| | OBJECTIVES | MAIN ACTIVITY | GROUP ACTIVITIES | PLENARY | OUTCOMES |
|---|---|---|---|---|---|
| **LESSON 9** | ● To know that seeds develop in the ovary. ● To know the functions of pollen, the stamen and the stigma in fertilisation. ● To know the role of insects in the process of pollination. | Interactive lesson with role-play on insect pollination. | Sort sentences to describe insect pollination. Design and make a model or collage of an insect-pollinated flower. | Review the Group activities. | ● Know that fertilisation of a flower takes place when pollen is transferred to the stigma. ● Know that seeds develop in the ovary. ● Know that insects can pollinate flowers. ● Know that certain insects and certain flowers are mutually dependent. |
| **LESSON 10** | ● To develop an understanding of life cycles. ● To know the life cycle of a butterfly. | Use a letter from an incompetent gardener to discuss insect life cycles. | Answer questions on insect life cycles. Write a critical letter to the incompetent gardener. | Discuss ideas for natural crop protection. | ● Have an extended understanding of life cycles. ● Know the life cycle of a butterfly. |
| **LESSON 11** | ● To know that some plants are pollinated by the wind. ● To know that the fruits of grasses play an important part in our diet. | Discuss wind pollination and the importance of cereals in our diet. | Answer questions on wind-pollinated flowers. Identify cereals in processed foods as seeds of particular plants. | Look at the causes of hay fever and information on other wind-pollinated plants. | ● Know that some plants are pollinated by the wind. ● Know that the fruits of some grasses (called 'cereals') play an important part in our diet. ● Can represent simple information in a tabular form. |
| **LESSON 12** | ● To know that if living things fail to reproduce they become extinct. | Use a game to learn about the life cycle of the song thrush and threats to its survival. | Make a poster to explain why the song thrush may become extinct. Make a charter of ways to help conserve the song thrush. | Discuss ideas to help the song thrush and information on other endangered British birds. | ● Know that if living things fail to reproduce they become extinct. ● Know that living things in our own environment are facing extinction through environmental change. ● Know that we can all do something to promote conservation. |
| **LESSON 13** | ● To revise the life cycles of the butterfly, thrush and green plant. ● To understand the meaning of the term 'mammal'. ● To know that mammals have life cycles. | Compare the life cycles of a plant and a thrush with that of a cat. | Answer questions on the mammalian life cycle. Draw a graph of data on gestation periods. | Discuss the graphs of gestation periods and information on other mammals. | ● Have consolidated their knowledge of life cycles. ● Know that a mammal is a class of animal whose young are fed on milk from the mother. |
| **LESSON 14** | ● To compare the life cycles of different animals. ● To develop knowledge of some other life cycles. | Discuss the similarities and differences between the life cycles of a cat and a thrush. Describe another life cycle. Make another comparison. | | Discuss the life cycles of other animals. | ● Know the similarities and differences between some animal life cycles. ● Find out about some other animal life cycles. |

| | OBJECTIVES | ACTIVITY 1 | ACTIVITY 2 |
|---|---|---|---|
| **ASSESSMENT 15** | ● To assess the children's knowledge of the life cycle of plants. ● To assess the children's knowledge of some animal life cycles. | Label a flower picture. Answer questions on methods of pollination and seed dispersal. | Answer questions on the life cycles of a butterfly and song thrush, and the value of several animal species to the gardener. |

# LESSON 1

## OBJECTIVES

- To know that flowers produce fruits and that fruits contain seeds.
- To revise the vocabulary of the main stages of development of a plant.
- To revise and extend knowledge of plants that humans use as foods.
- To know that flowering plants have life cycles.

### RESOURCES

**Vocabulary**

seed, flower, fruit, seed catalogue

**Main teaching activity:** An apple, orange, tomato and cucumber, plus a collection of fruits from other plants that the children will not identify as 'fruits' (such as acorns in cups, peas in a pod, a conker in its prickly shell); a knife, five long strips of card with Blu-Tack on the back (see Preparation), an A3 version of photocopiable page 64.
**Group activities: 1.** Seed catalogues or gardening books (one per pair or group of three children) containing pictures of vegetables; photocopiable page 64. **2.** Drawing materials, hand lenses.

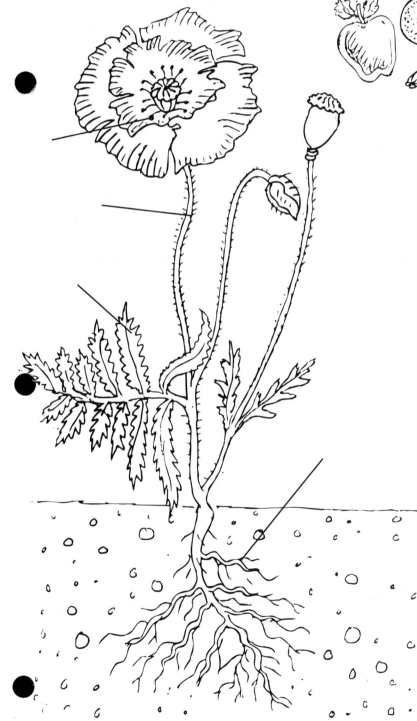

### PREPARATION

On the board or flip chart, prepare a diagram of a plant with roots, a stem, leaf, flower, seeds and a separate fruit, with label lines drawn ready for annotation (see illustration). Cut the apple, orange, cucumber and tomato in to sections to reveal the seeds. Rub some orange juice on the apple to prevent the cut surface from browning. On each of the five long strips of card, write one of the following sentences: *Seeds are planted in the ground. Stems and leaves grow up above the ground. Flowers grow on the stems. Fruits are formed from the flowers. Seeds grow within the fruits.*

### BACKGROUND

Although flowering plants vary widely in appearance, they are all built to the same basic plan. The children will recognise roots, stems, leaves and flowers from earlier school work. However, their concept of a 'fruit' will probably refer only to the succulent varieties they have seen in shops: apples, oranges, plums, cherries and so on. In botanical terms, the fruit is the ovary that contains the maturing fertilised seeds of the plant. All flowering plants produce fruits. The children will have eaten fruits that they thought of as 'vegetables': tomatoes, runner beans, mange tout and so on.

Many children grow up in an environment that is some distance from the source of the food they eat. They may even be unaware that potatoes grow underground! This lesson will help the children to consolidate their knowledge of the sources of plant food. It will also give them a basic overview of the life cycle of flowering plants that will put rest of this unit into context.

## INTRODUCTION

Tell the children that they are going to think about the food we grow to eat. Ask: *Do you know anyone who has ever grown any food to eat?* Ask any child who says 'Yes' to tell the class what was grown. They may have relatives who rent allotments or grow tomatoes on a balcony or patio.

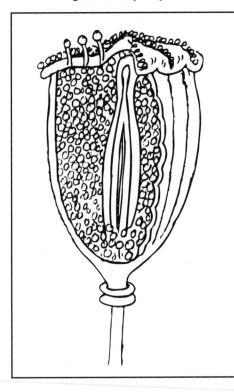

## MAIN TEACHING ACTIVITY

Tell the children that they are going to think about the parts of the plant that they eat. Point to the display diagram and ask the children to help you annotate the parts of the plant: root, stem, leaf, flower and seed. Now point to the fruit and ask: *What do you think we call this seed container?* Show the children the sections of apple, orange, cucumber and tomato that you have prepared, and point out the seeds. Elicit or reveal the answer that the seed container is called a 'fruit'. Emphasise that all flowering plants produce fruits.

Show the children some familiar seed containers that they might not have previously identified as fruits (see Resources). Keep one example back to use for assessment. In each case, ask the children to identify the seeds; stress that the whole seed container is a fruit, then ask: *Where does the fruit come from?* Establish that it was produced from the flower. Use the diagram to adapt a flower into another fruit.

Now display the enlarged version of page 64. Look at the first section. Ask: *Which part of these plants do we eat?* Elicit the correct answers in a discussion, and write the name of the appropriate plant part for the first few entries: Lettuce *leaves,* Potato *roots,* Tomato *fruit,* Celery *stem,* Cauliflower *flower.*

## GROUP ACTIVITIES

**1.** Give each child a copy of photocopiable page 64, but encourage the children to work together in pairs to discuss or look for the answers. Identify the secondary sources of information (seed catalogues and books) that they can use to resolve difficulties.
**2.** Ask each child to make a detailed, enlarged drawing of one of the sections of fruit that were shown to the class (apple, orange, cucumber and so on). Make sure each child has access to a hand lens to encourage detailed observation.

## DIFFERENTIATION

**1.** For some less able children, the pictures in a seed catalogue could be cut out. The children could sort them into groups of roots, stems, leaves, fruits and flowers, then stick the groups onto a backing sheet and label them. **2.** Children who finish their drawing quickly could repeat the activity with another fruit.

## ASSESSMENT

During the plenary session, show the children one further example of a seed container. Establish that they know it is a fruit which contains seeds and has developed from a flower.

## PLENARY

Discuss the answers to the photocopiable sheet. Show the class the children's drawings. Display the five sentences that describe the life cycle of a flowering plant in random order, and ask the children to help you arrange them in the order in which they happen. Display the children's pictures.

## OUTCOMES

● Know that flowers produce fruits and that fruits contain seeds.
● Recognise the parts of some plants that humans use as foods.
● Know the main stages in the life cycle of a flowering plant.

## LINKS

Art and design: making things.

# LESSON 2

| | |
|---|---|
| **Objectives** | ● To know that flowering plants have life cycles.<br>● To revise and extend knowledge of plants that humans use in processed foods. |
| **Resources** | The five sentences on card from Lesson 1, Blu-Tack, a collection of containers (tins, boxes etc) for processed foods, each with an 'Ingredients' label; a large, blank ruled table on the board or flip chart with three columns headed 'Processed food', 'Ingredients that we are sure come from plants' and 'Part of plant'; copies of this table (perhaps prepared on the class computer); children's dictionaries. |
| **Main activity** | Display the card sentence strips in random order, attached to a vertical surface. Remind the children of Lesson 1. Ask them to help you arrange the sentences in the order in which they happen. Rearrange the sentences into a circular pattern and discuss the term 'Life cycle'.<br>    Show the children the processed food containers and identify the 'Ingredients' lists. Show them the prepared table, then select a processed food container and complete a table entry – for example, the food *Baked beans* might have the ingredients *Beans, Tomatoes, Onion Powder, Sugar* and *Maize*; the corresponding plant parts would be *Seeds, Fruit, Roots, Stem* and *Seeds*. Ask the children to work in pairs, selecting one processed food container at a time and completing the table. Children for whom this is an appropriate task could look up ingredients that they believe to be plant parts in a class dictionary. They could use the printed definitions to check their ideas. |
| **Differentiation** | Less able children could be given a sheet with several lists of plant-derived ingredients from processed foods. They could read the lists, then match each set of ingredients to the appropriate processed food container. |
| **Assessment** | Test the children's understanding with a simple game. Display the five plant life cycle sentences in the correct circular pattern, then ask the children to shut their eyes. Remove a sentence. Ask the children to open their eyes and tell you what sentence has been removed. |
| **Plenary** | Discuss the children's answers in the table. Some ingredients (such as sugar) may originate from more than one type of plant. Whenever possible, stress the relationship between *flowers, fruits* and *seeds*. |
| **Outcomes** | ● Develop the concept of a life cycle in relation to a flowering plant.<br>● Know the parts of some plants that are used in processed foods. |

# LESSON 3

## OBJECTIVE
● To know that seeds must be dispersed to help new plants grow.

## RESOURCES

**Main teaching activity:** The five life cycle sentences on card from Lesson 1, a large poster of a woodland (see diagram); large pictures (from other sources) of a song thrush, a squirrel, a mouse, and the fruits or seeds shown on page 65, each mounted on card with Blu-Tack on the back.
**Group activities: 1.** A selection of art materials, including various papers, drinking straws, glue, scissors, adhesive tape, felt-tipped pens, and a quantity of something very light to act as seeds (such as milk bottle tops, plastic 'unit' cubes or dried bean seeds). **2.** Photocopiable page 65.

## PREPARATION

Display the five life cycle sentences from Lesson 1 in a circular sequence. Prepare a poster based on the diagram shown, and display it where it will be clearly visible and accessible. Fasten the six pictures of fruits or seeds to different trees on the poster.

## BACKGROUND

To help the children understand the process of seed dispersal, this lesson uses the familiar seeds of native British tree species. Many of these seeds are large and easy to handle, and have clear characteristics that aid dispersal.
    For plants to thrive, they need to have access to light, moisture and nutrients. Competition from other plants, including the parent, can delay growth or suffocate the emerging plant. Therefore, if seeds are transported and germinate away from the parent plant, they have a greater chance of survival and success. This is the reason why seeds are dispersed. There are three basic mechanisms of seed dispersal:

**1. Hoarded heavy seeds.** Trees that use this method of dispersal include the oak and beech. The tree produces large numbers of heavy seeds that fall to the ground around the parent tree. These seeds are a valuable winter food supply for woodland animals such as the badger and squirrel, who find and hoard the seeds (often storing them in small holes in the ground). Uneaten seeds may eventually germinate in a new location, some distance from the parent tree.

**2. Bird-sown seeds.** The hawthorn, rowan and elder are examples of trees that rely on birds for seed distribution. The birds eat the attractive fruits and defecate the undigested seeds in a new location. Songbirds often roost in positions where they have a clear view of their territory and potential predators. A good place to search for bird-sown seedlings is at the edge of woodland, beneath the branches where berry-eating birds have perched.

**3. Wind-blown seeds.** The seeds of the sycamore and ash will be easiest to find. Both have large appendages that help them to spin away from their parent tree in the wind. These seeds can be a useful food source for small mammals.

## INTRODUCTION

Using the five life cycle sentences on flowering plants from Lesson 1, draw the children's attention to the fact that the life cycle begins with seeds being sown and ends with the production of new seeds.

## MAIN TEACHING ACTIVITY

Tell the children that they are going to find out about how seeds are naturally sown in the ground. Explain that you are just going to talk about tree seeds, but that the seeds of other plants are sown in the same way. Refer to the woodland poster. Remove one seed picture from a tree and fasten it to the ground below. Ask: *Why won't this seed grow if it falls here?* Establish that the parent plant will shade the seed and deprive the infant plant of light and water. Put the seed back on the tree.

Introduce the term 'seed dispersal'. If the plant is to survive and reproduce, it needs to make sure that its seeds are spread out to reach better sites for growing. Write 'seed dispersal' on the board or flip chart. Keeping the lesson as interactive as possible, use the poster and the seed and animal pictures to demonstrate dispersal by birds, animals and the wind. Show how one seed of each dispersal type is moved to a suitable location and germinates. On the poster, draw a few leaves above the successful seed in its new location. The other seeds are eaten by animals or dropped in an inappropriate location. After demonstration of each method of dispersal, write the terms 'bird-sown seeds', 'heavy hoarded seeds' and 'wind-blown seeds' on the board or flip chart. At the end of the session, ask questions to check that the children understand these terms.

## GROUP ACTIVITIES

**1.** Working in pairs, the children can design and make a model fruit that will carry the 'seed' (a small weight) as far as possible using wind power. Discuss and agree on methods to make the test fair. Decisions will need to be taken about: the range and size of materials that can be used; the weight of the seed; and the method for testing the 'fruits' (including how the fruits will be released and how much time will be allowed for them to blow). Before the test, bring the children back together to discuss their designs. Ask them to predict which 'fruit' will go furthest. Emphasise that they must test their designs by careful observation and measurement. It might be wise to make 'clearing up' a condition before the competition takes place.
**2.** Give each child a copy of page 65 to complete individually.

## DIFFERENTIATION

**1.** Differentiation is built in to this activity. However, some children may find it difficult to imagine original design ideas. Make suggestions to get them started, such as: *How about designing a fruit like a kite, sail, helicopter rotors, propeller, cylinder, paper chain, bag, parachute, aeroplane?* Encourage early finishers to make their 'fruit' instantly recognisable with appropriate decoration. **2.** The children can use secondary sources to find out which of the methods other trees use to disperse their seeds.

## ASSESSMENT

Ask questions to check that the children understand both the reasons for and the methods of seed dispersal.

## PLENARY

Discuss the results of Group activity 1. Ask children to explain why some seeds travelled a long distance and why others were less successful.

## OUTCOME

● Know the reasons for and the basic methods of seed dispersal.

## LINKS

Lesson 4: germination of seeds.

# LESSON 4

## OBJECTIVES

● To know the factors that affect the germination of seeds.
● To practise and develop investigative skills.

## RESOURCES

**Main teaching activity:** The forest poster from Lesson 3; a large copy of the diagram shown.
**Group activities: 1.** Paper, writing materials. **2.** A variety of large seeds (such as runner beans, dwarf beans, nasturtiums); a variety of pairs of small flowerpots, some identical clear plastic containers and sheets of absorbent paper, a variety of peat-free composts, some garden soil from a single location, some small trowels or similar implements, containers for measuring small amounts of water, black paper, junk materials, elastic bands, labels.

## PREPARATION

On the board or flip chart, write the words 'conditions' and 'germinate'. Prepare a large diagram of how to germinate seeds without soil (see diagram). Organise the classroom so that the flowerpots can be filled with the minimum of mess. Make sure that all the resources are easy to see and access.

*Vocabulary*

seedlings, conditions, variable, constant

## BACKGROUND

At this stage, the children may have a good knowledge of the conditions that help seeds to germinate, but have limited experience of actually growing plants. However, the main purpose of this lesson is not to grow plants successfully but to devise a scientific experiment. The children are invited to choose from a range of materials in order to test their skill in experimental design. There is a risk of over-managing this kind of experience: if you limit the range of resources and provide just one size of flowerpot, one kind of seed, one kind of seed compost and so on, you may restrict the children's understanding of the process of scientific enquiry; they will all use the same pot, the same seeds and the same compost because that is all there is! Try to organise a good range of resources.

The best seeds to use are runner beans, dwarf beans and nasturtiums. All prefer warm conditions and are easy to obtain and handle. Let the children choose from these. For the growing medium, you could use a variety of seed composts bought from a garden centre. Try to use peat-free composts, since the RSPB are unhappy about the effects of peat extraction on bird habitats. Some groups could use garden soil dug from a single location. Other groups could grow the seeds between the side of a clear plastic container and a coiled sheet of absorbent paper, as shown in the diagram above. Watering the experiments fairly will need your support and encouragement. Insist that the children measure and record all that they do. They should revisit the experiment over a period of three or four weeks and record their results. Lessons 5 and 6 outline the further development of this investigation.

At the end of the experiment, the children may have some healthy plants. These could be used to create a small class garden. An old car tyre on a corner of the playground, filled with soil and compost, could be used to plant the seedlings in. You could make an attractive runner bean teepee, surrounded by dwarf beans and nasturtiums. Better still, after the summer holidays the plants will have nearly completed their life cycle and you will have the seeds for another class.

## INTRODUCTION

Tell the children that they are going to think about the conditions that are needed for seeds to germinate. Check that they remember the meaning of the word 'germinate'. Remind them of the lesson on seed dispersal. Point to the forest poster and ask: *Why were the fruits or seeds transported to a new place to grow? Why didn't they grow next to the parent tree?* Elicit the answer: 'The seed needed light and water'. If the answer 'warmth' is not forthcoming (it may not be apparent from the forest poster), ask the following: *When you have walked past other people's gardens or allotments, have you noticed any other things that might help seeds to grow quickly?* Look for the answer 'greenhouse' or 'cold frame' to establish that gardeners often use the additional warmth of the solar energy trapped under glass to help plants to grow. Reinforce the idea that the three things needed for seeds to germinate are warmth, light and moisture. Write these three words on the board or flip chart.

## MAIN TEACHING ACTIVITY

Ask the children to work in pairs, designing an experiment to prove that seeds need the right conditions in order to germinate. Their experiment should test one factor: warmth, moisture or light. Through questioning, make sure they understand that their test samples need to have the same number of seeds, type of seed, container, soil, depth of planting and so on – establish that there should be only one variant. Write appropriate sentences on the board or flip chart as a guide for Group activity 1, stressing the word 'same' – for example: *We are going to use two sets of the <u>same</u> kind of seed.* Now establish where sensible warm and cold or light and dark locations for the experiments could be.

Say that you will show the children one experimental design as an example. Ask: *Is soil necessary for seeds to germinate?* Show them the prepared diagram to demonstrate that it is possible to germinate the seeds without soil.

Let the children form pairs and decide which of the three criteria they are testing. Indicate the resources that can be used in the experiment, and how they are organised.

## GROUP ACTIVITIES

**1.** Ask the children to work with their partner, writing down a title for their experiment and an account of how it is organised. Ask them to highlight the word 'same' each time they write it. When they have finished, they can move on to Group activity 2.
**2.** Ask the children to discuss with their partner how they are going to do the experiment, select the materials they need to carry it out and then set it up. Make sure they label each flowerpot, so that they can identify their work. When they have finished, they can move on to Group activity 1.

## DIFFERENTIATION

**1 and 2.** The writing on the board or flip chart will help less able children with the written element of this task. Children who finish quickly could design flowerpot sleeves or notices to explain the purpose of their experiment.

## ASSESSMENT

During the group work, ask children why it is important to have only one factor that changes in the experiment.

## PLENARY

Draw the children's attention to the different approaches used in similar experiments. Remember to stress the importance of not disturbing the experiments. Finally, ask the children which sample of seeds will be the first to germinate and why.

## OUTCOMES

● Know the factors that affect the germination of seeds.
● Have practised and developed their investigative skills.

## LINKS

Lessons 5 and 6: germination of seeds.

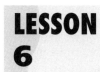

## LESSON 5

| Objective | ● To develop observational and recording skills. |
|---|---|
| Resources | The growing seeds from Lesson 4; rulers, hand lenses, paper, drawing and writing materials, digital camera (optional). |
| Main activity | A week after Lesson 4, remind the children that they are trying to find out how warmth, light and moisture affect the germination of seeds. Select one pot containing germinated seeds. *Look at these seedlings. By next week they may have grown. Next week, how will we remember what the seedlings were like at this time?* Stress the importance of looking carefully at any seeds that have germinated and making careful drawings. Now ask: *How will we know how much these seeds have grown next week?* Stress the importance of making careful measurements. *What parts of the plant could be measured?* List the parts that could be measured on the board or flip chart, eg the height of the plant above the soil or the length and width of the largest leaf. Ask the children to make detailed drawings and measurements of their germinated seeds. |
| Differentiation | Some children may find accurate drawing a difficult task. If you have access to a digital camera, this could be used to monitor their experiment. |
| Assessment | As they work, ask children: *Why do we need to look so carefully at our experiments? Why do we need to record carefully what has happened?* |
| Plenary | Ask the children, from their observations, to predict: *Which seedlings will have grown the tallest next week? Which seeds will still not have germinated next week?* Ask them to give reasons for their predictions. Continue the experiments for another week. |
| Outcomes | ● Understand the purpose of accurate observation.<br>● Understand the need for careful recording. |

## LESSON 6

| Objectives | ● To use evidence to identify a link between environmental conditions and seed germination.<br>● To identify patterns in their observations and draw simple appropriate conclusions. |
|---|---|
| Resources | The children's seed experiments from Lesson 4; plates or trays on which to empty the contents of 'failed' pots; paper towels, soap and a bowl for hand-washing. |
| Main activity | A week after Lesson 5, many of the seeds will have germinated and grown well in the warm, light and moist conditions. There may be limited growth in a cool or dry environment. Plants that may have been deprived of light may be weak and 'leggy'. Tell the children that this is the end of the experiment and the time to look carefully at all their seedlings. Encourage them to examine seeds that have not germinated. Make sure that they are aware of hygiene issues: they must wash their hands after handling soil or compost. Discuss with the children, and list on the board or flip chart, the things they need to do in order to complete the experiment: draw and measure both successful and unsuccessful seedlings; record their plant measurements; look at their pictures and measurements and decide what they have found out from the experiment; record their conclusions. |
| Assessment | As the children complete the work, ask them to state and explain their conclusions. |
| Plenary | Ask some pairs of children to show their seedlings and tell the rest of the class their conclusions. Ask the children to listen carefully and decide whether the conclusions were fair. Ask children who conducted similar experiments whether their conclusions were similar. There may be some general patterns – for example, the seeds in cool conditions or in dry conditions may have poor germination rates. |
| Outcomes | ● Can identify patterns from their observations.<br>● Can determine whether a test is fair. |

## LESSON 7

### OBJECTIVES
● To know that insects are attracted to flowers.
● To know the main parts of an insect-pollinated flower.

### RESOURCES
**Main teaching activity:** Large pictures of a bee and a cross-section of a flower (see Preparation), Blu-Tack, photocopiable page 66 (one copy per pair).
**Group activities: 1.** Copies of the questions at the bottom of photocopiable page 66 (one copy per child). **2.** Details of this activity on a board or flip chart.

## PREPARATION

There are two characters in the play 'Buzz to Ground Control'. Practise reading the playscript (page 66) using two voices, or with another adult or a confident child reading one of the parts. Make an enlarged copy of the foxglove cross-section picture on page 66 and display it on the board or flip chart. Make an enlarged copy of one of the bee pictures on page 66, paste it onto card, cut it out and stick some Blu-Tack on the back.

## BACKGROUND

**Vocabulary**

worker bee, hive, stigma, stamen, pollen, nectar

Flowers are the organs of plant reproduction. The children will already know that flowers develop into fruits (see Lesson 1). This lesson and the next two deal with the basic structure of insect-pollinated flowers, introducing the vocabulary 'petals', 'stamen', 'stigma', 'ovary', 'pollen' and 'nectar'. The functions of these parts are alluded to in the first lesson and explained fully in the subsequent lessons. This lesson concentrates on introducing all of the terms except *ovary*.

Pollen is an essential element in the reproductive process of plants. It is also a protein-rich food for insects. Pollen is produced in the stamens. It has to be transferred to the stigma, which connects to the ovary where fertilised seeds develop. Once attached to the stigma, the pollen grain puts out a long tube that reaches into the ovary at the base of the flower. Nectar is a sugar-based solution produced in a small gland near the ovary. Petals and nectar play no direct part in the reproductive process: their function is to attract insects. A great variety of insects are attracted to flowers and play a role in the transfer of pollen. The honey bee is used as an example in this lesson because most children will be familiar with it. Of the 250 different varieties of British bee, fewer than 30 live in colonies or hives as the honey bee does.

The main part of the lesson is a 'radio play' about two worker bees. It uses the image of an 'air traffic controller' guiding a bee to a successful destination. Worker bees are female. They collect food, store honey and care for developing eggs. When they visit flowers, they collect pollen in tiny sacs on their rear legs. Pollen also clings to the hairs on their bodies, and as a result is transferred between the stamens and stigmas of different flowers. The other members of a hive are the queen bee and the drones. The queen bee lays all the eggs, which have been fertilised by a male drone. Nectar is an essential food supply for bees. Worker bees will regurgitate excess nectar in the hive, where in a few days it is converted into honey. It is important to stress that insects depend on flowers and flowers depend on insects.

## INTRODUCTION

Tell the children that during the next few lessons, they will learn how flowers develop into fruits and seeds. Then ask: *Have you ever eaten honey? Where does honey come from?* (Bees.) *Have you ever been stung by a bee?* Ask the children what they know about bees. Elicit as much accurate information from them as you can. Explain that the rest of this lesson is concerned with worker bees – the kind of honey bee that they are most likely to see.

## MAIN TEACHING ACTIVITY

Give each pair of children a copy of page 66. Read the introduction to the play and ask questions to make sure that the children understand the context. Explain that bees do not really communicate over a long distance: once a worker bee finds food, she goes back to the hive and gives detailed instructions about where to find it – by dancing! Read the play aloud while the children follow the text.

Now ask two confident children to re-read the parts. Show the children the cut-out 'worker bee' and ask a third child to move the bee to a suitable part of the flower picture as the story develops. Ask the other children to listen to the play and watch the bee. Tell them to put up their hand during the reading if they think the bee is in the wrong place on the picture. Warn the readers that you will interrupt them if you see a hand raised.

If the play progresses well, with only a few interruptions, move on to the group work. If there are lots of interruptions, help the children to find a sensible solution and go through the reading in the same way for a final time. If necessary, take over moving the bee to the appropriate places.

## GROUP ACTIVITIES

**1.** The children can work individually through the exercise at the bottom of page 66.
**2.** The children can draw a worker bee (as shown on page 66) and a large speech bubble, then write what Buzz might have said about her adventure to the other worker bees back at the hive.

## DIFFERENTIATION

**1.** Give less able children a copy of the flower cross-section picture from page 66 only. Read through the text of page 66 with them. Ask them to highlight on the text the names of flower parts and write these in the appropriate places on the diagram. They could draw a worker bee and colour in parts of the diagram. More able children could go on to tackle Group activity 2 if they finish the sheet quickly. **2.** Some more able children might enjoy writing a continuation of the play in which Buzz returns to the hive and meets GCB; others could use secondary sources of information to find out more about honey bees.

## ASSESSMENT

In the plenary session, draw the children's attention to the large foxglove picture and ask them to name each part of the flower as you point to it. Ask them why insects need flowers.

## PLENARY

Ask children who completed Group activity 2 to read out what Buzz said on her return to the hive. If time allows, listen to a performance of the 'continued play'. Display the children's work.

### OUTCOMES

● Can name the main parts of an insect-pollinated flower.
● Knows about the activities of a worker bee.

### LINKS

Lessons 8 and 10: looking closely at insect pollination.

# LESSON 8

## OBJECTIVES

● To observe the structure of an insect-pollinated flower.
● To recognise flowers that attract insects.
● To observe the role of insects in pollination.

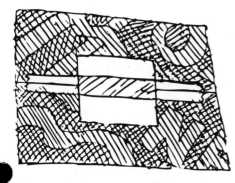

## RESOURCES

**Main teaching activity:** The foxglove picture from Lesson 7; scissors, card and clear sticky tape (see Preparation).
**Group activity:** Each child will need a clipboard, a pencil, a copy of photocopiable page 67 and a 'pollen poaching tool'; some spare pencils and 'pollen poaching tools' may be needed.

## PREPARATION

You will need to identify a safe area outside, but near to the classroom, where there are a number of insect-pollinated flowers for the children to study. If the location is not part of your school site, you will need to arrange additional adult supervision in accordance with your school or LEA policy.

The diagram above shows a 'pollen poaching tool'. Use a rectangle of thin scrap card about 10cm×5cm (such as part of a breakfast cereal box). Fold it and cut out a narrow rectangle along the fold, then stretch a piece of clear sticky tape across the aperture: you have made a sticky microscope slide. Make a few spare 'pollen poaching tools' and take them with you on the visit, in case some of the children drop or spoil their own.

Try the activity yourself. Don't put too much pressure on the flower when you remove the pollen, or you'll 'poach' more than the pollen. If possible, ask some parents, students or other adult volunteers to join you in the outdoor lesson. Make sure that you are following the safety procedures indicated in your school policy.

> ### Vocabulary
> pollen, stamens, pollination

## BACKGROUND

The purpose of this lesson is to consolidate the knowledge of flower parts introduced in Lesson 7. The children will be taken out of school to look for insects that are involved in pollinating flowers; to collect a sample of pollen; and to make a detailed drawing of an insect-pollinated flower. This is a very focused activity; the information the children collect will be used in Lesson 9.

## INTRODUCTION

Show the children the foxglove picture from Lesson 7. Use questions to recap on the names of the flower parts, what attracts insects to the flowers, and why the insects collect pollen and nectar.

## MAIN TEACHING ACTIVITY

Tell the children that they are going on a short outside visit, and that they are going to become 'pollen poachers'. Ask them what a poacher is. (A 'nature thief' might be an appropriate definition.) *How did Buzz the worker bee collect pollen in the previous lesson?* (She scraped the pollen into sacs on her back legs, and some stuck to the hairs on her body.) Demonstrate to the children how to make and use the 'pollen poaching tool', and let them make one each.

Show the children a copy of page 67. Tell them that they are going to:

1. Make a pollen poaching tool.
2. Walk together to a site where there are some insect-pollinated flowers.
3. With a partner, quietly watch one small area of flowers to see which insects visit them.
4. Individually, make a detailed drawing of a flower with petals, a stigma and stamens. It is important for the next lesson that both children in each pair draw a similar flower.
5. Finally, press the sticky surface of their 'pollen poaching tool' gently onto the stamens of the same flower as they have drawn – can they poach some pollen?

Give each child a copy of page 67, a clipboard and a pencil. They should attach the 'pollen poaching tool' to the clipboard sticky side up. Take them on the outdoor activity.

## GROUP ACTIVITY

Photocopiable page 67 will help to remind the children of the structure of the activity once they are outside the classroom. They should work in pairs as described above.

## DIFFERENTIATION

Try to provide extra adult support for the outdoor activity. With encouragement, children will produce excellent results. Many children will make very detailed drawings if they have enthusiastic support.

## ASSESSMENT

On returning to the classroom, sit the children in a circle. Ask them to describe the insects they saw visiting the flowers. *What parts of the flower did the insects visit? What do you think the insects were collecting?* Then ask: *Why do you think it is 'poaching' if we take pollen from flowers?* (Because the plants and insects need pollen and we don't!)

## PLENARY

Ask the children to look carefully at their 'pollen poaching tools'. Ask: *Who has poached a lot of pollen?* Ask a successful pair to describe what is on their pollen poaching tool. Finally, ask everyone to show their drawings. Carefully collect the drawings and the pollen poaching tools for the next lesson.

## OUTCOMES

- Have observed the structure of an insect-pollinated flower.
- Know some flowers that attract insects.
- Have observed the role of insects in the pollination process.

## LINKS

Lesson 9: the functions of the reproductive parts of a flower.

## LESSON 9

### OBJECTIVES

- To know that seeds develop in the ovary.
- To know the functions of pollen, the stamen and the stigma in fertilisation.
- To know the role of insects in the process of pollination.

### RESOURCES

**Main teaching activity:** A card with the word 'Ovary' on it, Blu-Tack, the pictures of a foxglove and a bee from Lesson 7, the children's drawings of flowers and 'pollen poaching tools' from Lesson 8.

**Group activities: 1.** Eight strips of card, each strip with one of the following sentences written on it: 'Pollen is made in the stamen of a flower'; 'Colourful petals attract insects to the flower'; 'The insect feeds on pollen and nectar'; 'Some pollen sticks to the body of the insect'; 'The insect carries the pollen.'; 'Pollen rubs off the insect's body onto the stigma.'; 'A tube grows from the stigma to the ovary.'; 'Fertile seeds grow in the ovary.' Blu-Tack, paper, writing materials. **2.** A well-organised collection of art materials: bright-coloured paper, junk materials, cardboard packaging, paints, paintbrushes, felt-tipped pens, glue and so on.

## PREPARATION

Look carefully at the children's drawings of flowers from Lesson 8. Make a note of particularly clear pictures of similar species of flower drawn by the children. Sit the class in a circle with the board or flip chart close behind you. Place the children's flower pictures and 'pollen poaching tools' in the middle of the circle.

*Vocabulary*

ovary, fertile, fertilisation, male, female

## BACKGROUND

Two forms of pollination by insect are described in this lesson:
**1. Self-pollination.** This is where pollen is transferred by an insect between the stamen and stigma of the same flower, or between flowers on the same plant.
**2. Cross-pollination.** This is where pollen is moved by an insect from the stamen of a flower on one plant to the stigma of a flower on another plant of the same species.

The Main teaching activity tries to build on the knowledge and experience of the children, using a visual method to explain pollination. However, some children may be puzzled by the nature of the process. They may ask difficult questions such as: *Can the pollen of buttercups be used by bean plants?* The answer is that this does not happen: the plant 'recognises' that the pollen has come from the wrong sort of plant. However, if the children have grown runner beans in a previous lesson, you could tell them: *If you grow a red-flowered runner bean close to a white-flowered runner bean, the seeds the plants produce may grow into plants whose flowers are not the same colour as those of the parent plant. This will show that pollen has been transported from one plant to the other, and the two strains of runner bean have 'crossbred'.*

The male and female parts of the flower are described in this lesson. The human reproductive organs are discussed in Unit 1, Lesson 10; parallels could be drawn between the mechanisms of sexual reproduction in plants and in animals.

## INTRODUCTION

Remind the children of their outdoor work in the previous lesson. Hold up a 'pollen poaching tool' and ask: *What did you collect on these sticky things in the last lesson?* (Pollen.) Pointing to the foxglove picture, ask: *On which part of the flower will the insect find the pollen?* (The stamen.) *What will the flower develop in to?* (A fruit with seeds.)

## MAIN TEACHING ACTIVITY

**1. The ovary.** Tell the children that they are going to find out what happens to a flower before it develops into a fruit. Encourage them to work out where on the flower the fruit is produced by asking questions based on their observation and knowledge. Name the part of the flower where the fruit develops as the 'ovary'. Blu-Tack the word 'ovary' to the foxglove picture.
**2. Self-pollination.** Using the foxglove picture, explain that before a fruit can develop, pollen has to move across from the stamen to the stigma. Restrict the context to a single plant. Explain that the stamen is the 'male' part of the flower and the stigma is the 'female' part. Establish through questioning that the pollen is transferred on the bodies of insects.
**3. The stigma.** Refer again to the foxglove picture. Explain that once the pollen is in contact with the stigma, it becomes attached to it. A tube develops from the stigma to the ovary. Draw this tube on the picture. The male reproductive cells in pollen grains will fuse with the female reproductive cells in the ovary – a process called 'fertilisation' – to produce fertile seeds. Write 'fertilisation' on the board or flip chart. At this point, the fruit begins to develop. The flower's purpose is complete and the petals, stigma and stamen will begin to shrivel up.

Revise and reinforce these ideas with quick-fire questions such as *What has to happen before the fruit can grow?* (Pollen has to be moved from the stamen to the stigma.)
**4. Cross-pollination.** Tell the children that there is another way that pollen can go from a stamen to a stigma. Find a pair of similar flowers drawn by two different children in the previous lesson. Ask them to stand up and hold their work on opposite sides of the class circle. Using one of the children's pollen poaching tools and the cut-out worker bee, talk through the reproductive process of the plant with the class. Use the sentences listed in Resources as your script. Holding the bee, 'carry' the pollen across the class circle from one flower to the other. Redirect the children's attention to the foxglove picture and remind them of the roles of the stigma and ovary. Stress that this kind of fertilisation can only take place between plants of the same species: a buttercup can't fertilise a rose.

Finally, select another pair of similar flowers drawn by different children. Repeat the process, with a third child reading the eight sentences while a fourth child carries the bee and pollen from one flower to another. Direct the attention of the class to the foxglove picture at the appropriate moment.

## GROUP ACTIVITIES

**1.** Display the eight sentences on strips of card in random order. Ask the children to discuss, in pairs, a sensible order for these sentences and to write them down in that order.
**2.** Ask the children to create a model or collage of an insect-pollinated flower.

### DIFFERENTIATION

**1.** Less able children could be given a copy of the sentences, each on a separate strip. They could sort the sentences into a sensible order, then paste them together.
**2.** When they have finished creating flowers, more able children could go on to Group activity 1 and then could mount their writing alongside their flower.

### ASSESSMENT

During the plenary session, ask: *Does the insect need the flower, or do the flowers need the insect?* (Both need each other.) *Explain your answer.*

### PLENARY

Look at and display the flowers created in Group activity 2. Ask their creators to name some of the flower parts. Discuss the various answers to Group activity 1. Use the sentence strips to make the possible versions clear to the children.

## OUTCOMES

- Know that fertilisation of a flower takes place when pollen is transferred to the stigma.
- Know that seeds develop in the ovary.
- Know that insects can pollinate flowers.
- Know that certain insects and certain flowers are mutually dependent.

## LINKS

Unit 2, Lesson 11: looking at wind pollination.

# LESSON 10

## OBJECTIVES

- To develop an understanding of life cycles.
- To know the life cycle of a butterfly.

## RESOURCES

**Main teaching activity:** The five sentences on card from Lesson 1; an A3 version or OHT of photocopiable page 68; a 'reader's letter' (see Preparation); four cards with the words 'adult', 'caterpillar' or 'larva', 'egg', and 'pupa', with Blu-Tack on the back of each card.
**Group activities: 1.** Photocopiable page 68 (one copy per child). **2.** Paper, writing materials.

## PREPARATION

Sit the children close to the board or flip chart. Attach the five sentences on strips of card from Lesson 1 to the board with Blu-Tack in random order. Make a large copy or OHT of the 'reader's letter' on page 56. Cover the final two paragraphs of the reply on the copy of page 68, so the children cannot read it.

## BACKGROUND

The focus of this lesson is the life cycle of a cabbage white butterfly. The life cycle of a parasitic insect, the ichneumon fly, is also discussed. Both insects have a similar pattern of development.
The cabbage white is one of the most common species of butterfly. There are two varieties: the large white and the small white. Females of both varieties can lay up to 200 eggs on brassica (cabbage) plants. They are thought to identify these plants by smell. The eggs hatch in about a

week. The larval or caterpillar stage of both species, which lasts about a month, can cause great damage to crops. The caterpillars are well-camouflaged against the green crop. They are not attacked by birds – probably because they taste bad.

The caterpillars go through several changes of skin (moults) in their rapid growth. They eat greedily in order to store enough food for their pupa or chrysalis stage. The pupa stage lasts two to three weeks, unless it is over-wintering. The adult butterfly that emerges feeds on pollen and nectar. It does not grow; its purpose is to mate and reproduce.

The ichneumon fly (pronounced *ick-new-mon*) is a parasite. It lays its eggs in the bodies of living caterpillars. The flies hatch and feed inside the caterpillar until they are ready to pupate and form yellow cocoons. The caterpillar dies at this stage. Organic gardeners attract ichneumon flies to the vicinity of their brassica crops by planting flowers nearby. Insecticides can destroy this beneficial predator, so exposing the crops to caterpillars.

## INTRODUCTION

Ask the children to help you put the sentences on the plant life cycle in the correct order. Rearrange them in a circular form on the board, and draw arrows between them to convey the idea of a cyclical pattern. Then ask the children: *What do we call this pattern?* (A life cycle.) Tell the children that they are going to learn about animal life cycles.

## MAIN TEACHING ACTIVITY

Tell the children that the 'reader's letter' (see page 56) was written to the editor of a gardening magazine. Display a copy of the letter and read it together, or read it out to the children. Ask questions about it to help the children understand why it was written. You may have to explain the term 'insecticide'.

Now display an enlarged version of the 'editor's reply' (page 68). Read through this with the children as far as the final two paragraphs (which you have covered up); save these for later. Ask questions to develop the children's understanding of the text, focusing on the life cycle of the

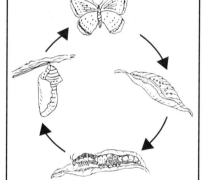

butterfly. The concept of 'pupation' may be strange to many children; it might be appropriate to re-read the paragraphs that focus on this stage.

Uncover the rest of the enlarged sheet and look at the pictures in the corners. In turn, hold up the cards with the words 'adult', 'caterpillar' or 'larva', 'egg' and 'pupa' and ask the children to help you place each under the appropriate picture. Draw arrows to indicate the life cycle (see diagram below).

Now read the final paragraphs of the editor's reply. Ask questions to help the children see that the life cycle of the ichneumon fly has similar stages to that of the butterfly.

Finally, draw the children's attention to the foolish behaviour of the gardener. *What do you think of the gardener? Was it sensible for him to spray the whole garden with insecticide? To grow so many cabbages? To pull them up and throw them in the dustbin?* This discussion will help children who complete Group activity 2.

## GROUP ACTIVITIES

**1.** Give out copies of page 68 and ask the children to work through it individually
**2.** Point out that the editor probably thought the gardener was quite stupid. Using the information on the sheet, the children can write a different reply that is far less polite. It could begin: *Dear Reader, I am amazed at how stupid you are...*

## DIFFERENTIATION

**1.** Less able children could cut out the pictures at the top of the sheet and arrange them in a life cycle pattern, then write a sentence under each one to explain what happens. **2.** Ask more able children to use secondary sources to find out more about the life cycle of the cabbage white butterfly: numbers of eggs laid, lifespan, similar butterflies and so on.

## ASSESSMENT

During the plenary session, ask the children to tell you: the four stages in the life cycle of a butterfly; the four stages in the life cycle of an ichneumon fly.

## PLENARY

Ask the children for some ideas to help the gardener protect next year's crop of cabbages. Ask children who have consulted secondary sources to share the information they have found.

## OUTCOMES
● Have an extended understanding of life cycles.
● Know the life cycle of a butterfly.

## LINKS
PSHE: how gardening involves responsible care for the environment.

> Dear Editor,
>   Please can you give me some advice? A few months ago, I planted about eighty cabbages in part of my garden. My family likes to eat fresh cabbage now and again. They grew well for a few weeks, then something started nibbling the leaves. I saw some tiny green caterpillars, so I sprayed the whole garden with insecticide to kill them.
>   Then we went on holiday for a few weeks. When we came back, there were no leaves left on the cabbage plants. I pulled up all the stalks that were left and threw them in the dustbin.
>   What did I do wrong?
>
> Yours sincerely,
>   A. Wally

# LESSON 11

## OBJECTIVES
● To know that some plants are pollinated by the wind.
● To know that the fruits from grasses play an important part in our diet.

## RESOURCES

**Main teaching activity:** The eight sentence strips from Lesson 9; a cornflakes box, the wrapper from a loaf of bread, empty processed food containers (one per pair of children); a flip chart or OHP, pens, an enlarged version of the table shown opposite; a few examples of wild or dried grasses, complete with flowers or seeds; if possible, some ears of wheat; a picture of sweetcorn (from a seed catalogue).

**Group activities: 1.** Photocopiable page 69 (one copy per child). **2.** Empty processed food containers, pencils, rulers, paper.

## PREPARATION
Prepare a copy of the table shown opposite on a flip chart or OHT.

## BACKGROUND
Many kinds of plant are pollinated by the wind. As insects play no part in this process, there is no need for the plant to develop petals or nectar in order to attract them. Wind-pollinated plants tend to have inconspicuous flowers; the children may not have realised that they have flowers at all.
For pollen to move from the stamen to the stigma, these organs need to be on the outside of the plant. The stigma will be unencumbered by petals and will often be 'feathery' in form, allowing the wind to pass through the structure. This increases the chance of the stigma catching passing pollen grains. The pollen of these plants is finer and lighter than that of insect-pollinated plants.
One large class of wind-pollinated plants is grasses. Children will be familiar with mown surfaces such as lawns and football pitches. The regular mowing nearly always prevents the grass from producing flowers and seeds. Grasses from hedgerows and field margins, which go through their life cycle undisturbed, are attractive examples of wind-pollinated plants. Some specially cultivated grasses play an important part in our diet: wheat, barley, oats, maize (corn or sweetcorn) and rye are common ingredients of processed foods such as bread and cereals.

**Vocabulary**
pollinated, cereal, wheat, maize, barley, oats, rye

## INTRODUCTION

Tell the children that they are going to learn about a group of plants that produce very important fruits and are not pollinated by insects. Ask: *What do I mean by 'pollinated by insects'?* (Insects transfer pollen from the stamen to the stigma.) Use the sentence strips from Lesson 9, placed in random order, to revise the process of insect pollination.

## MAIN TEACHING ACTIVITY

Ask: *How many of you have eaten some grass for breakfast?* Display a box of cornflakes and explain that breakfast cereals are made from the fruits of some grass plants. Establish that cornflakes are made from the fruit of the maize plant: 'sweetcorn' or 'corn on the cob'. Show the children a picture of 'sweetcorn' (from a seed catalogue). Now show them the wrapper from a loaf of bread. Establish that bread is made from the fruits of a grass (known as wheat) that have been ground into flour. Elicit or state the generic name for grass plants like wheat and maize: 'cereal'.

Give out a set of empty processed food containers so that each pair of children has one. Display the following table on a flip chart or OHT:

| Processed food | Wheat or flour | Maize (corn) | Barley | Oats | Rye |
| --- | --- | --- | --- | --- | --- |
| | | | | | |
| | | | | | |
| | | | | | |

Explain that several kinds of cereal are used in processed foods: wheat (or flour), maize (corn), barley, oats, and rye. Ask the children to look at the ingredients used in the processed food, and to raise their hands if they can see any cereals mentioned. Explain that, for example, 'corn syrup' is made from maize. Ask a few children to read out their cereal ingredients, and mark the chart. Ask some questions based on the data to check that the children understand the tabular form.

Now display the enlarged version of page 69 and look at the table. Remind the children of their work on insect-pollinated plants. *Does the insect-pollinated plant have flowers?* Write 'Yes' in the appropriate cell; with the children's help, complete each cell in the 'Insect-pollinated flower' column. Now ask the children what they think should be put in each cell in the 'Grasses and cereals' column. Write in the correct answers: grasses and cereals have flowers, pollen, a stigma, stamen and ovary, and fruits; but the plants do not have petals or scent, nor do they welcome insects. Explain that if farmers see lots of insects on a cereal crop, they often kill them with an insecticide spray to stop them damaging the crop.

Explain that we can only eat the fruits of grasses if the seeds have been fertilised, which means that the pollen has to travel from the stamen of one plant to the stigma of another. Pointing to the picture at the top of the enlarged sheet, ask: *How does pollen get moved from the stamen of one plant to the stigma of another?* Elicit the answer: 'By the wind.' Wave the wild or dried grasses dramatically, and remind the children how these are blown by the wind and the pollen is spread. Point to the flowers on the grasses. *Why are these light and feathery?* (To let the wind through.) *Why are there no petals?* (They don't need to attract insects.)

Finally, tell the children that many other plants are wind-pollinated. The stinging nettle and the birch tree are two examples that they may be familiar with.

## GROUP ACTIVITIES

**1.** Give the children a copy each of page 69 and ask them to complete it individually.
**2.** Ask pairs to read the ingredients listed on some processed food containers and look for the cereals. They should draw up a table similar to that shown above.

## DIFFERENTIATION

**1.** Able children who finish this activity quickly could use secondary sources to find out about other wind-pollinated plants, and how cereals are grown and harvested. **2.** Children who complete this activity could try to make detailed, labelled drawings of any wild grasses or cereals used as visual aids in the lesson.

## ASSESSMENT

At the end of the group work, ask the children to explain two different ways that plants can be pollinated, and why some breakfast foods are called 'cereals'.

## PLENARY

Ask the children what they think the answer to the last question on the sheet is: *What do you think causes hay fever?* (It is caused by wind-blown pollen from grasses.) Ask any children who used secondary sources to tell the class about other wind-pollinated plants and how cereals are grown and harvested.

## OUTCOMES

- Know that some plants are pollinated by the wind.
- Know that the fruits of some grasses (called 'cereals') play an important part in our diet.
- Can represent simple information in a tabular form.

## LINKS

Unit 1, Lessons 1, 2 and 3: looking at foods and cereals.

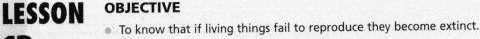

# LESSON 12

## OBJECTIVE

- To know that if living things fail to reproduce they become extinct.

## RESOURCES

**Main teaching activity:** Two OHTs or A3 copies of photocopiable page 70, pens for OHTs, pictures (from wildlife identification books) of a song thrush, sparrow hawk, magpie, crow, and squirrel, three large dice.
**Group activities: 1.** Paper, drawing and writing materials.
**2.** Paper, writing materials.

## PREPARATION

Organise two OHTs or A3 versions of page 70. On one copy, cover up the sentences in italics in the 'Risks' column.

## BACKGROUND

The song thrush is an indigenous British bird whose population is in steep decline. The four main reasons are:
**1. Loss of habitat.** The bird nests mainly in hedges and thickets. Increased farm mechanisation has meant an expansion in field sizes and loss of hedgerows and trees.
**2. Increased predation.** The numbers of domestic cats have increased in the UK in recent decades. The sparrow hawk too has recovered from its post-War decline (an effect of DDT insecticide poisoning). Populations of the predators of the infant bird (magpies, crows and squirrels) seem well-adapted to current environmental conditions.
**3. Reduced food supply.** The song thrush is an omnivore. Its diet mainly consists of worms, snails, insects and berries. Surveys show that the young bird is vulnerable to starvation when it leaves its nest. Often this period (early summer) is when the ground is hard. Worms are difficult to locate and seasonal berries are unavailable. It is thought that modern farming methods, insecticides and increased field drainage have reduced the supply of snails at this critical time in the bird's life.
**4. Tidier gardens.** It has never been easier to tidy the part of the environment that we manage. Tools to trim hedges, mow lawns and strim grass are widely used. There are few berries in the hedgerows, and no home in the garden for the insects that are an essential part of the bird's food chain.

Ways to encourage the song thrush include the following: plant hedges or thickets as nesting sites; allow hedge plants to develop berries for winter thrush food; avoid using insecticides and slug pellets – the thrush is a natural 'pest control'; use organic methods of cultivation that encourage worms and other small animals; allow parts of the environment to be naturally untidy.

## INTRODUCTION

Ask the children to define 'an endangered species'. Ask them to tell you about some endangered species they know about and why these species are in danger of extinction. Expect some exotic answers: the tiger, the blue whale and so on.

**Vocabulary**

extinction, habitat, predators, sparrow hawk, crow, magpie, brood, reproduce

## MAIN TEACHING ACTIVITY

Tell the children that they are going to look at the life cycle of the song thrush, an endangered British bird. Show them a picture of a song thrush. Display the first column of the enlarged 'Song thrush survival game'. Ask the children questions to illuminate the facts and terms in this column.

Now say that you are going to play a game with two teams: you versus the class. Uncover the whole game sheet (but keep the risks in italics covered). Explain the dangers faced by a song thrush at different stages of its life cycle. Show the children pictures of the predators of the bird: magpie, crow, sparrow hawk. Explain that life for all creatures is a lottery, and that a song thrush will often try to incubate two broods of three or four eggs in a year so that some will survive.

Explain the rules of the game (see page 70): the winning team is the one with the most surviving birds at the end. After each throw, teams can use the blank columns to record the progress of the game with symbols. For example, if the teacher throws a 1 on their first turn, the eggs from their first brood are all lost; if the children throw a 4, their first brood of eggs survive and move on to the chick stage; the teacher now throws for their second brood.

| Life cycle stages | Rules – How many dice can you throw? | Risks, predators, loss of habitat, food supplies | First teacher brood | Second teacher brood | First children brood | Second children brood |
|---|---|---|---|---|---|---|
| **Eggs in the nest** Mother builds nest, often about 2m from ground in hedges etc. Eggs incubated for 13 days until they hatch. | *Throw one dice. Your 3 eggs will hatch if you avoid the risks.* | 1 Nest raided by magpies, crows or squirrels. All die. | ⊠⊠⊠ | | | |
| | | *2 Increase in sparrow hawks. Mother ambushed on nest. All die.* | | | | |
| | | *3 Hedges dug up. Nest destroyed. All die.* | | | | |
| | | 4 | | | ☺☺☺ | |
| | | 5 | | | | |
| | | 6 | | | | |

When the first game has finished, play again, this time revealing and discussing the new risks (those in italics). They are mostly caused by human activity. Ask children to explain why few or no birds survived the second game. *What will happen to the song thrush if no young birds survive to become adults?* Emphasise the answer: *They will become extinct because they cannot reproduce.*

Ask the children for suggestions to reduce the risk to the song thrush. List their ideas on the board or flip chart for use in Group activity 1.

## GROUP ACTIVITIES

**1.** The children can make a poster to show other children in the school why the song thrush may become extinct.
**2.** They can make a scroll or charter to explain what could be done to help the song thrush.

## DIFFERENTIATION

**1 and 2.** Some children could use secondary sources to find out more about other British birds that may be endangered. The robin's population is also believed to be in steep decline.

## ASSESSMENT

At the end of the game, ask the whole class: *What happens to a species if it cannot reproduce itself?*

## PLENARY

Look at the results of the Group activities. Listen to any additional information on other birds.

## OUTCOMES

● Know that if living things fail to reproduce they become extinct.
● Know that living things in our immediate environment are facing extinction through environmental change.
● Know that we can all do something to promote conservation.

## LINKS

PSHE: responsibility towards the environment.

# LESSON 14

| | |
|---|---|
| **Objectives** | ● To compare the life cycles of different animals.<br>● To develop knowledge of some other life cycles. |
| **Resources** | The sentence strips and flip chart sheet 'Life cycle of a cat' from Lesson 13; a flip chart or board with a table as shown below, writing materials, paper, rulers, secondary sources of information on various animal life cycles (books, CD-ROMs etc). |
| **Main activity** | Use the sentence strips and the appropriate flip chart sheet from Lesson 13 to revise the life cycle of a cat. Show the children the following on a flip chart or board: |

| Similarities between the life cycles of a cat and a thrush | Differences between the life cycles of a cat and a thrush |
|---|---|
| Male and female adults need to mate to produce offspring. | The thrush chick grows in an egg in a nest. The baby kitten grows inside the mother. |

| | |
|---|---|
| | Discuss the similarities and differences between the life cycles of a cat and a song thrush, and list the suggestions on the table. The differences will be more obvious than the similarities, and will demand more space. Similarities may include: 'The chick in the egg and the kitten inside the mother are both kept warm.', 'The chick and the kitten both need feeding and protection by the adults.'<br>Show the children the secondary sources of information on other animal life cycles, and discuss the life cycle of one other creature (such as a frog). Write a set of sentences on the board or flip chart to describe this life cycle. Start with: 'Adult male and female frog mate.'<br>Ask the children to make a table to show the similarities and differences between the life cycles of the song thrush and the butterfly, or the cat and the butterfly. They can then use the secondary sources to investigate the life cycle of another animal, and write a set of sentences to describe that life cycle. |
| **Differentiation** | Provide less able children with a set of sentences that describe similarities and differences between two life cycles, and ask the children to sort them appropriately. Direct each child to appropriate secondary materials that match his or her ability. |
| **Assessment** | At the end of the lesson, ask the children to describe the similarities between the life cycles of the song thrush and the butterfly, or the cat and the butterfly. |
| **Plenary** | Listen to the children's descriptions of other life cycles. |
| **Outcomes** | ● Know the similarities and differences between some animal life cycles.<br>● Find out about some other animal life cycles. |

## ASSESSMENT

# LESSON 15

### OBJECTIVES
● To assess the children's knowledge of the life cycle of plants.
● To assess the children's knowledge of some animal life cycles.

### RESOURCES
The sentence strips from Lesson 13, photocopiable pages 72 and 73, pencils.

## PREPARATION

Make one copy per child of each assessment sheet.

## INTRODUCTION

Display the sentence strips from Lesson 13 in random order, and ask the children to rearrange them beneath the sentence 'Male and female cat mate' on the board or flip chart.

## ASSESSMENT ACTIVITY 1

Give out copies of photocopiable page 72 and let the children work through it individually.

### Answers

1b. Stamen; 1c. Petal; 1d. Ovary; 1e. The plant needs to be pollinated for fruits and seeds to be produced, and the insects help to do this; 2. Petals and scent (or nectar); 3a: Ash: wind-blown; 3b. Holly: bird-sown; 3c. Oak: heavy hoarded; 4. To have better access to moisture and light; 5. Most seeds may be eaten or fail to germinate because of lack of light, moisture, warmth or soil.

### Looking for levels

All the children should be able to answer questions 1, 2 and 3. Most children will complete the remainder of the sheet.

## ASSESSMENT ACTIVITY 2

Give out copies of photocopiable page 73 and let the children work through it individually.

### Answers

1. Male and female butterflies mate; The female lays eggs on a cabbage leaf; The eggs hatch into caterpillars or larvae; The caterpillar pupates into a chrysalis; A butterfly emerges from the chrysalis.
2. The male and female thrush mate; The female lays eggs in an nest; The eggs are incubated; Chicks hatch from the eggs; Chicks live in the nest, fed by the adults, until they are ready to fly; The young thrushes leave the nest; Male and female thrushes mate.
3a. The removal of hedges; 3b. The use of pellets or pesticides to kill slugs and snails and/or the draining of fields, leaving no moist ground for slugs and snails; 3c. There is less insect food for the song thrush; 3d. There are more predators of the song thrush.
4. Ichneumon flies and song thrushes eat garden pests, so that people can grow crops organically without using pesticides.

### Looking for levels

This sheet is more demanding than page 72. All the children should be able to answer questions 1 and 2. The most able children should provide cogent answers to questions 3 and 4.

## PLENARY

Discuss the answers to both sheets. Page 72 could be marked with the children at the end of the session. A discussion about the range of acceptable answers to the questions on both sheets will be informative for the teacher and the children.

# What plants do we eat?

1. A gardener listed all the seeds that were needed to grow plants in the garden. When the plants have grown, at least one part of each plant can be eaten.

   Next to each plant, write down the name of the part that we eat. If you are not sure of the answer, look for a picture of the plant in a seed catalogue.

| Plant | Part eaten | Plant | Part eaten |
|---|---|---|---|
| Lettuce | | Melon | |
| Potato | | Sweetcorn | |
| Celery | | Turnip | |
| Tomato | | Runner or French bean | |
| Cauliflower | | Broccoli | |
| Cabbage | | Brussels sprout | |
| Carrot | | Parsnip | |
| Beetroot | | Courgette | |
| Cucumber | | Radish | |
| Leek | | Onion | |

2. Look carefully in the seed catalogue for the names of plants you don't think you have eaten, but could eat. List three of these plants and the parts that you think you would eat.

| Plants I don't think I've eaten | Parts of the plant that are eaten |
|---|---|
| | |
| | |
| | |

3. A healthy diet contains a mixture of foods.
   Look at the plants listed in question 1, and any others you have seen in the seed catalogue. Now choose your favourite food plants to fill these spaces.

| Part of the plant I eat | Favourite plant |
|---|---|
| Root | |
| Stem | |
| Flower | |
| Fruit | |
| Seed | |

Name _____

# Seeds

| Tree | Fruit or seed |
|---|---|
| Oak | Has an acorn, often found in a cup. |
| Sycamore | Has double-winged keys. |
| Holly | The red fruits are near the stalk of a prickly leaf. |
| Rowan | Red fruits surrounded by feathery leaves. |
| Ash | Has long, narrow, wing-shaped keys. |
| Horse chestnut | A shiny, heavy 'conker' in a prickly shell. |

1. Look at how the fruits and seeds of each tree are described in the table above. Find the picture below that fits each description and write the name of the tree below it.

2. Think about the three ways that each seed could be dispersed: heavy hoarded, bird-sown or wind-blown. Below each seed picture, write how the seed would be dispersed.

3. Draw a cartoon creature beside each seed: a squirrel or badger next to the heavy hoarded seeds, a blackbird or song thrush next to the bird-sown seed and mice next to the wind-blown seeds.

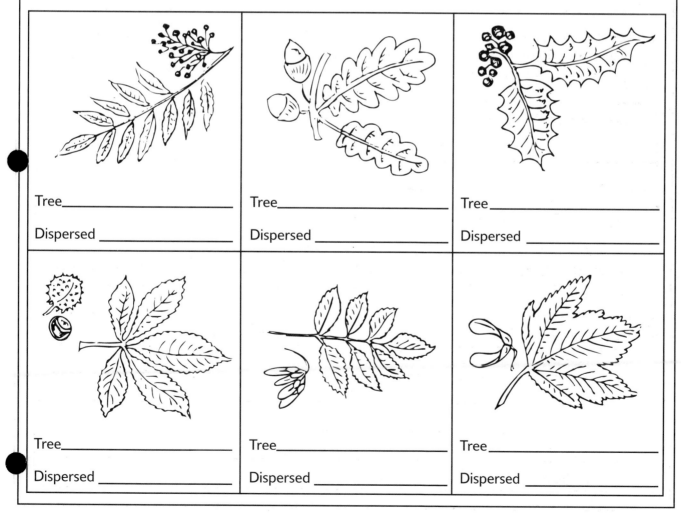

Tree_____

Dispersed _____

Tree_____

Dispersed _____

Tree_____

Dispersed _____

Tree_____

Dispersed _____

Tree_____

Dispersed _____

Tree_____

Dispersed _____

# Buzz's adventure

Read this story with your partner, one of you reading the part of Buzz and the other the part of GCB.

Buzz, a young worker bee, is on her first ever flight from the beehive. Buzz knows what pollen is, but not where to find it. GCB is another worker bee. She is directing other bees outside the hive to their destination by radio. Of course this does not happen, but use your imagination!

**Buzz** Buzz to Ground Control for Bees. Over! Buzz to Ground Control for Bees. Over!

**GCB** I hear you, Buzz. Please call me 'GCB'. Over.

**Buzz** Thanks for listening, GCB. I've a small problem. Over.

**GCB** What's the problem, Buzz? Over.

**Buzz** I'm sorry, but this is the first time I've flown out of the hive. The other bees in the hive showed me which way to go. *(Pause.)* I'm meant to be looking for flowers, but I don't know what flowers look like. Over.

**GCB** Oh, Buzz! Flowers are easy to spot. Look down into the fields. Flowers try to attract insects like us. Look for spots of bright colour near the ground. Over.

**Buzz** I can see lots of bright purple spots on the edge of the field below me. I'm flying down to investigate. Over.

**GCB** If the purple things are flowers, Buzz, they'll probably have a sweet scent as you get close to them. Over. *(There is a short pause as Buzz flies closer to the flower.)*

**Buzz** I'm hovering over the purple thing now, GCB. There is a sweet scent. It must be a flower! Where will I find the pollen I'm looking for? Is it on the purple bits? Over.

**GCB** No, the purple bits are the petals. They're just to attract you and other insects to the flower – and it's worked! Over.

**Buzz** Where is the pollen then? Over.

**GCB** If you look carefully, you will see some small stick-like things in the centre of the flower. There is often one stalk in the centre that is very different from the others. It's called the stigma. Can you see it? Over.

**Buzz** Yes, I'm going down to the stigma now. *(Pause.)* I'm looking at the stigma now, but there's no pollen on it. *(Pause.)* Where is the pollen? Over.

**GCB** You won't find much pollen on the stigma. Pollen is produced in the other stalks inside the flower. They're called stamens. Take a look at the stamens now. Look closely and tell me what you see. Over.

**Buzz** *(Pause.)* Oh yes! The stamens have got loads of pollen on them. There are some little sacs at the end of the stamens that are bursting with the stuff. I'll get to work straight away. Over.

**GCB** Start filling the pouches on your back legs, Buzz. Then I'll tell you where to find a real treat. Over.

**Buzz** Hey GCB, this is good fun! The pollen is sticking to all the hairs on my body, and the sacs on my legs are quite full. I will need to visit a few more flowers to fill them, though. *(Pause.)* Can I have my treat now? Over.

**GCB** Well done, Buzz. If you want your treat, look right inside the flower. Look into the space between the stamens and the stigma. Push between them and tell me what you find deep inside the flower. Over.

**Buzz** Grunt! Grunt! *(She pushes down between some stamens and the stigma.)* All the pollen is brushing off my body. *(Pause.)* Hey, there's a lovely sugary liquid in here. I know what this is, I've tasted it in the hive. It's nectar! Over.

**GCB** You're right! It's nectar. Drink as much as you possibly can. When you get back to the hive, you can regurgitate some nectar and other workers can turn it into honey!

**Buzz** Glug... glug... glug... Hey GCB, I'm full to the brim! I'm going to fly back to the hive now. Thanks for your help. Over.

**GCB** No problem, Buzz. Over and out!

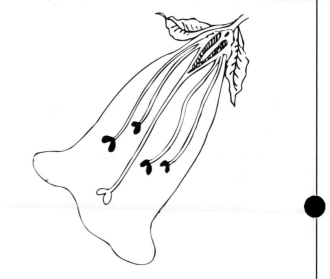

1. Can you work out the names of the parts of the flower that Buzz visited? Label the diagram with the names *petal, stigma* and *stamen*.
2. Where on the flower did Buzz discover pollen and nectar? Label those parts.

Answer these questions using full sentences.
3. How did Buzz know the correct direction to fly from the hive?
4. What are the two things that might attract an insect to a flower?
5. Why do bees collect pollen and take it back to their hive?
6. Where on the bee's body does the pollen go?
7. What is honey made from?

Name

 # A pollen poaching visit

Clip your 'pollen poaching tool' here. Make sure the sticky side faces upwards!

1. With a partner, look at the flowers that you think will attract insects. Watch carefully and quietly for a few minutes.
(a) What insects visited the flowers?

(b) What did the insects do?

2. With your partner, choose two similar flowers. Each draw a detailed picture of your flower in the space opposite.

3. When you have made a good drawing of your flower, use your pollen poaching tool to get some pollen from it. Be gentle – don't damage the flower!

# Growing cabbages

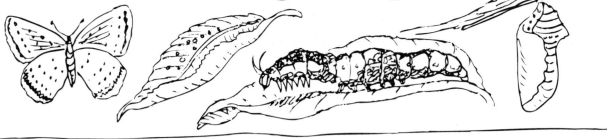

Dear Reader,

Thanks for telling us your problem. We are glad you are growing your own fresh food, but we think you have made a few mistakes.

Firstly, we think you are growing far too many cabbages. All those cabbages will be ready to eat at the same time. You'll need a big family to eat eighty!

The tiny green caterpillars you saw were probably from the Cabbage White butterfly. The female butterfly was attracted to your cabbages by their smell. If you had planted fewer cabbages and planted onions or garlic alongside them, the female might not have smelled your plants.

When the male and female butterflies mate, the female usually lays her cone-shaped yellow eggs underneath the cabbage leaves. After a short time, the eggs hatch out and tiny caterpillars begin to feed on the cabbage leaves. They grow quite quickly and spend most of the time underneath the cabbage leaves, where enemies can't find them and your spray won't reach them.

While you were on holiday, the caterpillars ate your cabbages and grew bigger, shedding their skin several times until they were ready to pupate. Then they crawled away to a safe, cool, dry place. At this stage, they fasten themselves to a stalk with a silken thread; after a few days, the shrivelled dry skin of the caterpillar drops off, leaving the pupa or chrysalis. Inside this dry silky shell, the butterfly develops. In two or three weeks, an adult butterfly emerges. It will fly off to feed on pollen and nectar.

When you sprayed your garden with insecticide, you probably missed the caterpillars but killed one of their deadly enemies. The ichneumon fly lays eggs in the bodies of caterpillars. Each egg hatches into a tiny larva that eats the caterpillar slowly from the inside. As the larva pupates, the caterpillar dies. If you grow flowers near your cabbages, you will encourage more ichneumon flies in that part of your garden and they will deal with the caterpillars.

It was sad that you pulled your damaged cabbages up. If you had left them in the ground, many would have grown new leaves. – *The Editor*

On a separate piece of paper, write sentences to answer these questions.

1. Which butterfly lays the eggs: the male or the female?
2. How does the butterfly find the cabbage plants?
3. What do the butterfly's eggs hatch into?
4. What happens to the caterpillar's skin as it grows bigger?
5. What does the caterpillar eventually change into?
6. What comes out of the chrysalis?
7. What do butterflies feed on?
8. Write down three sensible things the gardener could do next year to make sure the cabbages are not so badly damaged.
9. Copy or cut out the drawings on this sheet and arrange them in a life cycle pattern. Stick them down on another piece of paper.

Name _____

# Pollination

1. Complete this table by writing 'Yes' or 'No' in each cell.

| Does the plant have... | Insect-pollinated flower | Grasses and cereals |
| --- | --- | --- |
| flowers | | |
| pollen | | |
| stigma | | |
| stamen | | |
| ovary | | |
| fruit | | |
| petals | | |
| scent | | |
| Does the plant welcome insects? | | |

Answer these questions in sentences.

2. How does the pollen from the stamen of one grass plant travel to the stigma of another?

3. Why does an insect-pollinated plant need petals and scent?

4. Why don't cereals and grasses need petals or scent?

5. If a farmer saw lots of insects on a cereal crop, why might he or she use an insecticide?

6. Why are the stigmas on grasses and cereals often a feathery pattern on the tallest part of the flower?

7. Think about the food that some insects get from insect-pollinated plants. As well as pollen, can you think of something else that will not be found in grasses and cereals? (Clue: it is the main ingredient of honey.)

8. Some people suffer from 'hay fever'. It makes them sneeze and their eyes water. What do you think causes hay fever? (Clue: a hay field is full of flowering grasses.)

UNIT 2 ANIMALS & PLANTS

**100 SCIENCE LESSONS** ● **YEAR 5 / UNIT 2**

69

Name

# Song thrush survival game

| Life cycle stages | Rules – How many dice can you throw? | Risks, predators, loss of habitat, food supplies | First teacher brood | Second teacher brood | First children brood | Second children brood |
|---|---|---|---|---|---|---|
| **Eggs in the nest** Mother builds nest, often about 2m from ground in hedges etc. Eggs incubated for 13 days until they hatch. | *Throw one dice. Your 3 eggs will hatch if you avoid the risks.* | 1 Nest raided by magpies, crows or squirrels. All die. | | | | |
| | | 2 *Increase in sparrow hawks. Mother ambushed on nest. All die.* | | | | |
| | | 3 *Hedges dug up. Nest destroyed. All die.* | | | | |
| | | 4 | | | | |
| | | 5 | | | | |
| | | 6 | | | | |
| **Chick in nest** Lives in nest for 4 weeks after hatching. Both parents feed it worms and insects. | If you survived the egg stage, you have 3 tiny, blind chicks. *Throw one dice.* All chicks will live if you avoid the risks. | 1 Very cold and wet weather. Chicks freeze. All die. | | | | |
| | | 2 *All fields sprayed by insecticide. No insect food. All die.* | | | | |
| | | 3 | | | | |
| | | 4 | | | | |
| | | 5 | | | | |
| | | 6 | | | | |
| **Young bird** 4–12 weeks. Its summer diet is snails and insects. In autumn there will be berries too. | *Throw one dice for each surviving chick.* Any chick that avoids a risk will survive. | 1 Hot summer, no snails or worms to eat. Bird dies. | | | | |
| | | 2 Ambushed by predator: kestrel or sparrow hawk. Bird dies. | | | | |
| | | 3 *Increase in cat population. Bird caught and dies.* | | | | |
| | | 4 *Farmers use slug pellets and kill the snails. Bird starves and dies.* | | | | |
| | | 5 *Farmers kill weeds. Weeds feed insects. No insect food. Bird dies.* | | | | |
| | | 6 | | | | |
| **Adult** Survives winter. Finds mate. Looks for nesting habitat. | *Throw one dice for each surviving young bird.* If it survives it can find a mate. | 1 Very cold winter, can't find enough food. Bird dies. | | | | |
| | | 2 *Hedges cut, no winter berry food. Bird dies.* | | | | |
| | | 3 *Gardens too tidy. No insects or snails. Bird dies.* | | | | |
| | | 4 | | | | |
| | | 5 | | | | |
| | | 6 | | | | |

Each team takes it in turns to throw the dice. Each turn takes you to the next stage in the life cycle.
If you avoid the risks, you survive.
Start your second brood when your first brood die, or survive to become adults.
You only have two broods. There are three eggs in each brood.

**The team that has the most survivors wins.**

# The life cycle of a cat

1. These sentences tell you about the life cycle of a cat. Write them in the correct order.

*The kitten develops into a cat.*
*The embryo develops into a kitten inside the mother.*
*The kitten feeds on its mother's milk.*
*The kitten is born.*
*An egg is fertilised and develops into an embryo inside the mother.*
*The kitten feeds independently.*

The first sentence is written for you:

Male and female cat mate.

_____

_____

_____

_____

_____

Here is a gestation table.

| Animal | Days |
|--------|------|
| Cat | 65 |
| Human | 280 |
| Lion | 105 |
| Fox | 55 |
| Giraffe | 435 |
| Gorilla | 260 |
| Camel | 365 |
| Rabbit | 28 |
| Guinea pig | 63 |
| Cow | 280 |

The time of gestation is the number of days between the fertilisation of the egg and the live birth. 'Pregnancy' has a similar meaning to 'gestation'.

2. How many days does it take for a fox to grow inside its mother?

_____

3. Which animal is inside its mother for the same number of days as a human?

_____

4. Which of these animals is pregnant for the longest time?

_____

5. Which animal will give birth the shortest number of days from fertilisation?

_____

# Life cycles

1a. Look at this picture of a flower cut in half. Write these names of flower parts in the correct places: **petal**, **stamen**, **stigma**, **ovary**.

1b. In which of these four parts of the flower is pollen produced?

_____

1c. Which part attracts insects to the flower?

_____

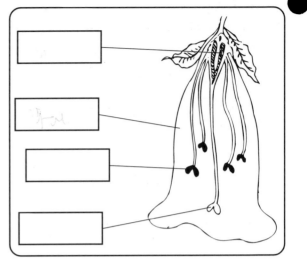

1d. In which part of the flower is a seed produced? _____

1e. Why do these flowers need to attract insects? _____

_____

2. An insect-pollinated flower has two things that a wind-pollinated flower does not need. What are they?

_____

3. The seeds of trees are dispersed in three main ways: heavy hoarded (moved by animals), bird-sown or wind-blown.

Look at these pictures of the fruits and seeds of trees. How is each tree's seed dispersed?

( Ash ) _____

( Holly ) _____

( Oak ) _____

4. Why do plants need to disperse their seeds?

_____

5. Why do many types of plant produce a great number of seeds?

_____

_____

# Life cycles

1. Here are some sentences about the life cycle of the cabbage white butterfly. Can you rearrange them in a more sensible order? The first sentence has been written for you.

| A butterfly emerges from the chrysalis. | *Male and female butterflies mate.* |
|---|---|
| The eggs hatch into caterpillars or larvae. | |
| Male and female butterflies mate. | |
| The caterpillar pupates into a chrysalis. | |
| The female lays eggs on a cabbage leaf. | |

2. Describe the life cycle of a song thrush. The first sentence has been written for you. Here are a few words that might help you: **egg**, **chick**, **hatch**, **food**.

*The male and female thrush mate.*

3. Human beings have changed the environment. There is a danger that these changes may make many creatures extinct.
Think about the song thrush: what it eats, its enemies and where it lives. Then complete this table.

| | The problem for the song thrush | What's causing the problem |
|---|---|---|
| a | There are fewer places for the thrush to make its nest. | |
| b | There are not enough slugs and snails around to feed it. | |
| c | | Farmers are using insecticides to kill insects on the crops they grow. |
| d | | Magpies, crows and squirrels seem to do well in the new environment. |

4. Why do some people believe that it is important to encourage ichneumon flies and song thrushes into fields and gardens?

# Water and the environment

## ORGANISATION (11 LESSONS)

| | OBJECTIVES | MAIN ACTIVITY | GROUP ACTIVITIES | PLENARY | OUTCOMES |
|---|---|---|---|---|---|
| **LESSON 1** | ● To know that water circulates through the environment. | Discuss the water cycle and how water is distributed on the Earth's surface. | Order sentences describing stages in the water cycle. Draw a pictorial graph to show the distribution of water on the Earth's surface. | Discuss the graphs. Consider the proportion of fresh water available to humanity. | ● Can describe the path of water in the water cycle and the changes that take place. |
| **LESSON 2** | ● To recognise things in our homes that create or remove water vapour. ● To know that water vapour is invisible but surrounds us. | List things in our homes that produce or remove water vapour. Use tables to classify and present this information. | | Discuss why excess water is extracted from our homes. | ● Know where water vapour is produced in our homes. |
| **LESSON 3** | ● To devise an experiment to show how wet materials can be dried efficiently. | A structured class experiment to test predictions about what factors affect the speed of drying. | | Discuss how some products are deliberately kept moist. | ● Know what conditions encourage water to become vapour. ● Know what conditions encourage wet things to dry. |
| **LESSON 4** | ● To know that the amount of water in a habitat varies. | Consider how to use rainwater over a year to prevent a garden pond drying out. | Answer questions on the pond problem. Design a school wildlife pond. | Children report on their wildlife pond designs. Discuss the effectiveness of these. | ● Can describe how the amount of water in a habitat varies. ● Can explain the purpose of reservoirs and why they are needed. |
| **LESSON 5** | ● To understand the catastrophic effects of floods and drought. | Use secondary sources to find out about and describe the effects of floods and droughts, and how floods can be prevented. | | Children share their reports and findings. | ● Understand some of the reasons for and effects of major floods and droughts. |
| **LESSON 6** | ● To know that we use a great deal of water and that water must be conserved. | Consider how much water is used in various activities and products in the home. Discuss ways of saving water. | Complete a sheet of tips for water saving. Make a poster to present ideas for saving water. | Discuss wasteful water-using practices. Discuss the effectiveness of the children's posters. | ● Recognise some activities that require a great amount of water. ● Can explain the need for water conservation. ● Can describe simple ways in which we can conserve water. |
| **LESSON 7** | ● To know that water can be polluted by waste from human activities. | Look at the biological indicators of how polluted an area of water is. | Fill in a table on water pollution indicators. Answer questions on biological indicators of water pollution. | Consider ways to prevent water pollution. Plan the equipment needed to check water pollution in local fresh water. | ● Can identify sources of water pollution. ● Know how water pollution can be assessed using biological indicators. ● Know some of the effects of water pollution. ● Know some ways to reduce water pollution. |
| **LESSON 8** | ● To use pollution indicators to monitor a local pond or stream. | Use observation and knowledge of biological pollution indicators to assess the health of a pond or stream. | | The children assess the water quality and explain their decision. | ● Can assess water quality in the local environment. |

## ORGANISATION (11 LESSONS)

| | OBJECTIVES | MAIN ACTIVITY | GROUP ACTIVITIES | PLENARY | OUTCOMES |
|---|---|---|---|---|---|
| LESSON 9 | ● To recognise some activities that cause air pollution. ● To recognise some effects on the environment of air pollution. ● To know some ways in which air pollution can be reduced. | Use role-play to consider the chain of events that cause acid rain and global warming. Consider ways of reducing air pollution. | Make a comic strip to explain the effects of air pollution. Make a poster encouraging people to reduce air pollution. | Discuss the children's ideas for ways to reduce air pollution. Could any of these be implemented in the classroom? | ● Recognise some activities that cause air pollution. ● Can describe some effects of air pollution on the environment. ● Can describe some ways in which air pollution can be reduced. |
| LESSON 10 | ● To know that human activities are affecting fish stocks. ● To understand why an indigenous fish species is in danger of extinction. ● To know that fish stocks need to be conserved if species are to survive. | Extract scientific information from a play about the dangers facing the wild salmon. | Continue the play with a further scene. Complete a table showing the dangers to the salmon at each stage of its life cycle. | Children perform their scenes. Discuss ways to conserve wild salmon. | ● Understand how human activities reduce fish stocks. ● Know the life cycle of an important indigenous fish species and understand some of the problems facing it. ● Can suggest some ways in which fish stocks can be conserved. |

| | OBJECTIVES | | ACTIVITY 1 | ACTIVITY 2 |
|---|---|---|---|---|
| ASSESSMENT 11 | ● To assess children's knowledge of the water cycle and where water appears in the environment. ● To assess the children's knowledge of the effects of human activity on the quality and distribution of water in the environment. | | Answer questions on the water cycle and water conservation. | Answer questions about water distribution, water pollution and the causes and consequences of air pollution. |

## LESSON 1

### OBJECTIVE

● To know that water circulates through the environment.

### RESOURCES

**Main teaching activity:** Colour pictures of the Earth and another planet, taken from space; enlarged copies of the two diagrams and the table of facts from photocopiable page 89, six strips of card (see Preparation), Blu-Tack.
**Group activities: 1.** Writing and drawing materials, paper. **2.** 1cm² squared paper, glue, plain or coloured mounting paper, drawing materials, scissors.

### PREPARATION

Display an enlarged copy of the water cycle diagram from page 89. Prepare six card strips, each with one of the following sentences: 'The heat of the sun evaporates water from the sea.'; 'The air from over the sea moves the water vapour over the land.'; 'Some of the water vapour in the air begins to condense into clouds.'; 'Rain or snow falls.'; 'Water runs into rivers, streams, lakes and ponds.'; 'Eventually the water finds its way back into the sea.'

### BACKGROUND

This lesson introduces the children to the water cycle. This is the process that moves water, a vital commodity for life, about the planet. The physical features that are part of this process, such as seas and rivers, will be studied as part of the geography curriculum; considering the distribution and care of this precious resource is relevant to PSHE.

Using the children's own experience of where water naturally occurs, the lesson directs their attention to the three physical states of water: liquid, solid (ice) and gas (water vapour). In the Plenary session, the children are made aware of how limited the planet's fresh water supplies are.

*Vocabulary*

evaporate, condense, naturally, water vapour, liquid, solid, gas

### INTRODUCTION

Show the children a colour picture of the Earth taken from space. Tell them that this is the only place in our solar system where life is known to survive. Show a colour picture of another planet and ask: *How does the Earth look different from other planets?* (It looks blue, the others do not.) *Why does the Earth look mainly blue when viewed from space?* (Most of the Earth's surface is covered with water.) Tell the children that they are going to learn more about water.

# LESSON 5

| Objective | ● To understand the catastrophic effects of flood and drought. |
|---|---|
| Resources | The pond picture from Lesson 4; secondary sources (such as newspaper cuttings and magazine articles) on catastrophic floods and droughts; writing materials. Write a list of questions on the board or flip chart: 'Where did the catastrophe happen?', 'What caused it to happen?', 'How many people were affected?', 'What was being done to help the victims?', 'If possible, what might be done to prevent a similar catastrophe from happening?' |
| Main activity | Using the pond picture from Lesson 4, remind the children how the gardener solved the problem of 'floods and droughts'. Point to the list of questions (see above). Reading from a secondary source, describe the catastrophic effects of an actual flood or drought. Discuss the answers to the displayed questions with the children.<br>  Give the children copies of news reports or other secondary sources on floods and droughts. Ask them to use the displayed questions to help them write a short report on the flood or drought described earlier. They can also use secondary sources to find out about methods of flood prevention, such as the Thames Barrier, sea defences and flood plains. |
| Differentiation | Less able children could be supplied with a focused resource sheet on a particular catastrophe to work from. |
| Assessment | During the group work, ask the children to explain the meanings of 'flood' and 'drought'. |
| Plenary | Ask some children to read out their reports of catastrophes and to share their information on methods of flood prevention. |
| Outcome | ● Understand some of the reasons for and effects of major floods and droughts. |

# LESSON 6

## OBJECTIVE

● To know that we use a great amount of water and that water must be conserved.

## RESOURCES

**Main teaching activity:** The water cycle and wildlife pond visual aids from Lessons 1 and 4; an A3 copy of photocopiable page 91; an empty litre bottle, a 10-litre bucket.
**Group activities: 1.** Photocopiable page 91 (one copy per child), writing materials. **2.** Paper, drawing and writing materials.

## PREPARATION

Prepare two separate charts as shown in the Main teaching activity.

## BACKGROUND

The consumption of water per person in Britain has increased rapidly over the decades since the 1950s. All the water that we use is abstracted from river systems or artesian sources. Much of the abstracted water is stored temporarily in reservoirs. The children will probably not realise how much water we use (between 300 and 700 litres per family per day), and that water is used in the manufacture and maintenance of most of the products we rely upon.

Excessive abstraction from rivers has caused environmental problems in many parts of Britain. River flows have been reduced and water tables have been lowered. Wildlife habitats for species as diverse as fish, frogs, otters and dragonflies have been depleted. The extra demand for water has put pressure on sewage treatment facilities and has led, as a consequence, to increased river pollution. Finally, the increase in demand for water has meant the construction of additional reservoirs and pipelines, many of which have altered the character of existing natural areas.

## INTRODUCTION

Ask the children: *Where does water from the tap come from?* Using the water cycle visual aid from Lesson 1, establish that our domestic water is rain-water which has been taken out of the water cycle, cleaned, and piped to our homes. *How do we make sure that we've got enough water to use even when it's not raining?* Use the visual aid of the pond and a barrel from Lesson 4 to establish that water has to be stored in reservoirs to ensure that we always have enough for our needs.

### Vocabulary

immersed,
conserve,
consume,
production,
recycle

## MAIN TEACHING ACTIVITY

Tell the children that they are going to find out how much water they use at home. Display an empty litre bottle and a 10-litre bucket, both clearly marked with their capacity, to help them judge quantities. On the board or flip chart, display this list of water-consuming activities:

**How much do we use?**
*A bowl of washing-up*
*A bath*
*A shower*
*Washing hands in a sink*
*A flush of the toilet*
*A washing machine load*

The answers are: 10 litres, 70 litres, 30 litres, 3 litres, 10 litres, 90 litres. Write these on the board in order of increasing quantity. Ask the children to guess from this list how much water is used for each activity. Write the correct answer alongside each activity. Check that the children understand how many full buckets of water would be needed in each case.
Now say that lots of water is used to make other things. Display a second list:

**How much water to:**
*make a car?*
*clean and prepare a frozen chicken?*
*make a kilogram of paper?*
*make a can of beer?*

The answers are: 78 000 litres, 26 litres, 250 litres and 10 litres. Display these in order of increasing quantity. Before asking the children to guess the volume of water used in each product, give them a simple indication of how water is used in the production:

**Car:** Water is an ingredient in the paint on a car, and used to cool and clean the metal, glass and plastic from which the car is made.
**Frozen chicken:** Dead chickens are immersed in boiling water to loosen their feathers, and their meat is cleaned with water before they are frozen.
**Paper:** The tiny particles that make paper are floated and kept separate by water until the paper is made.
**Beer:** Barley and hops are mixed with water, cooked, and fermented with yeast to make beer.

Explain to the children that we are using more water than ever before. *Where are we going to get the extra water from?* Elicit the answer that more water will have to be taken from rivers, and more reservoirs will have to be built. Stress the environmental consequences of this (see Background). Say that everyone needs to reduce their water consumption. Explain that car and paper manufacturers now have to recycle their water and use it again and again.
   Show the children an enlarged version of page 91. Look at each activity in turn and discuss ways in which water is wasted. Ask the children to suggest ways of saving water. Write a couple of answers in the appropriate cells of the table as an example for those children who attempt Group activity 1. When you have discussed each water-saving idea with the children, ask them to suggest three ideas that they could implement at home. Ask them how they could persuade other members of their family to save water.

## GROUP ACTIVITIES

**1.** Give the children a copy each of page 91 and ask them to complete it individually.
**2.** The children can design a poster (to display in school) that presents two or three good ideas for saving water.

## DIFFERENTIATION

**1.** The sheet could be made more challenging by omitting some of the information from the 'How to waste water' column. **2.** The children can use techniques appropriate to their stage of development.

## ASSESSMENT

During the Plenary, ask the children to identify things at home that use a lot of water. Ask them why we need to save water.

UNIT 3 **THE ENVIRONMENT**

## PLENARY

Ask the children who completed Group activity 1 to tell you which they think is the most wasteful activity listed on the sheet. Ask for their reasons. Look at the posters from Group activity 2. Ask the children how effective these posters are at suggesting water-saving ideas and at explaining why we should conserve water.

## OUTCOMES
● Recognise some activities that require a great amount of water.
● Can explain the need for water conservation.
● Can describe simple ways in which we can conserve water.

## LINKS
PSHE: care of the local and wider environment.

## LESSON 7

### OBJECTIVE
● To know that water can be polluted by waste from human activities.

### RESOURCES
**Main teaching activity:** An A3 version of photocopiable page 92; the table shown opposite, copied onto a flip chart or large piece of paper.
**Group activities: 1.** Copies of the table opposite (prepared by hand or on computer), writing materials. **2.** Photocopiable page 92 (one copy per child), paper, glue, scissors, writing materials.

### PREPARATION
Prepare the visual aids and sheets needed.

**Vocabulary**

pollution, polluted, algae, conditions, discarded, sewage, sludge worm, rat-tailed maggot, water louse, caddis fly larva, dragonfly nymph

### BACKGROUND
Even though fresh water resources are limited, human development has damaged much of this precious and vital resource. Many areas of waterway in Britain have been polluted by industrial and agricultural activity. The problem has often been compounded by ignorance and neglect. Organisations such as the National Rivers Authority have begun to make some improvement. They have successfully prosecuted industries and farmers who have failed to take proper action to prevent pollution, and have enforced compliance with 'anti-pollution' regulations.

Simple biological indicators, such as those described on page 92, can be used to determine the existence of pollution. Water containing a wide range of species is likely to be less polluted than water that carries a concentration of a narrow range of species.

### INTRODUCTION
Remind the children of the main points of the previous lessons: water is essential for our survival; fresh water resources are limited; we need to conserve water as the demand for it increases.

### MAIN TEACHING ACTIVITY
Tell the children that even though water is precious, human activity has been spoiling the resource. Ask them whether they know a word that describes dirty water ('Pollution'). Ask them whether they have seen or know of any polluted areas of water. Discuss their observations and knowledge. Show the children an enlarged version of photocopiable page 92 and read through the 'Frog's guide to ponds' with them.

Show the children a large copy of the table opposite. Using the information in the 'Frog's guide', show the children how the empty cells can be filled. For example, ask: *What did the frog say the water looked like in very polluted conditions?* (Lots of human litter and waste; liquids and junk from factories.) *What is living in very polluted water?* (Nothing.)

### GROUP ACTIVITIES
**1.** Give the children a copy each of the 'Is there pollution?' table. Ask them to use the information from the enlarged version of page 92 to complete the table.
**2.** Give the children a copy each of page 92 with scissors, paper and glue to complete.

| Is there pollution? | | |
|---|---|---|
| Clean or polluted? | What the water looks like | What is living in the water |
| Very polluted | | |
| Polluted with algae | | |
| Polluted with sewage | | |
| A little pollution | | |
| No pollution | | |

## DIFFERENTIATION

**1.** Some less able children could cut out the paragraphs from the 'Frog's guide' and paste them into the correct parts of the table. They could paste pictures of the creatures into the appropriate cells. Children who complete the task quickly could use secondary sources to find out what resources would be necessary to assess the level of pollution in a local pond or stream. **2.** Children who complete this task quickly could use secondary sources to find out more about the creatures mentioned on the sheet.

## ASSESSMENT

During the Plenary session, ask the children how they would find out whether a pond or stream was polluted. Ask them to tell you some of the main causes of pollution. (Industry, farming, sewage and thoughtless humans.)

## PLENARY

This session is a particularly important part of this lesson. Write the main causes of pollution on a board or flip chart: 'industry', 'farming', 'sewage' and 'thoughtless humans'. Ask the children what they would do to prevent pollution by each of these causes. Listen to the children's suggestions; then inform them that there are laws to prevent water pollution, and that these are gradually being enforced.

Ask the children what equipment they would need to check on water pollution in a local stream or pond. Ask them why they think the rat-tailed maggot has a strange tube extending from its nose. (This is a natural snorkel to breathe in air from the surface, as the creature lives in stagnant, oxygen-starved water.)

## OUTCOMES

- Can identify sources of water pollution.
- Know how water pollution can be assessed using biological indicators.
- Know some of the effects of water pollution.
- Know some ways to reduce water pollution.

## LINKS

PSHE: care of the local and wider environment.

## LESSON 8

| Objective | • To use pollution indicators to monitor a local pond or stream. |
|---|---|
| Resources | An enlarged, filled-in 'Is there pollution?' table from Lesson 7; pond-dipping nets, hand lenses, white plastic trays; copies of photocopiable page 93, clipboards, pencils. You will need a safe, accessible area of local waterway, with no deep water, for a 'pond-dipping' lesson. Check with your school or LEA policy on 'out of school' visits; organise appropriate supervision, first aid and so on. Inform parents of the arrangements and purpose of the visit. Ensure that the children are appropriately dressed for the activity. |
| Main activity | Tell the children they are going to investigate an area of local water for pollution. Use an enlarged, filled-in table from Lesson 7 to discuss the indicators they should look for. Demonstrate how to use the pond-dipping nets safely and effectively. The children should work in pairs for safety and practical effectiveness. There are usually three ways of catching a representative selection of water life: a slow horizontal sweep near the surface; a vertical sweep up the stems of water plants; a very slow sweep along the bottom of the waterway. Encourage the children to use all three methods. After each sweep, the net should be carefully emptied into a tray part-filled with stream or pond water. After observation and monitoring, the water creatures should be carefully returned to their environment. Show the children how to complete page 93, and carry out the visit to a pond or stream. |
| Differentiation | The sheet is organised so that one group can pond-dip while another surveys the local environment for evidence of pollution. |
| Assessment | On return to school, ask the children to explain the purpose of the two sections of the photocopiable sheet. |
| Plenary | Ask the children for their assessment of the water quality, and the reasons for their decision. If the water is polluted, plan the action that you and the children will take to inform the appropriate local authority. |
| Outcome | • Can assess water quality in the local environment. |

# LESSON 9

## OBJECTIVES

● To recognise some activities that cause air pollution.
● To recognise some effects on the environment of air pollution.
● To know some ways in which air pollution can be reduced.

## RESOURCES

**Main teaching activity:** Three visual aids (see Preparation), marker pens, a bucket and spade, a globe, a pair of swimming armbands.
**Group activities: 1 and 2.** Paper, writing and drawing materials.

## PREPARATION

Draw the three visual aids shown below on large pieces of paper or flip chart pages.

## BACKGROUND

There is now agreement among world scientists that climate changes are taking place due to global warming. 'Greenhouse' gases are trapping larger amounts of infra-red radiation from the Sun, warming the surface and atmosphere of the Earth. The three main 'greenhouse gases' are carbon dioxide, methane, and nitrous oxide. Carbon dioxide is the least potent of these, but by far the most abundant. The increased levels of carbon dioxide in the atmosphere are due to the burning of fossil fuels (coal, gas and oil). In Britain, fossil fuels are consumed by homes, vehicles, factories and power stations.

It is certain that one of the effects of the climate changes is a rise in sea level. This is due to the expansion of sea water as its temperature increases, and to the melting of some polar ice. Some islands and low-lying countries are already threatened by the rise in sea level. Parts of eastern Britain are likely to be affected too.

The burning of fossil fuels and emissions of sulphur dioxide pollution have caused acid rain locally and in nearby Scandinavian countries. Lakes and forest soils have undergone an increase in acidic conditions, with the result that many fish and trees have died.

This lesson establishes a clear chain of events between the creation of air pollution and damage to both the regional and the global environment.

## INTRODUCTION

Ask the children to tell you some of the causes of water pollution mentioned in Lesson 7. (Sewage, fertiliser from farms, industrial pollution and human carelessness.) Explain that you are going to show them how we are all accidentally polluting the air and damaging the habitats of other people and animals.

## MAIN TEACHING ACTIVITY

Show the children your first visual aid: a simple drawing of a house, power station, vehicles and factory (see above). Ask the children to tell you where air pollution might come from in this picture. Draw black clouds rising from the house chimney, power station, factory flues and vehicle exhaust as the children indicate these sources of air pollution.

Ask the children whether they have ever caused unnecessary air pollution. *Do you ever leave the TV on when you are not watching it? Do you ever leave a light on in an empty room? Do you ever leave the door open when the heating is on? Do you ever ask a parent to drive you somewhere when it would be easy to walk there?*

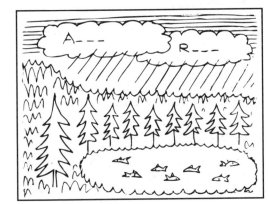

Most children will admit to these 'errors'. Choose a child with a good sense of humour. Ask this 'unfortunate child' to come to the front of the class, and say that you are going to act the part of a very angry teacher. Now overact! Explain that wasting electricity or heat, or making unnecessary car journeys, adds to air pollution. Tell the child that you are very angry because he or she has caused extra air pollution. Point to the black clouds on the visual aid, and say that air pollution damages the world in two ways.

Show the children a second visual aid: a simple drawing of a lake and wood beneath a black rain cloud, with the initials 'AR' on the cloud. Ask: *Has anyone heard the name for rain that has been spoiled by pollution?* Elicit the answer: 'Acid rain'. Explain that acid rain kills

trees and poisons fish. Tell the 'unfortunate child': *Leaving a TV on without watching it helps to cause more acid rain.* Explain why this is.

Still in role, tell the child that you are so angry with him or her for causing air pollution that you are going to send him or her to a desert island.

Reveal the third visual aid: a child with bucket and spade, standing on a desert island. The sun is shining, but a single black cloud of pollution (with the initials GW) is in the sky. Give the child a bucket and spade to hold. Say that air pollution causes another problem. Point to the cloud and the initials. Tell all the children that air pollution is making the whole world warmer. *Has anyone ever heard of the name of this problem?* (Global warming.)

Pick up a globe and point to the North and South Poles. *What is it like at the North and South Pole?* Establish that there is ice there. *What will happen to the ice as the world gets warmer?* Establish that the ice will melt and the water will go into the sea. Now point to the visual aid and ask: *What will happen to the water around the island if the ice at the North and South Poles is melting*? On the visual aid, draw a deepening sea that gradually covers the island and the child. Turn to the 'unfortunate child' and take away the bucket and spade. Explain that because he or she caused unnecessary air pollution, he or she won't need a bucket and spade any more. Give the child a pair of swimming armbands and ask them to 'swim' back to his or her seat.

Go through the chain of events again to remind the children that wasting heat and electricity and burning fuels can cause air pollution, which in turn causes acid rain and global warming. Remind the children that global warming is not a joke. Some children who live in flat countries close to the sea, such as Bangladesh, already know that the sea level is rising: their land is often flooded by the sea.

On the board or flip chart, list the children's ideas for ways to reduce air pollution. The list should include ways of reducing electricity consumption, conserving heat in buildings, reducing car use and producing power by sustainable means (such as solar energy).

## GROUP ACTIVITIES

**1.** Ask the children to make their own copies of the visual aids, then add stick characters and speech bubbles to create a comic strip explaining the effects of air pollution.
**2.** The children can make a poster to encourage people to reduce air pollution.

## DIFFERENTIATION

Both Group activities are differentiated by outcome.

## ASSESSMENT

At the start of the Plenary session, ask the children to list some of the activities that produce air pollution and explain the damage that is caused.

## PLENARY

Warn the children that there is evidence that polar ice is melting, and that our weather is gradually changing. Discuss their ideas for reducing air pollution. Ask them whether they have any ideas that could be implemented in the classroom.

## OUTCOMES

● Recognise some activities that cause air pollution.
● Can describe some effects of air pollution on the environment.
● Can describe some ways in which air pollution can be reduced.

## LINKS

Unit 2, Lesson 12: life processes of humans and other animals.
PSHE: responsibility for the environment.

# LESSON 10

## OBJECTIVES
● To know that human activities are affecting fish stocks.
● To understand why an indigenous fish species is in danger of extinction.
● To know that fish stocks need to be conserved if species are to survive.

## RESOURCES
**Main teaching activity:** Photocopiable page 94 (one copy per pair); an A3 copy of page 94; a copy of the chart shown below (see Preparation); a highlighter.
**Group activities: 1 and 2.** Writing materials, paper.

## PREPARATION
Practise reading the play 'A Fisherman's Tale' on page 94 with a confident child or adult. Copy the chart shown below onto a large sheet of paper or a flip chart.

## BACKGROUND

*Vocabulary*

salmon, fish farm, fish stocks, sand eel

The North Atlantic Wild Salmon is in danger of extinction. A huge decline in its population occurred at the end of the twentieth century. At least four factors are thought to have contributed to this decline:
1. Pollution of streams and rivers by agricultural, industrial and social waste.
2. Diseases contracted by the wild fish from their proximity to populations of fish-farmed salmon. Large numbers of the latter are reared intensively. They are prone to infectious and parasitic diseases.
3. Global warming is believed to be affecting the food chain of the wild salmon. While at sea, salmon feed on species that thrive in cold Arctic water.
4. Intensive 'forage farming' of fish species that are part of the salmon's food chain. Huge quantities of sand eels and other species are dredged from the floor of the ocean. They are dried, then used as 'fishmeal' in poultry and pig feeds, as pellets to feed farmed fish, as fertiliser, and as a fuel for power stations in some countries (such as Denmark).

The North Atlantic Salmon Conservation Plan is a project of detailed research into the plight of the fish, particularly their life at sea. Currently, a 'catch and release' policy is advocated for fishermen who catch the species. Releasing caught fish will prevent further depletion by fishing, and might allow the remaining salmon to spawn.

| Salmon life cycle | Problems |
|---|---|
| Eggs are laid in patches of gravel. | |
| Small fish live in a river. | |
| Young fish migrate to the sea. | |
| Fish growing in the sea. | |

There are good reasons for the conservation of salmon stocks. The large tourist industry in Scotland and Ireland is partly dependent on salmon fishing. Also, the salmon possesses behavioural skills that are only partially understood, such as the ability to return to the river where it spent its infancy.

## INTRODUCTION
Remind the children of the lessons in this unit that involved water pollution and global warming. Help them to remember the causes of both problems. Water pollution is caused by agricultural, industrial, and social waste. Global warming is caused by the burning of fossil fuels in homes, industries, vehicles and power stations.

## MAIN TEACHING ACTIVITY
Tell the children that they are going to learn about the danger of extinction facing a famous fish, the wild salmon. Explain that this fish used to be common in most rivers in Britain.

Give each pair of children a copy of page 94. Read the play aloud, with you and a confident child or another adult reading the two parts. Ask questions to make sure the children understand the text. Now display an enlarged version of the play. Ask the children to help you highlight words that give information about the life cycle of the salmon. Use a highlighter for this. Highlight phrases such as 'eight thousand eggs', 'patches of gravel' and 'the place where I hatched'. When all the appropriate phrases are highlighted, use them to discuss the life cycle of the wild salmon.

Show the children the flip chart or large sheet of paper marked with the table above. Ask them to tell you what problems human beings have caused for each stage of the wild salmon's life cycle. Discuss each stage of the development of the fish, but only fill in a couple of cells in the table as examples.

Finally, inform the children that in order to help the wild salmon increase in numbers, fishermen who catch them are being asked to release them again.

## GROUP ACTIVITIES

**1.** Ask the children to write a second short play, presenting a conversation between the fisherman and a friend when they meet at their holiday hotel later that day.
**2.** Ask the children to copy and fill in the table, using information from the play.

## DIFFERENTIATION

**1.** Children who have difficulty with writing a playscript could record their play on a cassette recorder. **2.** The problems facing the salmon are highlighted in bold text in the play. Less able children could cut out the bold sections of text from an enlarged version of page 94 and paste them into a copy of the table.

## ASSESSMENT

In the Plenary session, ask the class to explain the problems facing salmon at different stages of their life cycle.

## PLENARY

The class could listen to some of the plays written by the children. Finally, discuss how the children think wild salmon could be conserved. This is an important part of this lesson.

## OUTCOMES

● Understand how human activities reduce fish stocks.
● Know the life cycle of an important indigenous fish species and understand some of the problems facing it.
● Can suggest some ways in which fish stocks can be conserved.

## LINKS

PSHE: care of other living things.
Geography: rivers, seas and migration routes.

## ASSESSMENT

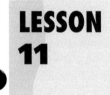

# LESSON 11

## OBJECTIVES

● To assess the children's knowledge of the water cycle and where water appears in the environment.
● To assess the children's knowledge of the effects of human activity on the quality and distribution of water in the environment.

## RESOURCES

Photocopiable pages 95 and 96, writing materials.

## INTRODUCTION

Start with a 'warm-up' of oral questions on the content of Lesson 10 (the demise of the wild salmon).

## ASSESSMENT ACTIVITY 1

Give the children a copy each of page 95 and let them complete the sheet individually.

**Answers**
A:1. evaporates; 2. water vapour;
3. condense; 4. rain and snow; 5. rivers and streams; 6. sea.

B:

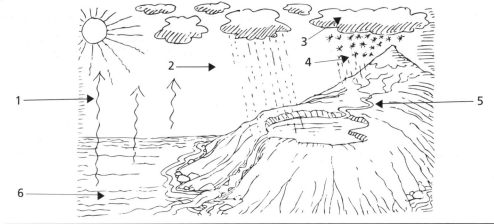

C:

| | How to waste water | How to save or conserve water |
|---|---|---|
| Cleaning teeth | Clean them while the tap is running. | Use a glass or cup of water as a mouth rinse. |
| Washing hands | Wash them under a running tap. | Use a small bowl or insert a plug. |
| Washing a car | Use a hose to wash and rinse the car. | Use a bucket. |

D: Sentences that imply: clean water fit for drinking is a precious commodity; excessive extraction from rivers and streams is causing environmental damage; increased demand leads to increased sewage and pollution; building extra reservoirs damages the appearance of a landscape.

**Looking for levels**
All the children should be able to complete parts A and B. Most children should be able to complete the rest of the sheet. The most able children will provide cogent answers to part D.

## ASSESSMENT ACTIVITY 2

Give the children a copy each of page 96 and let them complete the sheet individually.

**Answers**
A: 1. with water; 2. covered with ice or desert; 3. a small fraction of the Earth's surface.
B: Accept sentences that imply two of the following: humans pollute water through waste that emerges from factories; through excessive use of fertilisers by farmers; through sewage that enters the water.
C. A sensible order is as follows: I switch on the light in my bedroom; The electricity that makes my light work comes from a power station; The power stations make electricity by burning coal, oil or gas; The pollution from the power station helps to cause global warming. Ice at the North and South Poles melts; The seas and oceans are deeper; Low countries such as Bangladesh are flooded.

**Looking for levels**
This assessment sheet is more demanding than the first. All children should be able to attempt part A. Most children should be able to complete the rest of the sheet. The most able children will probably provide the most cogent answers to parts A and B.

## PLENARY

The answers to both sheets should be discussed. Page 95 could be marked with the children at the end of the session. A discussion about the range of acceptable answers to both sheets will be an informative process for the teacher and the children. Children may argue cogently that there is more than one sensible order for the sentences in part C of page 95.

# The Earth and its water

## Facts about the Earth's surface

| | |
|---|---:|
| Fraction of the Earth's surface that is covered by water | 71% |
| Fraction of the Earth's surface that is covered by ice | 3% |
| Fraction of the Earth's surface that is desert (very little water) | 10% |
| Fraction of the Earth's surface that nearly everybody lives on | 16% |

# A fisherman's tale (a play for two people)

*A fisherman is alone on holiday, fishing from the bank of a clean river. Suddenly the fishing line goes tight. After a long struggle, a huge salmon is pulled to the side of the river. The hook is taken from the mouth of the exhausted fish, which is dropped into a large net.*

**Fisherman**  What a brilliant fish. The largest I've ever caught! I've been trying to catch wild salmon for weeks! *(Pause as he admires the fish.)* No wonder they call you the 'King of the River'!

**Salmon**  *(Puffing and panting.)* King? I'm no king! I'm female. I'm the 'Queen of the River'! I've got eight thousand eggs inside me. If you kill me, you'll be killing all my babies too *(Pause.)* Let me go!

**Fisherman**  A talking fish – I don't believe it! *(Pause as he wonders what to say next.)* Excuse me, Your Majesty, but where were you going?

**Salmon**  *(Gradually puffing less.)* I was going to find some patches of gravel higher up the river. I was going back to the place where I hatched, to lay my eggs. Stupidly, I ate your fly and you caught me. Please let me go! Wild salmon like us are becoming extinct. Let me go!

**Fisherman**  *(Nodding.)* Extinct, I can believe that! I've been fishing here for weeks without catching any salmon. Why are you becoming extinct?

**Salmon**  **Many of the rivers where we lay our eggs have been polluted. Young salmon can only live in clean water where there are lots of insects, such as dragonfly nymphs, to feed on. You humans have allowed sewage, fertilisers and rubbish to pollute so many rivers. Let me go!**

**Fisherman**  This river isn't polluted, and you can lay lots of eggs. Why aren't there lots of salmon living here?

**Salmon**  After the eggs hatch out, we live in clean rivers like this for about six years. Then, when we are a bit bigger than your hand, we swim down the river to the sea. Let me go!

**Fisherman**  You live in fresh water *and* in sea water? That's clever. I didn't know that.

**Salmon**  **We swim down to the sea. We swim past the places where you keep large numbers of our cousins, the farmed salmon, inside prisons. We wild salmon try to keep well away from those poor creatures. The water around them is full of water lice and diseases that can kill us. Let me go!**

**Fisherman**  So lots of wild salmon die from diseases and pests they catch as they pass the fish farms? Is that why you're becoming extinct?

**Salmon**  Partly, yes. But there are other problems for us out at sea. *(Pause.)* **When we live in the sea, we have to eat sand eels and other tiny sea fish. These fish live in the colder parts of the sea. The sea has been getting a little warmer lately. These little fish don't like the new conditions. Let me go!**

**Fisherman**  Global warming is heating the seas – I knew that. But I didn't know it affected fish too.

**Salmon**  Well, it does! *(Pause.)* And there's another problem with our food supply. **Lots of fishing boats are catching the sand eels and tiny fish. They are taking millions of tons of the things out of the sea!** Sometimes these fishing boats scoop up wild salmon too! What do you want those tiny fish for? They're our food! Let me go!

**Fisherman**  I know about fishing. They catch the tiny fish, dry them and feed some of the bits to chickens and pigs. Other bits are fed to the salmon in the fish farms, and some is burned in things we call 'power stations' to make electricity.

**Salmon**  What a stupid waste! Can't they feed the pigs and chickens other stuff? And can't they make electricity in other ways? It's *our* food they're catching. We *will* become extinct! Let me go!

**Fisherman**  You really do have a lot of problems! Water pollution, fish farming, global warming, fishermen scooping up tons of sand eels and tiny fish... *(Pause while the fisherman thinks.)* I'd better put you back in the river, or there will be no more wild salmon to catch.

**Salmon**  *(As it is gently tipped from the net into the river.)* Thanks! I wish more people would listen like you.

**Fisherman**  Good luck, Your Majesty! I'm going back to the hotel to tell other fishermen about your problems.

# Water and the environment

**A. Use these words to complete the sentences below:**

sea, rivers and streams, rain and snow, water vapour, condense, evaporates

1. The heat of the sun _____ water from the sea.

2. Air over the sea moves _____ over the land.

3. Some of the water vapour in the air begins to _____ into clouds.

4. _____ falls to the ground.

5. Water runs into _____.

6. Eventually the water finds its way back to the _____.

**B. Label this diagram of the water cycle with the numbers of the sentences in part A.**

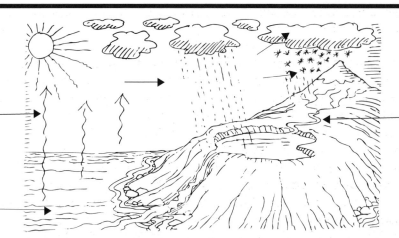

**C. Fill in this table by writing ways that we can waste or conserve water.**

|  | How to waste water | How to save or conserve water |
|---|---|---|
| Cleaning teeth |  |  |
| Washing hands |  |  |
| Washing a car |  |  |

**D. Write down two good reasons why we should try to conserve water.**

_____

_____

Name

# Water and the environment

A. Look at these facts about the Earth's surface:

| | |
|---|---|
| Fraction of the Earth's surface that is covered by water | 71% |
| Fraction of the Earth's surface that is covered by ice | 3% |
| Fraction of the Earth's surface that is desert (very little water) | 10% |
| Fraction of the Earth's surface that nearly all humans live on | 16% |

Use the table to complete these sentences:

1. Most of the surface of the Earth is covered _____

2. A lot of the land is difficult for humans to live on because it is _____

_____

3. Humans have to live on _____

B. Explain, using sentences, two ways in which humans pollute water apart from litter and rubbish.

_____

_____

C. Here are seven sentences that describe how switching on an electric light can help to cause flooding in Bangladesh. Write these sentences in a sensible order.

Ice at the North and South Poles melts.
I switch on a light in my bedroom.
Low countries such as Bangladesh are flooded.
The electricity that makes my light work comes from a power station.
The pollution from the power station helps to cause global warming.
The seas and oceans become deeper.
Most power stations make electricity by burning coal, oil or gas.

_____

_____

_____

_____

_____

_____

_____

# Gases, solids and liquids

## ORGANISATION (14 LESSONS)

| | OBJECTIVES | MAIN ACTIVITY | GROUP ACTIVITIES | PLENARY | OUTCOMES |
|---|---|---|---|---|---|
| **LESSON 1** | ● To know the characteristic features of the solid and liquid states of matter.<br>● To sort materials as solids and liquids.<br>● To describe the processes of melting and dissolving. | Review the children's knowledge of solids and liquids. Demonstrate melting and dissolving. Sort materials into solids and liquids. | | Sort materials as a class, summarising the key features of the solid and liquid states. | ● Can distinguish solids and liquids by their properties.<br>● Can give examples of melting and dissolving. |
| **LESSON 2** | ● To know that air is all around us.<br>● To know that air is a type of material called a gas.<br>● To know that air has mass. | Demonstrate some properties of air using a beach ball, a marble, a feather and a simple 'balloon balance'. | Identify and discuss devices that make use of the air. Use a sheet of paper to demonstrate that air is a material. | Review the group work. Summarise the physical properties of air. | ● Know that we are surrounded by air.<br>● Recognise that air is a material.<br>● Can demonstrate the presence of air.<br>● Can describe how the mass of air can be demonstrated. |
| **LESSON 3** | ● To know that porous materials are composed of solid particles or regions surrounded by gaps.<br>● To know that when porous materials are dry, the gaps are filled with air.<br>● To observe that water can displace the air from the gaps in porous materials. | Demonstrate the presence of air in a porous material by submerging Oasis in water. | Observe and draw the displacement of air from sponge by water. Observe and draw a piece of sponge using a magnifier. | Review the children's drawings. Use these to reinforce the idea of a porous material. | ● Can state that porous materials contain many air-filled holes.<br>● Can identify bubbles rising from a submerged piece of material as air that was in the spaces in the material.<br>● Recognise the need to repeat experiments in order to check observations. |
| **LESSON 4** | ● To know that soil contains air.<br>● To use measuring cylinders and jugs to measure volumes of water.<br>● To compare the volumes of air present in different soils. | Demonstrate a water displacement method for determining the volume of air in a soil sample. Discuss the need to repeat measurements for accuracy. | The children use the method to compare soil, sand and gravel samples. | Review the children's results and discuss their implications for gardening. | ● Can use measuring cylinders or jugs to measure water volumes.<br>● Can explain the importance of taking care when reading scales, and of repeating measurements in order to check results.<br>● Understand that in order for a comparison to be fair, all variables except the one being tested must be kept the same. |
| **LESSON 5** | ● To know that there are a variety of useful gases. | Use secondary sources to research the properties and uses of gases. Make a poster about each gas. | | Children display their posters and describe their findings. | ● Know that a number of gases exist.<br>● Can describe the uses of a variety of gases. |
| **LESSON 6** | ● To know that when a liquid evaporates, it forms a gas. | Demonstrate examples of evaporation. Groups research and write about the operation of 'drying machines' such as hairdryers. | | Groups present their findings. | ● Recognise that when a liquid evaporates, it forms a gas.<br>● Recognise that rate of evaporation depends on temperature.<br>● Recognise that rate of evaporation depends on air movement.<br>● Can explain how appliances that dry things (eg a hairdryer) work. |

## ORGANISATION (14 LESSONS)

| | OBJECTIVES | MAIN ACTIVITY | GROUP ACTIVITIES | PLENARY | OUTCOMES |
|---|---|---|---|---|---|
| LESSON 7 | ● To conduct an investigation into the factors affecting the rate of evaporation. | Groups devise and carry out experiments to investigate the factors that affect the rate at which water evaporates. | | Groups display their results as a chart or graph and report their findings to the class. | ● Can plan and carry out an investigation and record the results. |
| LESSON 8 | ● To know that gases do not have a fixed volume as solids and liquids do. ● To know that gases are more easily compressed (squashed) than solids and liquids. ● To know that gases and liquids can flow and change their shape, but continuous solids have a fixed shape. | Compare and contrast solid, liquid and gas samples. Make carbon dioxide and demonstrate that it is heavier than air. | Role-play molecules in gases, liquids and solids. Make cards summarising the properties of the different states. | Children show and discuss their 'state' cards. | ● Know that a gas can be poured and squashed, has no fixed shape or volume, and can spread out into the air when released from its container. ● Can describe the different properties of solids, liquids and gases. |
| LESSON 9 | ● To know that gases can be turned into liquids by cooling. ● To know that this process is called condensation. ● To know that water vapour is present in the air, but cannot be seen. | Demonstrate examples of condensation on cold items. Observe condensation of water vapour from cut flowers. | Observe condensation on cooled cling film over warm water. Identify places in a house where condensation might occur. | The children report on their observations and knowledge of condensation. | ● Recognise that when a gas condenses, a liquid is formed. ● Can identify where condensation takes place in the home. ● Recognise that water vapour is present in the air, but cannot be seen. |
| LESSON 10 | ● To know that when a liquid is heated to a certain temperature, it boils. ● To know that when a liquid boils, it changes into a gas. ● To know that water boils at 100°C. | Record temperature-time data for water heated to boiling point. Observe changes in the water's appearance. | Plot a graph using the data. Interpret the graph to identify significant facts. | Review the information gained and reinforce the concept of boiling point. | ● Recognise when a liquid is boiling. ● Recognise that the white cloud seen over boiling water is made up of condensed water droplets. ● Can interpret data from a graph. |
| LESSON 11 | ● To conduct an investigation into rates of melting. ● To know that the freezing/melting temperature of water is 0°C. ● To know that the temperature in the classroom is normally 18–22°C. | Record temperature-time data for an ice-water mixture. Consider factors that might affect the rate of melting. | Investigate (as a class) how the rate of melting depends on the number of ice cubes in a drink. | Review and combine the children's results to produce a class graph. | ● Know that ice melts at 0°C. ● Know that normal room temperature is 18–22°C. ● Can identify one or more factors that affect the rate at which ice melts. ● Can carry out an investigation. |
| LESSON 12 | ● To know that heating/cooling can cause materials to melt, boil, evaporate, freeze or condense. ● To know that some materials are natural and others are manufactured. ● To know that many materials are manufactured and processed by methods involving the use of heat. | Demonstrate candle-making. Discuss other manufacturing processes involving heating or cooling. Groups use secondary sources to research these processes and make charts. | | Groups display their charts and describe their findings. | ● Recognise examples of melting, boiling, freezing, evaporation and condensation. ● Recognise a range of natural and manufactured materials. ● Can describe processes in the making of materials. |
| LESSON 13 | ● To know where ice, liquid water and water vapour are found in the natural environment. ● To know about evaporation and condensation in the water cycle, and about freezing and melting in erosion. | Class discussion of water and its changes of state in the natural environment. Groups use secondary sources to research and make posters on topics such as rainfall, glaciers and icebergs. | | Groups present their posters and describe their findings to the class. | ● Know where water is found as a solid, as a liquid and as a gas in the environment. ● Can explain the part played by evaporation and condensation in the water cycle. |

| | OBJECTIVES | ACTIVITY 1 | ACTIVITY 2 |
|---|---|---|---|
| ASSESSMENT 14 | ● To assess the children's knowledge and understanding of gases, the differences between gases, liquids and solids, and changes of state. ● To assess the children's ability to explain observations and to draw conclusions from measurements. | Give examples of solids, liquids and gases and describe their properties. Identify the changes of state involved in melting, boiling, evaporating and condensing. | Interpret some simple temperature data in physical terms. |

# LESSON 1

| Objectives | • To know the characteristic features of the solid and liquid states of matter.<br>• To sort materials as solids and liquids.<br>• To describe the processes of melting and dissolving. |
|---|---|
| Resources | A wooden brick, a wax candle, sugar lumps, a jug of water; cards (one set per group) with the names of different solid and liquid materials (such as stone, wood, iron, ice, glass, water, cooking oil, paraffin, lava, mercury, milk, blood written on). |
| Main activity | Show the children the brick, candle, sugar lumps and water. Use these items to review their knowledge of solids and liquids from Year 4/Primary 5. Demonstrate melting by lighting the candle and observing the wax. Demonstrate dissolving by stirring a sugar lump into water. In their groups, give the children the cards to sort into solids and liquids. |
| Differentiation | Less able children could try to select examples of solids and liquids from the cards. More able children could describe the characteristic features of solids and liquids. |
| Assessment | Sort the cards as a class, reviewing the key properties of each material in turn. |
| Plenary | Ask each child to pick a solid and a liquid from the cards, then write one or two sentences about the properties of their chosen materials. Check that they understand that a solid has a fixed shape, but a liquid flows to take up the shape of its container. |
| Outcomes | • Can distinguish solids and liquids by their properties.<br>• Can give examples of melting and dissolving. |

# LESSON 2

## OBJECTIVES

- To know that air is all around us.
- To know that air is a type of material called a gas.
- To know that air has mass.

## RESOURCES

**Main teaching activity:** An inflatable beach ball and ball pump, a feather, a marble, an electric fan, two party balloons, thread, a wire coat-hanger, a digital balance (if available).
**Group activities: 1.** Paper, pencils. **2.** Blank A4 paper.

## PREPARATION

Inflate two party balloons and tie them to either side of a wire coat-hanger with thread. Suspend the coat-hanger from a string. Adjust the positions of the balloons until the coat-hanger balances horizontally (this needs some care). Position the electric fan where the children will feel it blowing air on their faces when they are sitting down at the start of the lesson.

## BACKGROUND

There are three common 'states' of matter: solid, liquid and gas. The different properties of matter in these three states can be explained by the arrangement and behaviour of the particles (molecules) from which the matter is composed. The molecular structure of matter is examined further in Lesson 8 (page 105).

The air is a mixture of gases. In the gaseous state, matter is so thin we can move through it, pushing it aside with little resistance. Most gases are invisible, though some have a colour and can thus be seen (for example, the poisonous gas chlorine is green).

Although air is invisible, we can easily detect that it is all around us by its effects. You can feel the movement of air when you blow on the back of your hand. When you blow up balloons or bicycle tyres, you are filling them with air. Air expands to fill the space available to it, and exerts a pressure on the walls of its container. It can be compressed into a smaller volume by increasing the pressure applied by the walls, for example by squashing a ball between your hands. The increased pressure of the air trapped inside the ball makes it feel springy. If you let the air out from an inflated tyre or a balloon, it escapes in a rush – making a steady hiss or a sudden bang.

The Earth is cloaked in a layer of mixed gases called the 'atmosphere'. We call this mixture of gases 'air'. The wind is the movement of air through the atmosphere, caused by slight differences in pressure around the Earth. The push of the wind flaps washing on a line, carrying away moisture. It lifts kites, powers sailboats and turns windmills. Air has mass. The air inside a typical classroom has about the same mass as the teacher!

> **Vocabulary**
>
> air, air resistance, deflate, gas, liquid, solid, inflate, weight, state

For us, the most important property of air is that 21% of it is the gas oxygen, which almost all living things need for respiration (see Unit 1, Lesson 5, page 17). Most of the rest of the atmosphere (78%) is the relatively unreactive gas nitrogen. The atmosphere also contains water vapour (in varying amounts), carbon dioxide (0.03%), tiny quantities of 'rare' gases such as argon (0.93%), and pollution products (for example, the gases sulphur dioxide and carbon monoxide) emitted by vehicles, power stations and factories.

## INTRODUCTION

The children should already be familiar with the differences between solids and liquids from work in Year 4/Primary 5. Ask them what they can feel blowing on their faces from the fan: *Is the sensation caused by a solid, a liquid or something else?* (It is caused by moving air, which is neither a solid nor a liquid.)

Ask them to think of some other ways that they can tell they are surrounded by air. If necessary, prompt them to talk about the sensation of moving through the air on a bicycle, the power of the wind to lift kites and turn windmills, and their need to breathe air in and out of their lungs. Build on the children's ideas to explain that air is not 'nothing', but a special kind of material called a 'gas'. Say that you will demonstrate to them that air flows, is springy (exerts a pressure), drags on moving objects, and has a mass of its own.

## MAIN TEACHING ACTIVITY

Inflate the beach ball. Explain how you are using the pump to fill the ball with air. Demonstrate how it becomes firmer and more 'bouncy' as you squeeze more air inside it. Discuss the use of a bicycle pump to inflate bicycle tyres, and the effect of getting a puncture.

Drop a marble, then drop a feather. Ask the children to explain why the feather falls more slowly than the marble. If they think it is just because of the weight difference, drop a pin to show that a light object can fall just as fast as a heavier one. Develop the idea that the large feather has to push more air aside than the marble or the pin, and so experiences more air 'resistance'; because it is light, this resistance can be as strong as the effect of gravity. Discuss the application of air resistance to slowing down the fall of a parachutist. (Unit 6 of *100 Science Lessons: Year 6* explores this in more depth.)

Ask the children whether air has mass (and thus weight). Many children will think that air is weightless, since it does not appear to fall. Explain that, although gases are much lighter than liquids and solids, they are not completely weightless: air settles on the surface of the Earth, which is why the air is 'thinner' at high altitudes. If the air had no mass, it would drift off into space. Show the children the 'balloon balance' and ask them to predict what will happen if you let the air out of one of the balloons. Pinch the neck of one balloon and puncture the pinched-off part with a pin. This will allow you to let the air out slowly. When the balloon is deflated, release the balance and let the children see whether their prediction was correct.

If you have a digital balance, you can demonstrate directly that a fully inflated balloon is slightly heavier than a deflated one. (**NB** You cannot use this method to 'weigh' the air inside the balloon directly, since the buoyancy of the inflated balloon needs to be allowed for.)

## GROUP ACTIVITIES

**1.** List and sketch the following things on the board or flip chart: a kite, a sailboat, a hand-held fan, a car tyre, a windmill, a football, a parachute, a hot air balloon, a sycamore seed, an aeroplane. Ask the children to think about these and discuss in their groups how air helps to make each thing work. Each child should then select an item and write one or more sentences on a sheet of paper to explain how it makes use of the air. Encourage them to write about as many items as they can.

**2.** Give each group a blank sheet of A4 paper. Ask them to think of as many ways as they can of using the paper to show that air exists. (For example, they might fan themselves with it, let it flutter to the ground, blow it across the table, make a tube and blow through it, make a paper aeroplane, and so on.)

## DIFFERENTIATION

**1.** Ask the less able children to give a simple explanation of one of the items shown on the board, such as how a kite or a sailboat works (the push of the wind). More able children will tackle a wider range of items involving more properties of gases, such as the spring (pressure) of the air squeezed inside a tyre. Challenge the most able by asking which items would work on the Moon. They should know or be able to find out that there is no air on the Moon, so any device that uses air in the atmosphere (such as sailboats, kites and planes) will not work. Air-filled items such as tyres and balls will work on the Moon, but they will need to be filled with air (or another gas) brought from the Earth.

**2.** Prompt the least able children to use the paper as a fan. The most able children will generate a wide range of imaginative ideas.

### ASSESSMENT

Check that the children understand that air is not 'nothing', but is a material with its own mass that can affect objects within it. The children's writing about the items drawn on the board or flip chart will reveal their level of understanding of the air as a gas.

### PLENARY

Ask representatives from each group to read out some of their writing about the items on the board. Ask each group to demonstrate one method of showing the presence of air with the sheet of paper. Use the children's writing and demonstrations to summarise the key learning points: air is all around us; air is a gas; air has mass.

### OUTCOMES

- Know that we are surrounded by air.
- Recognise that air is a material.
- Can demonstrate the presence of air.
- Can describe how the mass of air can be demonstrated.

### LINKS

Unit 6, Lessons 7 and 8: the force of the wind.

## LESSON 3

### OBJECTIVES

- To know that porous materials are composed of solid particles or regions surrounded by gaps.
- To know that when porous materials are dry, the gaps are filled with air.
- To observe that water can displace the air from the gaps in porous materials.

### RESOURCES

**Main teaching activity:** A jar full of marbles, a sand bucket, dry sand, a plastic jug, a piece of dry Oasis (from a florist or garden centre), a wooden spoon or ruler, a large clear plastic tank, water.
**Group activities: 1 and 2.** A water tray, pieces of natural and synthetic sponge, samples of any other porous materials you have (such as Oasis, sand, cotton wool, fabrics, foam rubber), magnifying glasses or low-power microscopes (if available), paper, pencils.

### PREPARATION

Fill the sand bucket to the brim with dry sand and level off the surface. Stand the bucket in a tray next to a plastic jug full of water. Three-quarters fill the plastic tank with water and stand it where all the children can see it. Lay out pieces of sponge, magnifying glasses, paper and pencils ready for the Group activities.

*Vocabulary*

solid, pores, porous, absorb, air bubble, displace

### BACKGROUND

Solids such as metals, glass and most dense rocks are continuous: there are no pores, gaps, or spaces within the structure of the material. Continuous solids do not contain air, and usually do not absorb water when they are made wet. But many other common materials, such as powders, sand, sponge, foam plastic, paper, card and most fabrics, are porous. A porous material contains many tiny holes or gaps that surround the solid particles or regions that make up the bulk of the material. When a porous material is dry, these pores are filled with air. When it is immersed in water, the air is displaced and rises as bubbles to the water surface as the water soaks into the material.

### INTRODUCTION

Show the children the bucket full to the brim with sand. Ask whether they think it is possible to get anything else into the bucket. Some children may say that it is not possible, because the bucket is already full. Slowly pour some water on to the surface, so that it is absorbed into the sand without spilling over the edge. Ask the children where the water has gone. Explain that it has 'fitted in' to the spaces between the sand grains. Ask what was in these spaces before the water entered them (air, which is a gas). Ask what happened to the air as the water filled the spaces (it was displaced into the air above the bucket).

Use the jar of marbles to demonstrate what happens when water is poured into a porous material. The children will see the water filling the gaps between the marbles. Explain that the marbles are just like the particles of sand, but on a larger scale.

## MAIN TEACHING ACTIVITY

Show the children a piece of dry Oasis. Explain how it is used by florists to hold water for an arrangement of flowers. Like sand, Oasis is a porous material with many holes. Ask the children to try to think of an experiment to prove that the pores in dry Oasis are filled with air. The water-filled tank may trigger some ideas. With the children observing, rapidly submerge the Oasis in the water tank. Hold it under the surface with a wooden spoon or ruler. Ask the children to describe what they see (a mass of air bubbles streaming upwards from the Oasis). Ask what the bubbles are. Explain that they are air bubbles displaced by the water from the pores on the Oasis. Discuss the importance of repeating scientific experiments to confirm that the observed results are reproducible and not a fluke. Repeat the experiment with a second piece of dry Oasis.

## GROUP ACTIVITIES

**1.** Ask a child to submerge a piece of sponge in the water tray while the rest of the group observe what happens. They should repeat the test at least once more to confirm what they have seen. Each child should draw a labelled sketch of his or her observations and write a brief account of the experiment.

**2.** Ask the children in their groups to observe the structure of a piece of sponge through a magnifying glass or low-power microscope. Both natural and synthetic sponges can be studied. The children should sketch what they see and label the pores as 'filled with air'. Encourage them to go on to examine other porous materials.

## DIFFERENTIATION

**1.** The children's attainment will be differentiated by the detail of their drawings, and by the level of understanding expressed in their written accounts. All the children should be able to state that the dry sponge is full of holes and that these are full of air, which is a gas. Ask the more able children to explain why the air bubbles rise when a porous material is submerged. (Air is lighter than water, so it floats to the surface.)

**2.** Less able children can concentrate on observing and sketching a piece of sponge. More able children can observe and sketch a wider range of porous materials, including Oasis, sand, cotton wool and fabrics. Their sketches should show the different characteristic features of these materials.

## ASSESSMENT

Check that all the children understand that the gaps in porous materials are not 'empty', but are filled with air. Note whether the more able children can explain how the water displaces the air from the pores as the sponge is submerged.

## PLENARY

Ask representatives from the groups to show their sketches of the different materials and to describe the differences they observed. Use the children's observations and ideas to summarise the key learning point: that some solid materials contain air.

## OUTCOMES

● Can state that porous materials contain many air-filled holes.
● Can identify bubbles rising from a submerged piece of solid material as air that was in the spaces in the material.
● Recognise the need to repeat experiments in order to check observations.

## LINKS

Unit 4, Lesson 4: looking at the volumes of air in different soils.

# LESSON 4

## OBJECTIVES
● To know that soil contains air.
● To use measuring cylinders and jugs to measure volumes of water.
● To compare the volumes of air present in different soils.

### RESOURCES

**Main teaching activity and Group activity:** A soil sample; buckets of gravel, sand, and garden soil; three empty buckets; trowels and/or spades; stickers or felt-tipped pens; plastic beakers, measuring jugs and cylinders; water, photocopiable page 115, pencils.

### PREPARATION

Set out three plastic beakers, a measuring cylinder or jug and a trowel for each group. Make one copy per child of page 115.

### BACKGROUND

The children learned in the previous lesson that porous materials contain air. Soil is also porous. The presence of air in soil is significant for the various things that live there. The children will have observed how air can be displaced from porous materials by water. In this investigation, they will measure the amount of air in different soil samples by using the displacement technique. When water is poured onto a soil sample, the volume of air displaced is equal to the volume of water absorbed. The children can therefore equate their measurement of the volume of water a sample absorbs to the volume of air it contained initially. Water volumes can be measured with a measuring cylinder calibrated in millilitres.

The volume of air a soil sample contains is a measure of its porosity (how porous it is), which affects the rate at which the soil drains. Sandy soils are more porous, and so drain more quickly, than clay soils. They are therefore less likely to become waterlogged in wet weather.

**NB** The children should always wash their hands after handling materials in a science investigation.

### Vocabulary

soil, particles, pores, porous, absorb, volume, millilitre, measuring scale

### INTRODUCTION

Show the children a soil sample and ask them what living things they might find in it. (Worms and other minibeasts, plant roots, microbes.) Ask the children which of these living things need to breathe air. (Small animals, some microbes.) *How do they manage to breathe in the soil?* The children should recall your demonstration in Lesson 2 that porous materials such as sand contain air. *Do you think there is air in soil? How much? Do all soils contain the same amount of air? Can you think of a method for measuring the amount of air in soil?* Try to lead the children towards devising an approach based on displacing the air with water, developing from their observations in the previous lesson.

### MAIN TEACHING ACTIVITY

Demonstrate the method to the children. Two-thirds fill a plastic beaker with gravel from the bucket. Use a sticker or felt-tipped pen to mark the level of the gravel surface. Fill a measuring jug with water. Show the children the scale on the jug, and remind them that water volumes can be measured in millilitres. Note the initial reading on the jug (for example, 1000ml). Slowly pour water from the jug onto the gravel sample until the gravel is saturated (the water level just reaches the gravel surface, and does not fall again). The children will observe air bubbles rising through the water in the beaker as the air is displaced from the gravel. Note the new reading on the jug (for example, 550ml) and explain that the volume of water poured onto the gravel is equal to the difference between the initial and final readings on the jug (1000ml–550ml=450ml). Make sure the children understand that this volume is equal to the volume of air that was in the gravel initially.

Discuss the accuracy of the measurement. Explain the importance of standing the jug on a level surface and putting your eye close to the scale when making a reading. Explain that to check the reliability of a measurement, it is always good practice to repeat it at least once. Empty the wet gravel into an empty bucket and refill the beaker with a dry sample. Discuss the importance of filling the beaker to the same level as before, so that the volumes of the two samples are the same. Repeat the measurement and take an average of the results to obtain a 'best' estimate.

## GROUP ACTIVITY

Divide the children into groups and ask them to use this method to compare the volumes of air in three different samples: gravel, sand and garden soil. Each child should record the results of the group's experiments on a copy of page 115.

## DIFFERENTIATION

All the groups should make measurements, aiming to use all three basic samples. More able groups might like to extend their investigations to a range of soil samples taken from different locations. These could be collected from around the school or brought in by the children from their own gardens.

## ASSESSMENT

Check that the children are taking appropriate care with their measurements and recording. They should be able to explain that in order for their comparisons to be 'fair', they need to use the same volume of dry soil for each test.

## PLENARY

Ask representatives from each group to hold up their record sheets and describe their findings. *Which sample held the most water? Which held the least? Are the results consistent between different groups? Can the figures be compared directly, or did the different groups use different amounts of soil for their tests?* The children will probably have found that the gravel held the most water and is therefore the most porous material. The sand is the next most porous material, and the garden soil the least porous. Discuss the use of gravel to make a dry, well-drained surface for garden paths and driveways. *Why do gardeners sometimes dig sand into sticky clay soils?* (To improve the drainage.)

## OUTCOMES

● Can use measuring cylinders or jugs to measure water volumes.
● Can explain the importance of taking care when reading scales, and of repeating measurements in order to check results.
● Understand that in order for a comparison to be fair, all variables except the one being tested must be kept the same.

## LINKS

Unit 3, Lesson 1: water in the environment.

## LESSON 5

| Objective | ● To know that there are a variety of useful gases. |
|---|---|
| Resources | A selection of secondary sources that the children can use to research the properties and uses of gases: science encyclopaedias, CD-ROMs and videos; posters and pamphlets produced by industrial gas companies; a pack of cards (one per group) with the names of different gases: oxygen, carbon dioxide, nitrogen, helium, natural gas, hydrogen, chlorine etc; large sheets of paper, felt-tipped pens. |
| Main activity | Remind the children of the composition of air. Ask them whether they can name any other gases that are not normally present in air. They may be familiar with helium (used in party balloons) and 'natural gas' (mostly methane; used for cooking and heating). Divide the class into groups and give each group a card naming a gas. Ask the groups to use the secondary sources to research the properties and uses of their named gas. Each group should record their findings on a poster. |
| Differentiation | Less able children can find one use for a more familiar gas, such as oxygen. More able children can find a range of properties and uses for a number of less familiar gases, such as hydrogen and chlorine. |
| Assessment | Ask the children (working individually) to pick a gas and write one or two sentences about its uses in their science notebooks. Check that they understand that a gas is a material similar to the air, and that different gases have different properties. |
| Plenary | Each group should display the poster they have prepared and describe their findings to the rest of the class. |
| Outcomes | ● Know that a number of gases exist.<br>● Can describe the uses of a variety of gases. |

# LESSON 6

| | |
|---|---|
| **Objective** | ● To know that when a liquid evaporates, it forms a gas. |
| **Resources** | Perfume, a dish, a battery-powered fan, cotton handkerchiefs, a hairdryer, string, clothes pegs; catalogues and magazines with pictures of hairdryers, tumble dryers and other 'drying machines'. |
| **Main activity** | Demonstrate the evaporation process by putting a little perfume in a dish. Waft the smell towards the children with the fan. Discuss examples of the evaporation of water, including washing drying on the line, puddles disappearing and people drying in the sun after a swim. Wet a handkerchief and hang it on a line. Discuss how the rate of evaporation depends on temperature and air flow. Demonstrate the effect of the hairdryer. Ask groups to find pictures of different 'drying machines' and write about how they work. |
| **Differentiation** | Less able children could focus on explaining where the water goes when something dries out. More able children could discuss the factors that affect the rate of drying, including air flow, surface area and temperature. |
| **Assessment** | Ask the children to explain what happens to the water when something dries out. Check that they understand that the water is not 'vanishing', but is changing into an invisible gas that becomes part of the air. |
| **Plenary** | A representative from each group can display their pictures and read their writing about a drying machine. |
| **Outcomes** | ● Recognise that when a liquid evaporates, it forms a gas.<br>● Recognise that rate of evaporation depends on temperature.<br>● Recognise that rate of evaporation depends on air movements.<br>● Can explain how appliances that dry things (eg a hairdryer) work. |

# LESSON 7

| | |
|---|---|
| **Objective** | ● To conduct an investigation into the factors affecting the rate of evaporation. |
| **Resources** | Cotton handkerchiefs, paper, string, clothes pegs, various containers, rulers, graph paper, pencils, timers. |
| **Main activity** | Ask the children to devise their own experiments to investigate the factors that affect the rate of evaporation of water. |
| **Differentiation** | Less able children could compare the drying time of a screwed-up wet handkerchief with that of one hung on a line, or the drying times of sheets of wet paper placed in different locations. More able children could plot graphs of the depth of water over time in open containers left in different locations. For fair comparisons, the exposed surface areas should be the same. The effect of changing the exposed surface area could also be investigated. |
| **Assessment** | Ask the children to explain how they planned their investigations. Did they predict how the drying time would depend on the location? Were their predictions confirmed? Make sure that they understand the importance of changing only one variable at a time when they are investigating the effect of a single factor. |
| **Plenary** | Each group should report their findings to the rest of the class and display them as a chart or graph. |
| **Outcome** | ● Can plan and carry out an investigation and record the results. |

# LESSON 8

## OBJECTIVES

● To know that gases do not have a fixed volume as solids and liquids do.
● To know that gases are more easily compressed (squashed) than solids and liquids.
● To know that gases and liquids can flow and change their shape, but continuous solids have a fixed shape.

## RESOURCES

**Main teaching activity:** An inflatable beach toy and pump, a small candle, a fireproof container such as a biscuit tin, a large plastic lemonade bottle, a small plastic funnel, sodium bicarbonate (baking powder), vinegar, party balloons, a solid wooden brick or ball, plastic beakers.
**Group activities: 1.** The playground or school hall. **2.** Three small plastic lemonade bottles per group, each filled to the brim with sand, water or air and with the tops screwed on tight, A4 sheets of card, felt-tipped pens.

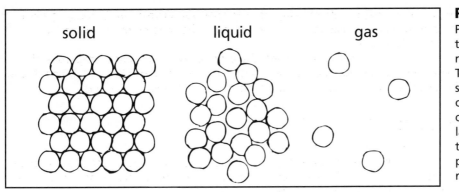

| solid | liquid | gas |

**PREPARATION**
Partly inflate a party balloon, then hold the neck under a running tap to fill it with water. Tie off the neck. Partly inflate a second balloon with air and tie off the neck. Put two teaspoons of sodium bicarbonate into the large empty lemonade bottle (use the funnel to help). Set out the plastic bottles, cards and pens ready for the Group activities.

*Vocabulary*

gas, compress, expand, space, flow, pour, rigid, fluid, liquid, solid

## BACKGROUND

Many of the properties of gases can be illustrated with an inflatable beach toy. When you inflate the toy, air from the pump (or your lungs) is squashed inside it. There seems to be no set amount of air required to occupy the space – the air simply expands and changes shape to fill the space available. The inflated toy is squashy and springy. If you pull out the stopper, the air flows out and expands into the surrounding atmosphere. In contrast, liquids and solids occupy (more or less) fixed volumes: they do not expand to fill the space available, and are far less compressible (squashy) than gases. Liquids can be poured, and change shape as they flow from one container to another. Solids are rigid and do not pour. A continuous piece of solid, such as a brick or a stone, has a fixed shape that does not change as it is moved from place to place. An applied force (such as a hammer blow) may change the shape of a solid, but gravity alone is not usually strong enough to do so.

The contrasting properties of gases, liquids and solids can be explained with a simple picture of the tiny particles from which they are made (see illustration above). These particles (molecules) are much too small to see even with a powerful microscope, but experiments prove that they exist. In a solid, the particles are linked together by strong forces. Individual particles cannot move over each other, so a solid is rigid and strong. In a liquid, the particles have more freedom of movement. Forces hold the particles close together, so the liquid has a fixed volume; but because the particles can tumble over each other (rather like grains of sand), the liquid pours and flows. In a gas, the particles are widely separated and move around almost independently. The wide separation explains why gases are light, have no strength to resist stretching or bending forces, and are easily compressed. The independent motion of particles explains why a gas expands to fill whatever space is available.

## INTRODUCTION

Pump up the beach toy in front of the children. Remind them that you are filling it with a gas called 'air'. Ask them to consider how the toy would be different if it were filled with a liquid or a solid (it would be much heavier and less squeezy; if it were filled with a solid, it would be hard and rigid).

## MAIN TEACHING ACTIVITY

Show the children the air-filled and water-filled balloons and the wooden brick. Use these items to compare and contrast the properties of gases, liquids and solids. Write words that describe these properties ('light', 'heavy', 'strong', 'weak', 'rigid', 'fluid') on the board.

Explain that, although you cannot see most gases, it is possible to demonstrate that they can expand, pour and flow. For example, you can feel and hear the air flowing out of an inflated beach toy when you remove the stopper. Explain that you are going to make the gas carbon dioxide by pouring a little vinegar onto some sodium bicarbonate in the lemonade bottle. Pour about an eggcup full of vinegar through the funnel. The children will observe the mixture fizzing and foaming as the gas is produced. Stretch the neck of a party balloon over the open bottleneck: the balloon will be partly inflated by the expanding gas.

Light a candle inside an open biscuit tin. Explain that carbon dioxide is heavier than air, so you can pour it out of the bottle. Remove the balloon and slowly pour the gas from the bottle into the tin (be careful not to pour out the vinegar). The carbon dioxide will extinguish the candle flame. During the experiment, stress the need for safety; tell the children that they should not try to repeat school science experiments at home.

## GROUP ACTIVITIES

**1.** Ask the children to imagine that they are the particles in a solid, liquid or a gas. Get each group to describe and act out (perhaps in the playground or school hall) the motion of the particles in the different states. To represent a solid, the children should link arms to form a rigid shape. In the liquid state, they should remain close together but move around, changing places, so that the group flows and changes shape. In the gas state, the children should spread out, rushing around in all directions.

**2.** Ask each group to prepare a set of three cards that summarise the different properties of solids, liquids and gases. Encourage them to use the descriptive words written on the board, and to examine the three lemonade bottles on their table in order to develop their ideas.

## DIFFERENTIATION

**1.** This activity should be accessible to all the children.
**2.** Less able children should be able to list at least one characteristic for each state (for example: gases are light, liquids pour, solids have a fixed shape). Challenge more able children to use the particle model to account for the properties they identify.

## ASSESSMENT

Check that all the children can identify whether a container is filled with a gas, a liquid or a solid. Ask them to describe a difference between a gas and a liquid, between a gas and a solid, and between a liquid and a solid.

## PLENARY

Ask a representative from each group to talk through the information they have included on one of their 'state' cards. Use the children's ideas to summarise the key learning points.

## OUTCOMES

● Know that a gas can be poured and squashed, has no fixed shape or volume, and can spread out into the air when released from its container.
● Can describe the different properties of solids, liquids and gases.

## LINKS

Unit 4, Lesson 9: condensation.

# LESSON 9

## OBJECTIVES

● To know that gases can be turned into liquids by cooling.
● To know that this process is called condensation.
● To know that water vapour is present in the air, but cannot be seen.

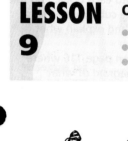

## RESOURCES

**Main teaching activity:** A picture of people or animals with steaming breath; a refrigerator, a small mirror, a pair of spectacles, a can of fizzy drink, cut flowers in a narrow-necked vase, a polythene bag, modelling clay, rubber bands.
**Group activities: 1.** Plastic bowls, warm water, cling film, ice cubes, paper, pencils.
**2.** Photocopiable page 116, pencils.

## PREPARATION

Cool the mirror, spectacles and can of drink in the refrigerator for half an hour before the lesson. Make sure there is a good supply of ice cubes available. Set out a plastic bowl and piece of cling film for each group, and a copy of page 116 for each child.

*Vocabulary*

condense, condensation, water vapour, changing state, liquid, gas

## BACKGROUND

Condensation is the process by which a gas changes into a liquid. It is the reverse of evaporation. Children will be familiar with the condensation that takes place on a cold glass or metal surface when it is brought into a warm room; the surface of a drink can or bottle taken from the fridge becomes wet with condensation. Spectacles 'steam up' with condensation when you come indoors on a cold day. Cool surfaces such as windows and mirrors become covered with water droplets in kitchens and bathrooms when there is a lot of water vapour in the air.

As a result of the evaporation of water from the soil, lakes, rivers and oceans, water vapour is always present in the atmosphere. Warm air can hold more water vapour than cooler air. This is why condensation is observed when warm air comes into contact with a cooler surface: the air

## MAIN TEACHING ACTIVITY

Show the children the pan of water on the stove. Tell them that you are going to investigate the way its temperature rises as it is brought to the boil. Stir the water with the thermometer probe and draw the children's attention to the temperature display. Remind them that temperatures are measured in degrees Celsius. Appoint a child to act as recorder, and position him or her by the whiteboard with a marker pen. (Alternatively, use a data-logger to record results directly onto the PC screen.) Record the current water temperature (at 0 minutes) and start the clock. At 1 minute, record the temperature again and turn on the stove. Continue recording the temperature at one-minute intervals until the water has been boiling for two or three minutes. Stir the water with the probe before each reading to make sure that the temperature is fairly uniform throughout the pan.

Draw the children's attention to the change in the appearance of the water as it comes to the boil. You could explain that the small bubbles that appear as the water is warmed are bubbles of air that had been dissolved in the cold water. Larger bubbles of steam don't start to form until the water boils.

## GROUP ACTIVITIES

**1.** Give each child a sheet of plain paper and a sheet of graph paper. Ask them to draw a table and copy the results recorded on the whiteboard into it. Then explain how they can transfer these results onto a graph (with suitable axes) to show how the temperature of the water changes as time passed. Discuss what axes are appropriate (see example below).
**2.** Ask each group to locate a particular value from the graph. Values that can be assigned to different groups include:
- the starting temperature of the water
- the time the hotplate was turned on
- the time when the water reached 70°C
- the 'boiling point' temperature of the water
- the time when the water started to boil.

## DIFFERENTIATION

**1.** Less able children will need considerable guidance in constructing axes for a graph and transferring the data to it from the table. If you used a data-logger, you could print out the graphs that were displayed on the screen for the children to interpret, thus avoiding the difficulties of the children producing their own graphs.
**2.** Ask less able children to locate the time when the water started to boil. More able children can be challenged individually to locate and label all the significant points.

## ASSESSMENT

Check that the children know that when a liquid boils it changes into a gas, and that the boiling point of water is 100°C. Can the representative for each group indicate in which region of the temperature–time graph the water is boiling?

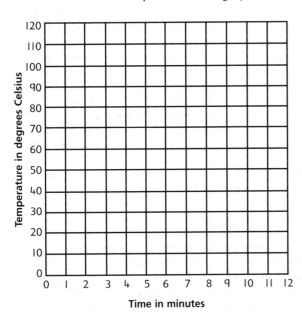

Time in minutes

## PLENARY

Ask a representative from each group to display their graph and explain how they located the required temperatures or times. Discuss the boiling process with the help of the graphs, and emphasise the key learning points. You could challenge more able children to find out from secondary sources why it is difficult to boil an egg or make a good cup of tea at the top of Mount Everest. (The atmospheric pressure is lower, so water boils at a lower temperature.)

## OUTCOMES

- Recognise when a liquid is boiling.
- Recognise that the white cloud seen over boiling water is made up of condensed water droplets.
- Can interpret data from a graph.

# LESSON 11

## OBJECTIVES

- To conduct an investigation into rates of melting.
- To know that the freezing/melting temperature of water is 0°C.
- To know that the temperature in the classroom is normally 18–22°C.

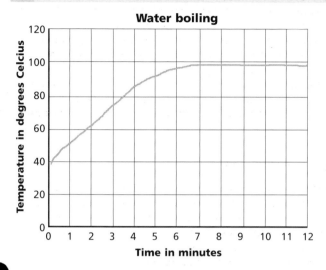

**Water boiling** (graph: Temperature in degrees Celcius vs Time in minutes)

## RESOURCES

**Main teaching activity:** an ICT temperature sensor linked to a computer, a clear plastic beaker, ice cubes, water.
**Group activity:** Plastic beakers, digital thermometers, timers (to measure up to 30 minutes), ice cubes, water, ruled or squared A4 paper, pencils.

## PREPARATION

Set up a temperature sensor and a computer with a screen displaying temperature against time. Select a time interval for the time display, so that a temperature graph is plotted over a 30-minute period on the monitor. Set out plastic beakers, thermometers, timers, paper, pencils and a sheet of ruled or squared A4 paper for each group. Have a supply of ice cubes ready for use.

*Vocabulary*

ice, melt, melting point, temperature, rate of melting, changing state

## BACKGROUND

Melting is the process by which a material changes its state from solid to liquid at a constant temperature. Children will be familiar with melting ice, candle wax and chocolate. At normal atmospheric pressure at sea level, ice melts to liquid water at 0°C. Normal room temperature is 18–22°C. Ice straight from the deep-freeze has a temperature of about –20°C. In a warm room, ice gradually heats up until its surface temperature is 0°C. The ice surface then starts to melt to liquid water. The temperature of the ice–water mixture does not rise above 0°C until all the ice has melted. While there is still ice present, the heat transferred from the surroundings goes into breaking the bonds between the water particles (molecules) that hold them rigidly together in solid ice. When these bonds are broken, the molecules move freely in the liquid state. The rate at which the ice melts depends on the temperature of the surroundings and the insulating properties of the container in which it is held.

## INTRODUCTION

Show the children an ice cube in a clear plastic beaker and discuss the melting process. Ask them to describe any other examples of melting they are familiar with. Explain that they are going to investigate how long an ice cube keeps a drink cold for before it melts.

## MAIN TEACHING ACTIVITY

Take a beaker of iced water from the fridge. Start the computer display with the sensor in air. Indicate to the children that the monitor is displaying the temperature of the room. Plunge the sensor into the iced water and observe how the temperature graph falls to, and remains at, 0°C. Stir the mixture every few minutes with the sensor. Explain that this is necessary to keep the temperature uniform (even) throughout the mixture.

Ask the children to predict what will happen to the temperature as time passes. *Will it rise or fall as the ice melts?* (The temperature will stay around 0°C while there is ice in the water. Only when all the ice has melted will the temperature of the water start to rise towards room temperature.) Ask the children to list factors that they think will affect the time taken for the ice to melt in a drink. Prompt them to consider the amount of ice (number of ice cubes), the amount of liquid, the temperature of the room, the insulating properties of the container and the initial temperature of the drink before ice was added. Tell them that they are going to conduct a fair test, in groups, to see how the melting time depends on the number of ice cubes.

## GROUP ACTIVITY

Ask each group to prepare a record sheet for their experiment, using ruled or squared paper. They will need to record the initial water temperature in °C, the number of ice cubes used and the temperature at one-minute intervals. Each group should have an identical beaker of water at the same (chilled) temperature. Ask the groups to measure and note the water temperature with their thermometers. Explain that all the water samples must start at the same temperature in order for the test to be fair. Take a tray of ice cubes from the fridge. Add one cube to the first group's beaker, two cubes to the second group's, three to the third group's and so on. Ask the children to record the temperature of the ice–water mixture on their record sheet at one-minute intervals, until the ice has melted and the water temperature has started to rise.

## DIFFERENTIATION

Less able pupils can just write their results on the record sheet. More able pupils can plot graphs as they go along. Ask them to label distinct regions on the graph (the time period during which solid ice is present, the period when the water is starting to warm towards room temperature). Children who would like to take the investigation further can investigate the effect of changing other factors – for example, the initial temperature of the water.

## ASSESSMENT

Check that every child can describe melting as the process in which a solid changes into a liquid, and can give examples such as a melting ice-lolly. Ask them to give the melting temperature of ice and to describe one or more factors that affect the rate at which ice melts, for example the temperature of the surroundings.

## PLENARY

Ask each group to use their data to determine a melting time for their ice sample. Combine the results to produce a class graph of melting times for different numbers of ice cubes. Discuss how the test was kept fair, so that valid comparisons could be made.

## OUTCOMES

- Know that ice melts at 0°C.
- Know that normal room temperature is 18–22°C.
- Can identify one or more factors that affect the rate at which ice melts.
- Can carry out an investigation.

## LESSON 12

| | |
|---|---|
| **Objectives** | ● To know that heating/cooling can cause materials to melt, boil, evaporate, freeze or condense.<br>● To know that some materials are natural and others are manufactured.<br>● To know that many materials are manufactured and processed by methods involving the use of heat. |
| **Resources** | A wax candle-making kit; a selection of secondary sources that children can use to research the manufacture and processing of materials (these could include: science encyclopaedias and CD-ROMs; posters, pamphlets and videotapes produced by industrial companies); large sheets of card, felt-tipped pens. |
| **Main activity** | Demonstrate the candle-making process. Explain that you are using heat to melt the wax so that it can be poured into a mould. When it cools, it 'freezes' solid again. Discuss the role of heat in extracting or manufacturing new materials from natural materials, and in processing them. For example, metals are extracted from ores by heating the ores in furnaces. Petrol and paraffin are extracted from crude oil by heating the oil so that the petrol and oil evaporate as gases, then cooling them so that they condense back to liquids. Salt is extracted from sea water by allowing the heat of the Sun to evaporate the water, leaving the salt behind.<br>   Divide the class into groups. Issue each group with a large card to make a wall chart. Ask the groups to use secondary sources to research examples of industrial processes that use melting, freezing, condensation, evaporation or boiling. Materials to study could include metals, glass, plastics, oil and petrol, frozen or dried foods, sea-salt, wines and spirits, scents and cosmetics. Each group should record their findings on a card. |
| **Differentiation** | Less able children could find examples of how melting is used to shape or mould materials. More able children could find separate examples of how melting, freezing, evaporation, condensation and boiling are used to change or process materials. |
| **Assessment** | Ask each child to pick a manufactured material and write a few sentences describing the action of heat in its production or processing. |
| **Plenary** | Each group should display the chart they have prepared and describe their findings to the rest of the class. |
| **Outcomes** | ● Recognise examples of melting, boiling, freezing, evaporation and condensation.<br>● Recognise a range of natural and manufactured materials.<br>● Can describe processes in the making of materials. |

| Objectives | ● To know where ice, liquid water and water vapour are found in the natural environment.<br>● To know about evaporation and condensation in the water cycle, and about freezing and melting in erosion. |
|---|---|
| **Resources** | Secondary sources of information on the water cycle and the role of water in physical processes in the environment; felt-tipped pens, large sheets of paper. |
| **Main activity** | Prompt the children to describe locations where ice, liquid water and water vapour are found in nature. Ask them to describe situations in which natural changes of state take place (such as evaporation from rivers and oceans, lakes freezing in winter and glaciers melting in summer). Divide the class into groups. Ask the groups to use secondary sources to research different aspects of water in the environment. Possible topics might include rainfall, erosion, glaciers, the water cycle, floods and icebergs. Each group should prepare a poster on their chosen topic. |
| **Differentiation** | Less able children could describe where ice, liquid water and water vapour occur naturally. More able children could describe processes in which changes of state are significant, such as the water cycle, erosion and glaciation. |
| **Assessment** | Ask each child to pick a topic and write one or two paragraphs about it. Check that the children understand that water occurs in three states in nature. |
| **Plenary** | Each group should display their poster and describe their findings to the rest of the class. |
| **Outcomes** | ● Know where water is found as a solid, as a liquid and as a gas in the environment.<br>● Can explain the part played by evaporation and condensation in the water cycle. |

**UNIT 4 MATERIALS**

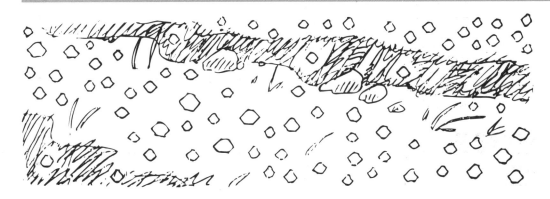

**ASSESSMENT**

## LESSON 14

### OBJECTIVES

● To assess the children's knowledge and understanding of gases, the differences between gases, liquids and solids, and changes of state.
● To assess the children's ability to explain observations and to draw conclusions from measurements.

### RESOURCES

Photocopiable pages 117 and 118, pencils, pens.

### INTRODUCTION

Use a brief 'question and answer' session to review the key learning points of the unit. Draw the children's attention to the posters, charts and experiments displayed around the room to remind them of the investigations they have made. They should recall the following facts:
● We are surrounded by a mixture of gases that we call 'air'. Air has mass.
● Soil and other porous materials contain air. The amount of air in soil can be measured by displacing it with water.
● There are a range of useful gases – for example, carbon dioxide is used in fizzy drinks and helium in balloons.
● Solids, liquids and gases have different properties.
● Melting, boiling, evaporation, freezing and condensation are reversible processes in which materials change from one state to another.
● Ice melts at 0°C. Water boils at 100°C.
● Changes caused by heat are used to manufacture and process materials.

## ASSESSMENT ACTIVITY 1

Use photocopiable page 117 to test the children's knowledge and understanding. Let them complete it individually. You will probably need to review and mark the sheets yourself to get a proper appreciation of each child's attainment. If you wish to give the children a numerical mark, you could award one mark for each correct answer. This gives 15 marks altogether.

### Answers

The following is a sample answer; accept any correct examples of gases, liquids and solids and their properties.

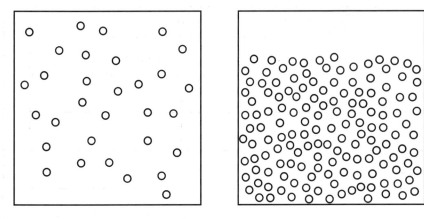

| melting | solid | → | liquid |
| boiling | liquid | → | gas |
| evaporating | liquid | → | gas |
| condensing | gas | → | liquid |
| freezing | liquid | → | solid |

### Looking for levels

All children, including the less able, should be able to give an example of a gas, a liquid and a solid and identify the start and end states for both boiling and freezing. Most children should be able to describe one or more 'special' properties of each of the three states of matter. They should also know the start and end states involved in evaporation and condensation. More able children will produce accurate sketches of the particle arrangements in each of the three states.

## ASSESSMENT ACTIVITY 2

Give each child a copy of photocopiable page 118. This sheet focuses on interpreting a simple set of measurements to draw conclusions and make predictions, based on knowledge and understanding acquired during the unit. You could award up to four marks for each answer, giving a possible total of 16 marks.

### Answers

1. Sophie stirs the drink to make sure that the temperature is 'even' or 'constant' throughout the liquid.
2. Drink B is the one with ice, since an ice–water mixture has a temperature of 0°C.
3. Beakers A and B, because condensation of water vapour from the air takes place on surfaces that are colder than the surroundings.
4. The temperature of beaker A will rise; that of beaker B will stay the same [since it still contains ice]; that of beaker C will stay the same [since it is at room temperature]; that of beaker D will fall.

### Looking for levels

All the children should give correct answers to questions 1 and 2. Some children should answer question 3 correctly and explain it as above. More able children will predict correctly in their answer to question 4.

## PLENARY

Review the question papers with the class, discussing each question and the different answers given by the children in turn.

# Soil investigation

## Sample 1

Description _____

| | Jug readings in millilitres | | |
|---|---|---|---|
| | Start | Finish | Start – finish |
| Test 1 | | | |
| Test 2 | | | |
| Average of test 1 and test 2 | | | |

## Sample 2

Description _____

| | Jug readings in millilitres | | |
|---|---|---|---|
| | Start | Finish | Start – finish |
| Test 1 | | | |
| Test 2 | | | |
| Average of test 1 and test 2 | | | |

## Sample 3

Description _____

| | Jug readings in millilitres | | |
|---|---|---|---|
| | Start | Finish | Start – finish |
| Test 1 | | | |
| Test 2 | | | |
| Average of test 1 and test 2 | | | |

# Condensation

Where in this home might you observe condensation?
Draw circles around the labels.
Can you explain why water sometimes condenses in these places?
Write on the back of the sheet.

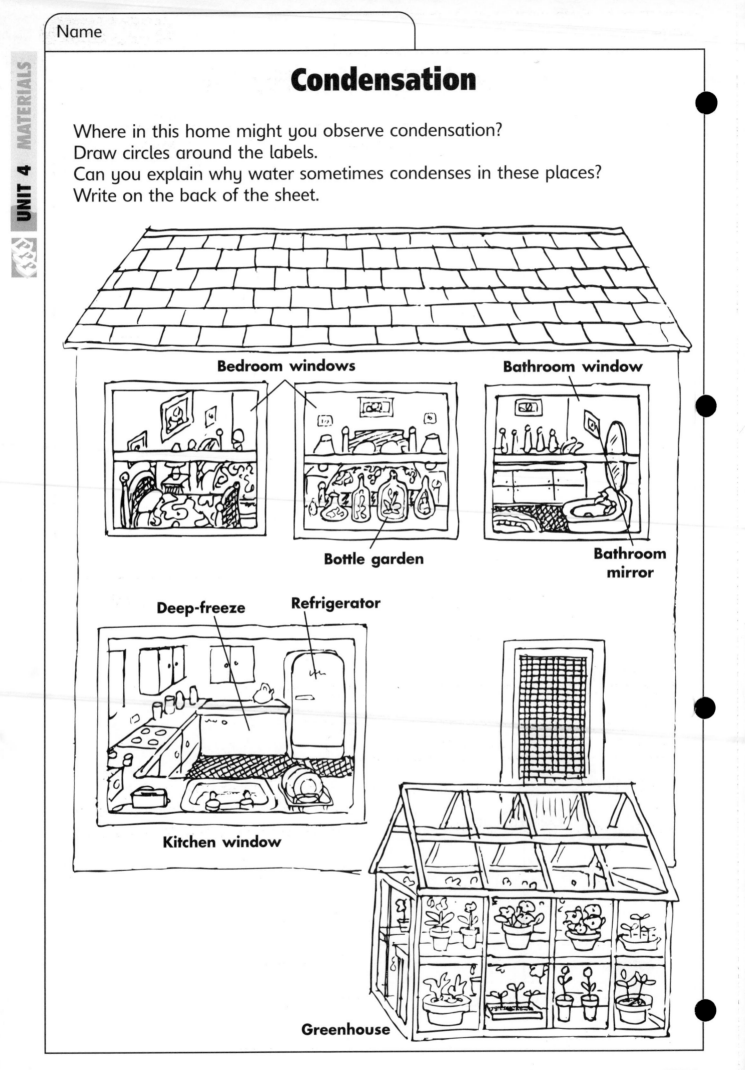

Bedroom windows

Bathroom window

Bottle garden

Bathroom mirror

Deep-freeze

Refrigerator

Kitchen window

Greenhouse

# Gases, solids and liquids

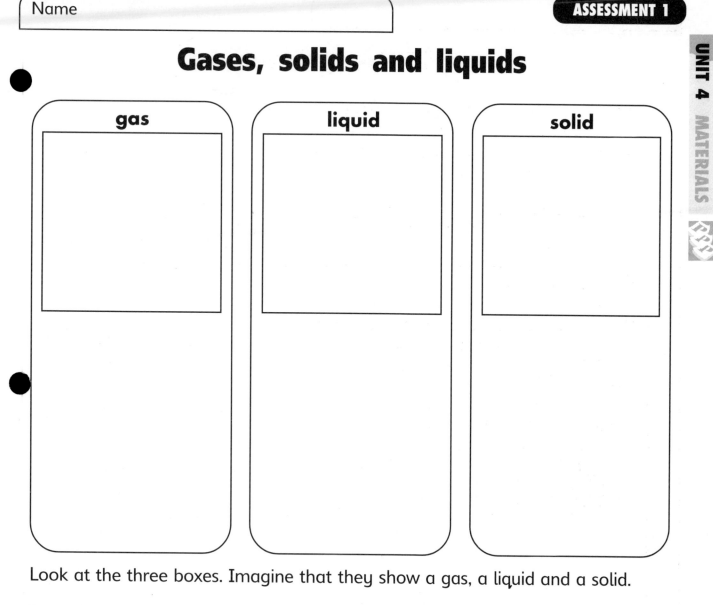

| gas | liquid | solid |

Look at the three boxes. Imagine that they show a gas, a liquid and a solid.

In each box, write and draw:

1. An example of a material or substance in that state.

2. One special property of the state (gas, liquid or solid).

3. A sketch of the particles in that material.

The following words are used to describe materials (for example, water) changing from one state to another. Fill in the blank spaces with the names of the states involved: **gas**, **liquid** or **solid**. The first one has been done for you.

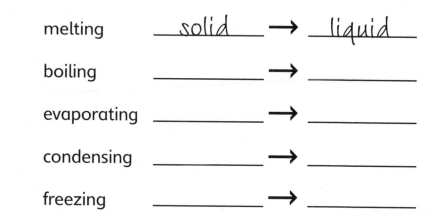

melting      _solid_ → _liquid_

boiling      _____ → _____

evaporating      _____ → _____

condensing      _____ → _____

freezing      _____ → _____

Name

# Gases, solids and liquids

Sophie uses a digital thermometer to measure the temperatures of four drinks in beakers. She stirs the drinks carefully before each measurement. These are her results:

| Beaker | Temperature |
|--------|-------------|
| A | 9°C |
| B | 0°C |
| C | 20°C |
| D | 38°C |

The temperature of the classroom in which the beakers are standing is 20°C.

1. Explain why Sophie stirs each drink before measuring its temperature.

_____

_____

2. One drink has ice in it.

Which drink is this? _____

Explain how you know. _____

_____

_____

3. There is condensation on the outside of two of the beakers.

Which beakers are these? _____

Explain why there is no condensation on the other two beakers.

_____

_____

4. Sophie leaves the beakers standing for 10 minutes. There is still some ice in one of the drinks. She repeats her temperature measurements, using the same method as before. Predict how the temperature of each drink will have changed – will it have risen ↑, fallen ↓ or stayed the same?

A                    B                    C                    D

# Making and using electricity

## ORGANISATION (8 LESSONS)

| | OBJECTIVES | MAIN ACTIVITY | GROUP ACTIVITIES | PLENARY | OUTCOMES |
|---|---|---|---|---|---|
| LESSON 1 | ● To know that in a battery, different chemicals are brought together to produce electricity. ● To make observations and draw conclusions from them. | Discuss how we can tell that electricity is present. Consider places where electricity is used to make light, sound or movement. | Use headphones to detect electricity. Make a salt water battery. Carry out a survey of where batteries are used and what types are used. | Compare the advantages of different ways of detecting electricity. | ● Know that chemicals in batteries react to generate electricity. ● Can use bulbs, buzzers and headphones to detect the presence of electricity. |
| LESSON 2 | ● To know how an electromagnet can be constructed and used. ● To ask scientific questions that can be tested. | Demonstrate how to make an electromagnet. Deduce what materials can be used to make an electromagnet. Consider what factors might affect the strength of electromagnets. | Ask and investigate a question about what factors affect the strength of an electromagnet. Use secondary sources to find out about different uses of electromagnets. | Discuss the children's findings and why electromagnets are used in various contexts. | ● Know how to make an electromagnet. ● Can describe some uses of electromagnets. ● Can ask and investigate a scientific question. |
| LESSON 3 | ● To know that magnets and wires carrying electricity affect each other. ● To decide what to do and what evidence to collect in an investigation. | Consider a compass needle as a magnet. Demonstrate that a piece or coil of copper wire on its own has no effect on a compass needle. | Investigate the effect that pieces and coils of wire carrying electricity have on a magnet. Discuss situations in which a compass might give a false direction reading. | Discuss the Group activities. By considering the forces involved, lead into the idea of the electric motor. | ● Can describe how electricity passing through a wire can affect a compass. ● Can describe how the movement of a magnet in a coil can make a current of electricity. |
| LESSON 4 | ● To know how an electric motor works. ● To know some uses of electric motors. | Demonstrate how a small electric motor works. Discuss the size and power of different electric motors. | Find examples of places where electric motors are used. Make a poster illustrating how an electric motor works or one use of an electric motor. | Discuss examples of electric motors, considering power sources and outputs. | ● Can describe how an electric motor works. ● Can describe a wide range of uses for electric motors. |
| LESSON 5 | ● To use electric motors in toys. ● To understand circuit drawings including motors. | Use a circuit drawing as the basis for a toy including an electric motor. | | Discuss the models. Look at other ways of using motors to drive machinery. | ● Can interpret circuit drawings and overcome practical problems to use electric motors in 'real life' situations. |
| LESSON 6 | ● To know that magnets and wires carrying electricity affect each other. ● To understand how this effect is used in power generation. ● To realise that power generation has environmental implications. | Look at how one type of power station generates electricity and draw an energy flow diagram. | Find out about another type of power station and draw an energy flow diagram. Find out about the environmental impact of different types of power station. | Review the Group activities. Link to energy conservation and ways of using less electricity. | ● Understand how a generator produces electricity and relate this to changes in energy. ● Know that electricity generation has environmental implications, and link this to the need for energy conservation. |
| LESSON 7 | ● To know that 'environmentally friendly' power sources exist. ● To understand some of the ways they are used. | Introduce the idea of renewable energy sources. Look at solar power as an alternative to batteries. Research other types of 'environmentally friendly' power. | | Talk about how and why renewable energy sources are used. How might the children's everyday energy use be reduced or made more environmentally friendly? | ● Can discuss energy use and its impact on the environment in an informed way. |

## ORGANISATION (8 LESSONS)

| OBJECTIVES | ACTIVITY 1 | ACTIVITY 2 |
|---|---|---|
| ● To assess the children's knowledge of situations where electricity is used. ● To assess the children's knowledge and understanding of energy changes in power stations and electric motors. | Identify equipment that uses electricity. Identify alternative ways of powering some equipment. Consider environmental benefits of using alternatives to electricity. | Recognise and label the energy changes taking place in a power station. Describe the construction of an electric motor and the energy changes in it. Name possible sources of electricity to power a motor, and describe an advantage of rechargeable batteries. |

**Please note that the term 'battery' is used throughout this unit. While it is technically correct to speak of electricity as being produced by a 'cell', and a 'battery' as being an electricity-producing device composed of a number of 'cells', the introduction of the term 'cell' at this stage may cause confusion.**

# LESSON 1

## OBJECTIVES

● To know that in a battery, different chemicals are brought together to produce electricity.
● To make observations and draw conclusions from them.

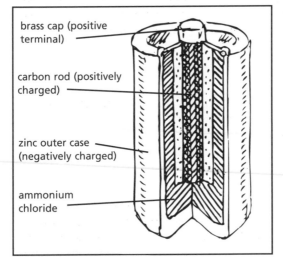

brass cap (positive terminal)

carbon rod (positively charged)

zinc outer case (negatively charged)

ammonium chloride

### RESOURCES

**Group activities: 1.** Photocopiable page 129 (one copy per group), batteries, headphones (one set per group – the ones given away in flight bags could be used), beakers of salt solution, copper coins, aluminium foil, crocodile clips and wires, bulbs. **2.** Paper, pencils; a computer and data-handling program (optional).

### PREPARATION

Have warm water available for making the salt solution. A stronger solution can be made with warm water than with cold water. Alternatively, make up the solution in advance with boiling water and allow it to cool.
**Safety note:** Remind the children **never** to try out electricity experiments with mains electricity or car batteries, and **never** to test batteries by putting them on the tongue to feel it tingling.

**Vocabulary**

powerful/weak battery, chemicals, reaction

### BACKGROUND

Batteries release electricity as a result of a gradual chemical reaction. When all the chemicals have been used up, the battery is said to be 'flat'. This lesson looks at another mixture of chemicals – not those in modern batteries – that can be used to make electricity. In Lesson 5, the children will look at another way of making electricity: by using energy to generate it in a power station. At primary school level, electricity is usually detected by observing what it does: lighting a bulb, working a buzzer and so on. In this lesson, because the amount of electricity the chemical reaction will produce is not enough to operate a bulb or a buzzer, the children will use headphones to detect the crackling sounds produced by the electricity. The stronger the salt solution, the better this will work.

### INTRODUCTION

Remind the children of their work on switches in Year 4/Primary 5. Discuss why switches may be needed in circuits. Ask where the electricity that the switches are controlling comes from. *Where else does electricity come from?* Discuss the suggestions made. The children will be aware of mains electricity at home and at school, and of batteries in toys and torches; they may also be aware of car batteries, rechargeable batteries and lightning. Discuss which sources of electricity they can use in experiments in school, reminding them that mains electricity and electricity from car batteries is too powerful to be used safely in school.

### MAIN TEACHING ACTIVITY

*We know lots of places that electricity comes from, but how can we tell when electricity is there?* Discuss the fact that we cannot see electricity: we can only see the effect it has on other things. Ask the children what electricity can do so that we know it is there. Discuss places, at home and in school, where electricity is used to make light, sound or movement. *Where in your experiments have you detected electricity by light or sound?* (Bulbs lighting up, buzzers sounding.) Tell them that today they are going to use a new way of detecting electricity; they are also going to make a simple battery.

## GROUP ACTIVITIES

**1.** Each group can use a copy of page 129 to help them build their own battery using salt water, copper coins and aluminium foil, then use headphones to check for the presence of electricity. They should draw a diagram to show how they made the battery. Ask them to explain (in writing) how they could tell it made electricity. *Was it a powerful battery or a weak battery? How could you tell?* (When the headphones are connected to a normal battery, a crackling sound is heard. The same sound can be heard from the salt water battery. When the salt water battery is connected to the bulb, nothing happens: the battery is too weak to light up a bulb.)
**2.** Groups can carry out a survey to find out where the children and their families use batteries, and what type of batteries they use ('ordinary', 'long life' or 'rechargeable'). Remind them to include batteries for mobile phones, calculators and wrist-watches. Each group can discuss what questions to ask, then one child from each group can ask other children the questions. This can run concurrently with Group activity 1. The children could use data-handling software to draw pie charts.

## DIFFERENTIATION

**1.** With less able children, you may prefer to demonstrate making the battery to one group at a time while the rest of the class work on Group activity 2. The children could write one sentence to say what they heard in the headphones, and one sentence to say what happened to the bulb. More able children could try to predict what would happen if a lot of these batteries were connected together, like 'ordinary' batteries.

## ASSESSMENT

During the group work, ask the children to explain why they heard a crackling sound when the headphones were connected to the aluminium and the copper coin in salt water, and why the bulb would not light up.

## PLENARY

Discuss with the children what they heard through the headphones. *Do you think this is a good way of detecting electricity? What advantages does it have over using a bulb or a buzzer?* (It can be used to detect smaller amounts of electricity.) *When would it be better to use a bulb or a buzzer?* (Where there is enough electricity, using a bulb or a buzzer is more convenient because you do not need to be wearing headphones – so more than one person can detect the electricity at a time).

Discuss the types of battery. Long life batteries are better for the user and the environment than ordinary batteries, as they do not need replacing so often. Rechargeable batteries are the best of all, as it takes much less energy to recharge a battery than to make a new one.

## OUTCOMES

● Know that chemicals in batteries react to generate electricity.
● Can use bulbs, buzzers and headphones to detect the presence of electricity.

## LINKS

Unit 5, Lesson 2: the flow of electric current.
ICT: electric circuits.

## LESSON 2

### OBJECTIVES

● To know how an electromagnet can be constructed and used.
● To ask scientific questions that can be tested.

### RESOURCES

**Main teaching activity:** Thin, insulated copper wire suitable for winding into coils; rods made of different materials (such as nails, pencils, pens); small paper clips or pins, a battery.
**Group activities: 1.** Large, thick iron nails or other iron cores; copper wire, crocodile clips and leads, batteries, paper clips or pins. **2.** Secondary information sources about electromagnets.

### PREPARATION

Make a coil of insulated copper wire that can be placed around different core materials to form an electromagnet (see diagram).

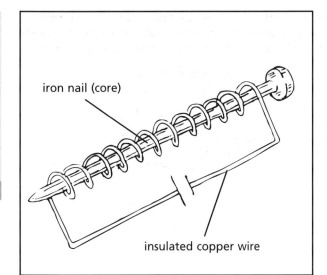

iron nail (core)

insulated copper wire

## BACKGROUND

This lesson looks at how electricity can be used to make temporary magnets known as electromagnets. Following lessons in this unit look at other ways in which electricity and magnets can affect each other.

Electromagnets are made by winding insulated copper wire around a soft iron core (see diagram). When an electric current flows through the wire, the iron core becomes a magnet. When the current is switched off, the core stops being a magnet. Electromagnets are used in places where a magnet needs to be turned on and off (such as an electric bell or a scrapyard crane), or where the strength of a magnet needs to be varied (such as a loudspeaker or a telephone earpiece, where different sounds are produced by varying the strength of the magnet). The core of the electromagnet is always made of soft iron because this can be magnetised and demagnetised much more rapidly than steel, so the magnet can be turned on and off faster.

*Vocabulary*

electromagnet, core, magnetic and non-magnetic materials

## INTRODUCTION

Tell the children that they are going to look at some uses of electricity that may be new to them. The first thing they are going to do is to use electricity to make a magnet. *How can you tell if you have made a magnet?* Recap on what type of things a magnet will be attracted to, and what it will be able to pick up.

## MAIN TEACHING ACTIVITY

Show the children how to make an electromagnet by winding many turns of insulated wire around an iron core such as a nail. Connect the ends of the wire to the terminals of a battery. Demonstrate that the electromagnet can be used to pick up small paper clips or pins. Try using several different magnetic and non-magnetic materials for the core. Encourage the children to predict which materials will become electromagnets. List the objects that become electromagnets and those that don't. Help the children to see that only magnetic materials can become electromagnets.

*Do you think all electromagnets will be as strong as each other?* If the children are not sure, ask them to think back to work they have done on magnets. *Can you think of a question about the strength of electromagnets that you could test?* Encourage the children to think of an investigation they could carry out.

## GROUP ACTIVITIES

**1.** Groups can focus on an appropriate question about the strength of electromagnets, then plan and carry out an investigation to find out what affects the strength of electromagnets. Discuss ways to ensure that the test is fair. They may find, for example, that increasing the number of turns in the coil of wire increases the strength of the magnet; or that increasing the number of batteries increases the strength of the magnet (however, with the range of voltages available, this effect may not be clear).

**2.** The children can use secondary sources to write a short talk (one or two minutes) on the uses of electromagnets. They should decide whether to cover many different uses of electromagnets or to cover one or two uses in greater detail.

## DIFFERENTIATION

**2.** Adjust the complexity of the secondary sources provided to suit different children.

## ASSESSMENT

Ask some children to present to other groups or to the class what they have found out about the factors affecting the strength of an electromagnet, and others to present their short talks on the uses of electromagnets. Look for recognition of how an electromagnet may be useful where a permanent magnet would not be, and that the strength of an electromagnet can be varied.

## PLENARY

Discuss what different groups of children have found out about the factors affecting the strength of electromagnets. Encourage the children to explain how they reached their conclusions from the observations or measurements they made. Ask some children to present their short talks on the uses of electromagnets. Discuss some of the places where electromagnets are used (see Background), encouraging the children to think about why electromagnets are used instead of permanent magnets.

## OUTCOMES

● Know how to make an electromagnet.
● Can describe some uses of electromagnets.
● Can ask and investigate a scientific question.

## LINKS

Unit 5, Lesson 3: looking at magnetic fields.

# LESSON 3

## OBJECTIVES

● To know that magnets and wires carrying electricity affect each other.
● To decide what to do and what evidence to collect in an investigation.

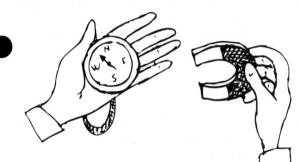

## RESOURCES

**Main teaching activity:** A small compass, magnets, a piece of and a coil of copper wire.
**Group activities: 1.** Photocopiable page 130 (one copy per child), batteries, copper wire, crocodile clips and leads, compasses.

## PREPARATION

Make room at the front of the class for all the children to gather close enough to see the needle of a small compass.

Vocabulary

compass, coil, magnetic, non-magnetic

## BACKGROUND

When electricity flows through a wire, it causes a magnetic field to form around the wire. This makes the wire behave like a magnet. It is this magnetic field that makes a coil of wire with an electric current passing through it able to turn an iron core into a magnet. The wire can also affect other nearby magnets, such as compasses. This connection between electricity in wires and magnetic fields also means that moving a magnet in and out of a coil of wire makes an electric current flow in the wire. This is how electricity is produced in generators and power stations. The amount of electricity that can be produced using the wire coils and magnets available in schools is so tiny that specialised equipment (an ammeter) would be needed to measure it. For this reason, this lesson concentrates on demonstrating the effect electricity in a wire has on a magnet.

## INTRODUCTION

Remind the children of some of the things that electricity can do, such as make a lightbulb glow and turn an iron bar into a magnet. In this lesson, they are going to learn about the effect that electricity can have on magnets – and the effect that magnets can have on electricity. These are very important effects, because they are used in electric motors and power stations (as the children will see in later lessons).

## MAIN TEACHING ACTIVITY

Show the children a small compass. *Who knows what this is? Can you explain how it works?* Make sure the children know that a compass is actually a small magnet that is free to turn around. *What sort of things might make the needle turn?* If necessary, help the children to work out that since the compass is a small magnet, it will be affected by magnetic materials and by other magnets. Demonstrate this.

*What effect do you think this wire, on its own, will have on the compass?* They may well believe that it will make the compass move, because it is metal. Demonstrate that the wire has no effect at all on the compass, and explain that this is because the wire is made of copper, which is non-magnetic. *Will a coil of copper wire affect the compass?* Again, show that it doesn't. Tell the children that now they know the wire does not affect the magnet (the compass), you want them to investigate how the electricity in the wire affects it.

## GROUP ACTIVITIES

**1.** The children can work in groups, with individual copies of page 130, to find out how electricity affects magnets. (A battery will almost certainly affect the compass, since most batteries of the type you are likely to use contain nickel, which is a magnetic material. You can make sure the battery will not affect the results by keeping it a long way from the compass. Electricity in a straight wire may make the needle move a small amount. Electricity in a coil of wire will make it move further. Increasing the number of turns on the coil increases the effect on the needle.)

**2.** Discuss the answers to these questions:

● *A person uses a torch to read a compass. Will the compass point in the correct direction?* (Probably not, as the batteries in the torch will affect the compass.)

● *A person stands under an electricity power cable and reads a compass. Will it give the correct direction?* (No: the electricity in the power cable will affect the compass.)

## DIFFERENTIATION

**1.** Less able children could discuss the answers to the questions on page 130, then write a sentence or two to record the things that make the needle move. More able children could discuss whether there are any other factors that might affect how far the needle moves. (The number of batteries and the distance between the coil and the compass.) **2.** Less able children could discuss the second question only. Encourage them to draw parallels between the electricity in their wire and the electricity in the power cable. More able children could try to think of other situations where electricity and magnets might affect each other.

## ASSESSMENT

During Group activity 1, ask the children to explain what they have found out about the effect of electricity on magnets.

## PLENARY

Discuss what the children have found out about the effect that electricity has on magnets. Encourage them to discuss the questions in Group activity 2, explaining why they reached the conclusions they did. Explain that the magnet in Group activity 1 moved because the electricity in the wire 'pushed' it (or 'there is a force between the electricity in the wire and the magnet', if the children are ready for this idea). Ask the children to speculate about what might happen if the wire could move but the magnet was held still. Use the example of a child pushing a door: if the door were held still and the child was on roller skates, it would be the child that moved. Explain that this is how electric motors work; they will look at this in the next lesson.

## OUTCOMES

● Know how electricity passing through a wire can affect a compass.
● Know how the movement of a magnet in a coil can make a current of electricity.
● Can decide what to do and what evidence to collect to answer questions in an investigation.

## LINKS

Geography: using a compass.

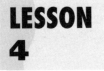

# LESSON 4

## OBJECTIVES

● To know how an electric motor works.
● To know some uses of electric motors.

## RESOURCES

**Main teaching activity:** A small electric motor.
**Group activities: 1.** Secondary sources about electric motors, paper, writing materials. **2.** Plain A4 paper, felt-tipped pens or coloured pencils.

## PREPARATION

Obtain a small electric motor. The motors of cars in electric racing tracks are ideal, since their workings are usually visible and they are designed to run well at different speeds when different voltages are used to power them. Check that your chosen motor works at different speeds from different-voltage batteries.

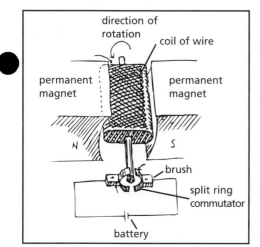

direction of
rotation

coil of wire

permanent
magnet

permanent
magnet

N

S

brush

split ring
commutator

battery

## BACKGROUND

An electric motor consists of a coil of wire that is free to rotate between two magnets. When electricity flows through the coil, a magnetic field is created around it. The force between the permanent magnets and the magnetic field from the coil of wire makes the coil spin round. The coil is fixed to an axle that turns whenever the coil turns; the axle can be used to turn wheels or other machinery. The greater the electric current, or the stronger the permanent magnets, the more powerful the motor will be.

Electric motors are used in many ways in the home and in almost every industry. Some of these motors are battery-powered (such as motors in toys and starter motors in cars), but most use mains electricity. They vary in size and power, from the tiny motors in toys to the powerful motors used in large cranes. In the home, mains-powered motors turn fans in hairdryers and fan heaters, and turn the moving parts in washing machines, tumble dryers, food mixers, cassette players, turntables and video recorders.

*Vocabulary*

electric motor, coil, axle

## INTRODUCTION

Remind the children how electricity in a coil of wire makes a magnet move. Explain again that they used electricity in a wire to move a magnet – but if the magnet were fixed and the wire free to move, it would be the wire that moved instead. Repeat the example of the door and the child on roller skates. Explain that this is what happens in electric motors: the magnets are held still, but the coil of wire is free to move.

## MAIN TEACHING ACTIVITY

Show the children the small electric motor. Show them where the magnets and the wires carrying electricity are. Can they guess from the toy car which way the movement will take place in the motor? Connect batteries across the motor to show it working, and to show how the turning of the coil of wire is used to make the wheels on the toy car turn.

Discuss ways of making the motor more powerful. Explain that if more electricity is used, the wires need to be bigger and so the whole motor is bigger. What are the largest and smallest electric motors they can think of? (For example: large motors in powerful cranes, small motors in toys.) Discuss some uses of large and small electric motors. *What provides the electricity? How powerful are they? How dangerous are they?*

## GROUP ACTIVITIES

**1.** Working in groups, the children should think of places where electric motors are used and list them under the headings 'Home', 'School' and 'Work/Industry'. They can use secondary sources of information, and try to think of a range of different-sized motors.
**2.** Ask the children to choose one use of an electric motor and produce an illustrated poster showing either how the motor works or where it is used and what its purpose is.

## DIFFERENTIATION

**1.** The children can work in mixed-ability groups. Give more able children a challenge: *Write a sentence about the smallest/largest/most unusual motor you can think of.*

## ASSESSMENT

How many different uses of electric motors have the children found? Do they know what these motors all do?

## PLENARY

Look at the range of places where motors are used. List the places the children found in Group activity 1. *Where have you found the most motors? Where are most small motors used? Where are most large motors used? How many use batteries? How many use mains electricity?* Recap on how motors work, considering the changes that would have to be made to the wires and magnets to turn a small motor like the one in a toy car into a large, powerful motor.

## OUTCOMES

● Can describe how an electric motor works.
● Can describe a wide range of uses for electric motors.

# LESSON 5

| Objectives | ● To use electric motors in toys.<br>● To understand circuit drawings including motors. |
|---|---|
| Resources | A large copy of the circuit drawing shown below; small electric motors, fans (or propellers) that clip onto a motor axle, batteries, wires, switches, modelling materials. |
| Main activity | The children use the circuit drawing to make a toy in which an electric motor is used to drive a propeller or fan. This mechanism can be used in toys such as racing cars (where the car is 'blown' along by the propeller) and windmills (where the sails are attached to the blades of the fan). The children have to decide where to put the battery and the switch, and what power to use (the higher the voltage, the faster the motor runs). |
| Differentiation | Less able children could be given a model or design to copy. More able children could be encouraged to invent a number of different toys. |
| Assessment | Ask the children to write brief descriptions of what they did and why. Look for skill in choosing the correct power for the battery and sensible positions for the battery and switch. |
| Plenary | Look at the models. Discuss any problems encountered and how they could be overcome. Discuss how motors can be used to power things other than fans and propellers. If you have suitable kits available, show how motors can be attached to drive belts and gearboxes to increase the range of things they can be used to power. |
| Outcome | ● Can interpret circuit drawings and overcome practical problems to use electric motors in 'real life' situations. |

# LESSON 6

## OBJECTIVES

- To know that magnets and wires carrying electricity affect each other.
- To understand how this effect is used in power generation.
- To realise that power generation has environmental implications.

## RESOURCES

**Main teaching activity:** The small electric motor from Lesson 4; secondary sources (books, videos, posters) on how a particular type of power station works.
**Group activities:** Secondary sources on different types of power station and their environmental impact.

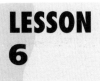

**Vocabulary**

electricity generation, power station, fossil fuels

## BACKGROUND

Electricity generators and power stations are basically electric motors working in reverse. In an electric motor, the interaction between permanent magnets and an electric current in a coil of wire causes the coil of wire to move. In an electricity generator, a coil of wire is rotated between permanent magnets. The interaction between the permanent magnets and the moving coil of wire causes an electric current to be produced in the wire.

## INTRODUCTION

Use a small motor to recap on how electric motors work (see Background). Explain that the mains electricity we use is generated in power stations. The electricity generators in power stations are really just like huge electric motors working in reverse (see Background again). In most types of power station, fuel is burned to make steam that turns turbines in order to turn coils of wire between magnets.

## MAIN TEACHING ACTIVITY

Describe how one particular type of power station works – for example, in a coal-fired power station, the coal is burned to heat water and make it turn to steam. The steam is used to push the turbines which generate the electricity around. Use an energy flow diagram to discuss the energy changes that take place at different stages in the power station. In this example, an appropriate energy flow diagram is shown on page 127.

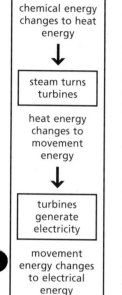

coal in

↓

coal burned to
heat water

chemical energy
changes to heat
energy

↓

steam turns
turbines

heat energy
changes to
movement
energy

↓

turbines
generate
electricity

movement
energy changes
to electrical
energy

↓

electricity out

## GROUP ACTIVITIES

**1.** The children can use secondary sources to find out about a different type of power station, describe briefly how it works and draw an energy flow diagram.

**2.** They can use secondary sources to look at the impact that different types of power station have on the environment.

## DIFFERENTIATION

**1.** Less able children could cut out pictures of different types of power station and label each one with the type or source of energy going in (such as coal) and the type of energy coming out (electricity). More able children could research and discuss which type of power station might be judged the 'best' from an environmental point of view. *Are some types of power station more suitable for certain places than others?* (For example, a hydroelectric power station would be best in a hilly region with a strong river.)

## ASSESSMENT

Look at the children's diagrams of energy changes in power stations. Look for recognition of the different types of energy at different stages. Some children may show an understanding of the changes taking place.

## PLENARY

Discuss the similarities and differences between the energy changes taking place in different power stations. Emphasise that all power stations make electrical energy from a different type of energy. Discuss the impact that electricity generation has on the environment: hot water pumped into rivers damages wildlife; waste gases from the burning of fossil fuels contributes to global warming; nuclear power generation produces waste products that remain dangerous for a long time. Discuss ways of using less electricity, and make the connection with energy conservation.

## OUTCOMES

● Understand how a generator produces electricity and relate this to changes in energy.
● Know that electricity generation has environmental implications, and link this to the need for energy conservation.

## LINKS

Unit 3, Lesson 9: the environmental impact of different industries.

## LESSON 7

| Objectives | ● To know that 'environmentally friendly' power sources exist.<br>● To understand some of the ways they are used. |
|---|---|
| Resources | A battery-powered calculator, a solar-powered calculator, Lego solar-powered kits; pictures of wind turbines and houses with solar panels; secondary sources of information on renewable energy. Educational resources can be obtained from the Centre for Alternative Technology at Machynlleth, Wales (tel: 01654 702400). |
| Main activity | Discuss where the power comes from to drive the battery-powered calculator and the solar-powered calculator. Introduce the idea of renewable energy sources being 'environmentally friendly', because they use an energy source which is being replaced. Look at the solar-powered Lego model. Discuss which is better for the environment: this kit or one powered by a battery. The children can use secondary sources to research, and write about, other types of 'environmentally friendly' power and what they can be used for. |
| Differentiation | Differentiate this activity through the complexity of the secondary sources different children use. |
| Assessment | Look for children whose writing shows understanding of the difference between renewable and non-renewable energy sources, and why the former are better for the environment. |
| Plenary | Discuss the types of 'environmentally friendly' power the children have researched. Encourage the children to talk about whether they think we should try to use energy in a more environmentally friendly way, and why. Talk about the types of energy they use in their everyday lives. How might they be able to use less energy, or to use energy in a more environmentally friendly way? |
| Outcome | ● Can discuss energy use and its impact on the environment in an informed way. |

# LESSON 8

## OBJECTIVES

● To assess the children's knowledge of situations where electricity is used.
● To assess the children's knowledge and understanding of energy changes in power stations and electric motors.

## RESOURCES

Photocopiable pages 131 and 132, writing materials.

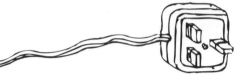

## INTRODUCTION

You may wish to start the lesson with the Assessment activities, or to start with a 'question and answer' session or short quiz to reinforce the children's knowledge of the topics covered in this unit, giving them the opportunity to ask questions about things they are unsure of.

## ASSESSMENT ACTIVITY 1

Give each child a copy of page 131 to work through individually. The completed assessment sheets can be marked by you and returned, or the children can swap them and mark each other's.

### Answers

1. The washing machine, hairdryer, torch, kettle and TV should be circled; 2. Washing machine, hairdryer; 3. Calculator, toy; 4. A calculator might be powered by solar power, a toy might be powered by clockwork; 5. Torches are used when it is dark, so solar panels wouldn't work; 6. The alternatives use renewable power sources, so the power can be used again and again without running out. The alternatives cause very little pollution compared with conventional electricity power stations; 7. Wind power or water power.

### Looking for levels

All the children should answer questions 1 and 3. Most children will answer questions 2, 4 and 5. More able children will answer questions 6 and 7.

## ASSESSMENT ACTIVITY 2

Give each child a copy of page 132 to work through individually. The completed sheets can be marked by you and returned, or used as a starting-point for further discussion.

### Answers

1. Chemical energy changes to heat energy. Heat energy changes to movement energy. Movement energy changes to electrical energy; 2. Magnets (or permanent magnets); 3. Movement energy; 4. Using weaker magnets or attaching the wire coil to a less powerful electricity source; 5. Mains electricity, ordinary batteries or rechargeable batteries; 6. Rechargeable batteries are cheaper in the long term: they last longer, so use fewer chemicals per hour of battery use, or they do not have to be disposed of as often, so produce less harmful waste per hour of battery use.

### Looking for levels

All the children should be able to answer questions 2 and 5. Most of the children will be able to answer questions 1, 3 and 6. More able children will be able to answer question 4.

## PLENARY

You may wish to go over the answers to the Assessment activities with the children, or to recap on some of the other topics covered in this unit. You could perhaps do this in the form of a class quiz, with each child contributing one or more questions and answers.

From this unit, most children will have reinforced their knowledge of circuits and gained an understanding of the energy changes taking place in batteries, motors and power stations. They will have learned that electricity, magnets and movement are connected, and that this connection is why generators and motors work. They will have thought about the impact that battery use and electricity generation have on the environment. Some children will have made less progress, but will know some of the situations in which batteries and electric motors are used and have some knowledge of the impact that these have on the environment. Some children will have made more progress: they will be able to explain how batteries, electromagnets and motors work and the factors that affect how powerful they are. They will show a thorough understanding of the ways that electricity generation and battery use affect the environment, and be able to suggest ways of minimising their harmful effects.

# Detecting and making electricity

Look very carefully at the plug on the end of your headphones.

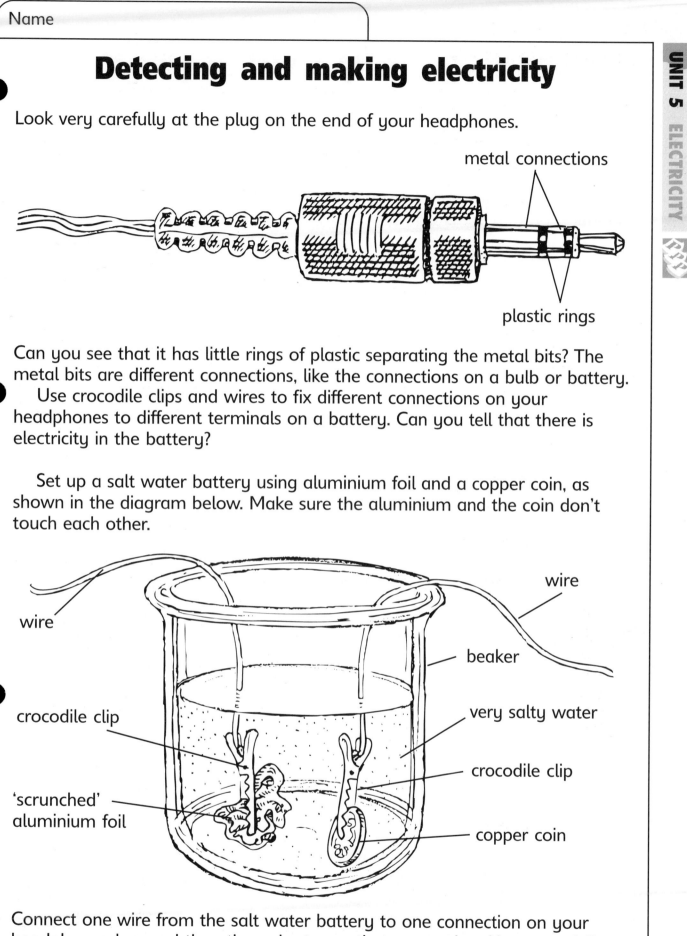

metal connections

plastic rings

Can you see that it has little rings of plastic separating the metal bits? The metal bits are different connections, like the connections on a bulb or battery.
    Use crocodile clips and wires to fix different connections on your headphones to different terminals on a battery. Can you tell that there is electricity in the battery?

    Set up a salt water battery using aluminium foil and a copper coin, as shown in the diagram below. Make sure the aluminium and the coin don't touch each other.

wire

wire

crocodile clip

beaker

very salty water

crocodile clip

'scrunched' aluminium foil

copper coin

Connect one wire from the salt water battery to one connection on your headphone plug, and the other wire to another connection. Listen carefully.
    Connect the wires from your salt water battery to opposite sides of a bulb. Look very carefully. What do you notice?

Name

# Does electricity affect magnets?

For this investigation, you will need: a battery, lots of wire, crocodile clips, a compass.

You already know that a piece of wire or a coil of wire on its own does not affect the compass. Now find out whether a battery on its own affects the compass.

1. What did you do?

2. What did you notice?

3. Can you explain this?

Connect the battery to a short piece of wire.

4. What will you do to make sure that the battery does not have any direct effect on your results?

5. Does the electricity in the wire affect the compass?

Now plan an investigation to see whether electricity in a coil of wire affects the compass.

6. Does the number of turns in the coil make any difference?

7. Use a separate sheet of paper to record what you did and the results.

# Making and using electricity

1. Put a circle around the things that use electricity from a battery or the mains.

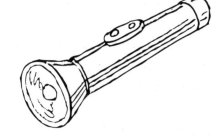

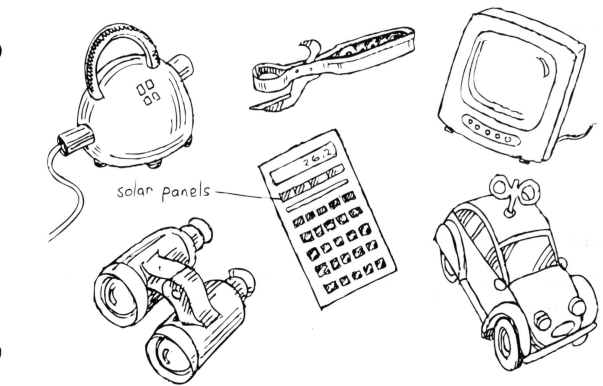

solar panels

Answer these questions on the back of the sheet.

2. List the things that have an electric motor in them.

3. Which items are sometimes powered by batteries and sometimes by some other method?

4. What other methods might be used?

5. Why isn't solar power used for torches?

6. Why are the alternatives to mains and battery electricity better the environment?

7. Name one other type of 'environmentally friendly' power.

# Making and using electricity

1. Label the energy changes that happen at each stage in a coal-fired power station.

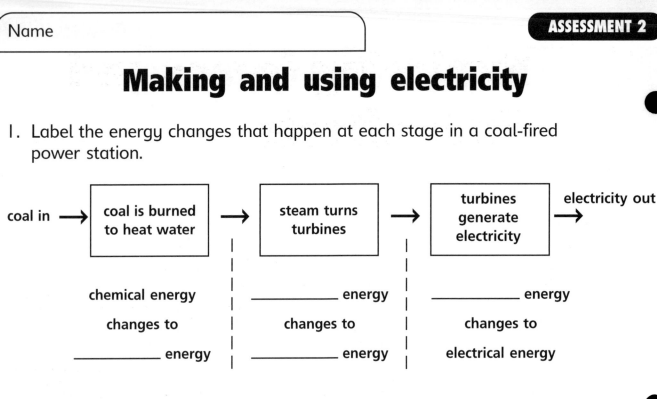

coal in → | coal is burned to heat water | → | steam turns turbines | → | turbines generate electricity | → electricity out

chemical energy changes to _____ energy

_____ energy changes to _____ energy

_____ energy changes to electrical energy

The electricity from the power station is used to power an electric motor.

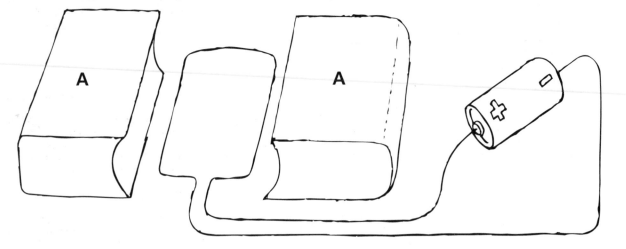

2. What are the parts labelled A? _____

3. When electricity flows through the coil of wire, what kind of energy comes from the motor? _____

4. Name one change that would make the electric motor less powerful.

_____

5. Name three possible sources for the electricity used to run the motor.

_____

6. Give one advantage of rechargeable batteries. _____

_____

# Exploring forces and their effects

## ORGANISATION (12 LESSONS)

| | OBJECTIVES | MAIN ACTIVITY | GROUP ACTIVITIES | PLENARY | OUTCOMES |
|---|---|---|---|---|---|
| **LESSON 1** | ● To know a variety of structures are used to support the weight of objects.<br>● To ask scientific questions, plan how to answer them and decide what evidence to collect. | Ask questions about the strength of shapes used to build different structures. Look at possible shapes for beams and ask questions about which are stronger. | Decide on one question to ask about structural components. Plan and carry out an investigation to find the answer. | Report back on findings. Draw conclusions about the strength of different-shaped structural components. | ● Can plan and carry out a test.<br>● Can compare the strength of different structural components. |
| **LESSON 2** | ● To know that a variety of structures are used to support the weight of objects.<br>● To use knowledge of structural components to build a load-carrying structure.<br>● To test a design, making modifications in a systematic way in the light of evidence collected. | The children design and build a load-carrying platform, using weights during construction to identify points where the structure needs to be strengthened. | | Test all the platforms for their load-carrying capacity. The children identify good points in each design. | ● Can use scientific knowledge to build a load-carrying platform.<br>● Can assess and modify their design and construction. |
| **LESSON 3** | ● To revise how friction can be reduced by lubricants.<br>● To conduct an investigation: ask a scientific question that can be tested, decide what evidence to collect, collect and record data appropriately, then identify and describe patterns in the data. | Review differences in friction forces between rough and smooth surfaces. Introduce the idea that it requires more energy to overcome the friction between rough surfaces. | Plan and carry out an investigation to see whether putting liquids on surfaces changes the friction on that surface. Look for patterns in the results. | Groups report back on findings and explain patterns in the results and conclusions drawn. Relate these findings back to the idea of energy use. | ● Know that lubricants reduce friction.<br>● Can decide how to test a scientific question.<br>● Can identify patterns in the results. |
| **LESSON 4** | ● To know that friction can be reduced by many liquid lubricants. | The children use secondary sources to find out about situations where reducing friction is useful or harmful. Make information cards and warning notices. | | Children present warning notices and information cards. Discuss friction forces and energy in engines with and without lubricant oil. | ● Recognise the importance of oil in reducing friction.<br>● Recognise that reducing friction can be harmful as well as helpful. |
| **LESSON 5** | ● To know that everything falls down and this is due to gravity.<br>● To know that falling materials can be used to measure time.<br>● To identify the significant features of a gravity-controlled timer.<br>● To evaluate a sand timer and a water clock and describe their limitations. | Discuss important features of a sand timer. The children consider what materials would be suitable to make a timer from, how these would affect the design, and what things the timer could time. | Build a sand timer and/or water clock. Use it to time, and compare it with a stopwatch. Discuss the limitations and advantages of each. | Discuss suggestions for improving the design of 'poor' timers. Discuss the limitations and advantages of sand and water timers. | ● Can design, make and use a sand timer and/or a water clock.<br>● Can recognise strengths and weaknesses in a design. |
| **LESSON 6** | ● To define the significant features of a good waterwheel.<br>● To know that falling water can be used to provide energy for work.<br>● To use scientific knowledge to design a waterwheel. | Look at a model waterwheel and discuss how it works to raise a weight. Discuss what is meant by a 'good' waterwheel. Discuss what features of a waterwheel could be improved. | The children design and build a waterwheel, then test it to see how closely it performs to the design | Some children explain their designs and choice of materials. Discuss any problems, and how the wheels could be improved. | ● Know that the energy of moving water can be converted into useful mechanical energy in a turning wheel.<br>● Can use scientific knowledge to identify the significant features of a waterwheel to be designed. |

## ORGANISATION (12 LESSONS)

| | OBJECTIVES | MAIN ACTIVITY | GROUP ACTIVITIES | PLENARY | OUTCOMES |
|---|---|---|---|---|---|
| **LESSON 7** | ● To know that the force of the wind can be used to provide energy for work. | Compare three types of windmill. Make energy flow charts for a variety of situations where energy comes from the wind. | | Recap on energy changes involving wind energy. Discuss how the amount of work done by a windmill can be increased. | ● Know that moving air can be used as an energy source. |
| **LESSON 8** | ● To know that changes in the direction and strength of the wind can be measured. ● To identify significant features of a wind direction and strength meter. ● To think of a variety of designs and choose the best one for a specified purpose. ● To test a design by making a series of observations, and adjust the design where necessary. | Identify the key features of an instrument to measure wind direction and strength. Discuss possible designs and consider how easy they would be to build. | Build a combined wind direction and wind strength meter. Test how well it works. | Look at the children's instruments and compare them with real wind-recording instruments. | ● Can find the direction of the wind and measure its force. ● Can specify the key features of a wind meter. ● Can produce a design to meet specifications, test it and suggest improvements in the light of observations. |
| **LESSON 9** | ● To know that when an object is pushed, an opposing push back can be felt. ● To decide what evidence to collect in an investigation. ● To explain results, using scientific knowledge and understanding. | Make a balloon racer on a string. Investigate the factors that affect how far along the string the racer travels. | | Discuss the forces acting on the racer and the energy involved. | ● Recognise action and reaction in a pair of forces. ● Recognise a change from stored energy to movement energy. ● Can explain the results of an experiment in scientific terms. |
| **LESSON 10** | ● To use the force of moving air. ● To know that when an object is pushed, an opposing push back can be felt. ● To design a balloon-powered toy car. ● To evaluate the limitations of their own and other designs. | Design and build a balloon-powered toy car. Predict, then test, factors that will affect how far the toy car will travel. | | Discuss the forces acting on the car and why some cars travel further than others. Discuss real vehicles propelled by gases. | ● Recognise action and reaction in a pair of forces. ● Recognise a change from stored energy to movement energy. ● Can evaluate a design and make suggestions for improvement. |
| **LESSON 11** | ● To know that energy stored in an elastic band can be turned into movement energy. ● To ask scientific questions, plan an investigation to find the answers and decide what evidence to collect. | Discuss how an elastic band 'crawler' works and what factors might make it work well. The children make a 'crawler' and test how well it works, making measurements and presenting the results. | | Discuss the limitations of elastic band power. Discuss situations where it would or would not be useful. | ● Recognise a change from stored energy to movement energy. ● Can decide what factors might affect how well the 'crawler' works. ● Can plan what to do and what evidence to collect in order to test an idea. |

| | OBJECTIVES | ACTIVITY 1 | ACTIVITY 2 |
|---|---|---|---|
| **ASSESSMENT 12** | ● To assess the children's knowledge of the forces affecting moving water. ● To assess the children's knowledge of how stretched elastic bands provide a force and of the factors affecting the strength of the force. ● To assess the children's ability to describe physical processes in terms of energy changes. | Identify the factors affecting how far water from a hosepipe will go, and describe an investigation to demonstrate the effect of nozzle size. Describe the energy changes taking place when a water jet hits a waterwheel, and the effect on the waterwheel. | To identify things that have stored elastic energy and moving energy. To identify the forces acting in one situation. To identify factors that affect how far an arrow fired from a bow travels, and describe the energy changes that take place. |

**This unit concentrates on the effects of forces. It introduces the involvement of energy, a key theme within the Scottish 5–14 National Guidelines for Science. However, the ideas in this unit are presented in a way that will enable teachers in England to choose additional work in Year 5 to meet the requirements of the QCA *Science Scheme of Work* Unit 5/6H: 'Enquiry in environmental and technological contexts'. All the practical activities are of an investigation or design type to develop the children's problem-solving and evaluation skills. They encourage the children to work out for themselves what to do – and then to look critically at their designs and results, and those of others, attempting to identify and improve upon limitations in the designs and in the results obtained. Because such activities will take the children longer than the practical activities in other units, the full lesson plans in this unit only have one Group activity.**

# LESSON 1

## OBJECTIVES

● To know that a variety of structures are used to support the weight of objects.
● To ask scientific questions, plan how to answer them and decide what evidence to collect.

## RESOURCES

**Main teaching activity:** Pictures of bridges constructed from different materials and in different shapes; pictures of typical Victorian iron architecture, showing iron frameworks; A4 paper, adhesive tape, strips and fasteners from construction kits (or strips of strong cardboard and paper fasteners), a large sheet of paper, a marker pen.
**Group activity:** A4 paper, adhesive tape, strips and fasteners from construction kits (or strips of strong cardboard and paper fasteners), weights, rulers, photocopiable page 147 (one per child).

## PREPARATION

Put the large sheet of paper in a prominent position to display the children's questions about structures. Enlarge the pictures if necessary.

## BACKGROUND

In all their design work in this unit, the children have to consider whether a material they choose is appropriate for the intended task. Therefore the unit starts with two lessons that encourage the children to look critically at a particular characteristic of components (in this case, strength) and then to choose a suitable component for a particular task.

*Vocabulary*

structures, components, beams, arches

## INTRODUCTION

Explain that in this unit, we are going to think about how we make good designs for things. We are surrounded by things that scientists and engineers have designed. Ask the children to suggest examples. Explain that whenever a scientist or engineer builds something, he or she has to be sure of using materials that will not break or fall apart later. So materials have to be tested to check that they will be suitable. Tell the children that their first design task will be to build something strong, and that in this lesson, they will start by testing some materials to find out how strong they are.

## MAIN TEACHING ACTIVITY

Show the children some pictures of bridges, both flat and arched. Discuss what the bridges are made from, and what shape they are. Identify and sketch the shape of each bridge. Encourage the children to ask different questions about which shapes are stronger and to predict the answers.

Look at pictures of some early iron structures (Victorian piers, bridges and railway station roofs are ideal). Identify some of the shapes used in them, such as squares, rectangles and triangles. Encourage the children to ask questions about which shapes are strongest. Look at the shapes of the beams themselves: *Are they round, square, I-shaped? Does it matter what shape they are?*

Show the children how to make rolled (round) or folded (square) beams out of paper, and how these can be bent into arches and held in place with Sellotape. Show them how different shapes (squares, triangles and so on) can be made using a construction kit (or strong cardboard strips and paper fasteners). Explain that they will be making some of these structural components and testing their strength.

## GROUP ACTIVITY

Working in groups, the children should decide on one question that they can ask about structures and find the answer to by testing. For example: *Can square beams hold up more weight than round beams?* or *Can we put more weight on a flat beam than on an arched one?* They should plan an investigation to find the answer, writing down what they intend to do and what measurements or observations they intend to make. They should then carry out their investigation and decide on a suitable way to record their results.

## DIFFERENTIATION

Help less able children to find a suitable question to investigate, or let them choose one of the following: *What shapes are hardest to distort (pull or push out of shape)?* (Try a selection of straight-sided shapes: triangles, squares, rectangles, hexagons and so on.) *Can a flat beam hold up more weight than a round beam? Which holds up more weight, a flat beam or an arch?* (Find out whether it matters which way up the arch is.) Help them to plan the investigation.

More able children could find out whether there is any difference in the strength of particular structural components if they are used different ways round. For example: *Can a square beam support more weight if it is stood on its end or if it is laid on its side?*

## ASSESSMENT

Ask the children to explain to others what they have investigated, using scientific terms to explain the tests they have carried out. They should say whether or not their investigation gave them an answer to their original question.

## PLENARY

Ask groups to report to the class on what their investigation showed them about the strength of different structural components. Draw up two columns on the board: 'strong components' and 'weak components'. They should have found out that triangles are hard to distort (look for triangles in the structures you showed earlier), and that square or round beams are stronger than flat beams. Some children may have found out that flat beams on their side are very strong. *If round beams are so strong, why don't we use round beams in buildings?* (Because they are harder to fix between flat surfaces.)

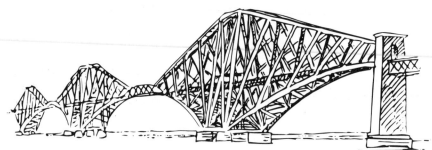

## OUTCOMES

● Can plan and carry out a test.
● Can compare the strength of different structural components.

## LINKS

History: how building methods have changed over time.

# LESSON 2

| | | |
|---|---|---|
| **Objectives** | ● To know that a variety of structures are used to support the weight of objects.<br>● To use knowledge of structural components to build a load-carrying structure.<br>● To test a design, making modifications in a systematic way in the light of evidence collected. | |
| **Resources** | Ample supplies of paper, adhesive tape, scissors, weights.<br>**Safety:** Warn the children to keep their fingers and toes well clear of possible falling weights when testing. | |
| **Main activity** | Groups design and build a weight-carrying platform for a crane. They should use weights during their building to identify weak points in the structure, and modify their design accordingly. Warn them not to test their platform to destruction at this time. | |
| **Differentiation** | Help less able children to plan the platform they will build, and to decide how to test it for weak points during construction. If appropriate, give them some pictures of real structures of a similar type. Ask more able children to consider whether they could use any of what they found out in Lesson 1 about beams being stronger some ways round than others. (Paper beams can support more weight end-on than on their sides, provided they are supported so they do not twist.) | |
| **Assessment** | Discuss each design with the group who made it. Test each platform to see how much weight it supports. | |
| **Plenary** | Test all the platforms (to destruction!) for their weight-carrying capacity. Ask the children to identify good points in the design of each platform.<br>**Safety:** Use a board to contain weights when the platforms collapse. | |
| **Outcomes** | ● Can use scientific knowledge to build a load-carrying platform.<br>● Can assess and modify their design and construction. | |

## LESSON 3

### OBJECTIVES
● To revise how friction can be reduced by lubricants.
● To conduct an investigation: ask a scientific question that can be tested, decide what evidence to collect, collect and record data appropriately, then identify and describe patterns in the data.

### RESOURCES

**Introduction:** A block, string.
**Main teaching activity:** A block, examples of rough and smooth surfaces, a force meter.
**Group activity:** Blocks, slopes, force meters, stopwatches, liquids (water, oil, washing-up liquid and so on).
**Safety:** Be aware that some children may have allergic skin reactions to some detergents.

### PREPARATION

Set up a block with a force meter attached, and a variety of different surfaces. The children may have used similar equipment to find out about friction in Year 4/Primary 5. Have a flip chart or board close by to record the children's ideas and questions.

### BACKGROUND

This lesson and the next are used to revise what the children know about friction, to demonstrate that certain liquids (called 'lubricants') can reduce friction, and to introduce the idea that forces and energy are related. The children probably know already that there is more friction between rough surfaces than between smooth ones (see *100 Science Lessons: Year 4/ Primary 5*). For example, we have to use more energy sliding a sledge over rough ground than over smooth snow, so the friction force that opposes its movement must be greater.

### INTRODUCTION

Pull a block across the desk on a piece of string. *Think back and tell me what you know about the forces involved when the block is being pulled.* If necessary, remind the children that a force is a push or a pull. They should remember that there is a force from you making the block move, and a friction force slowing the block down. If not, lead them towards this conclusion.

### MAIN TEACHING ACTIVITY

Show the children a rough surface and a smooth surface. *What do you remember about the friction forces?* If necessary, discuss how the block slides more easily on smoother surfaces, showing that the friction force is less. *Do I have to use up any energy to make the block keep moving?* If they are not sure, use the example of making a heavy sledge keep moving. *Do I use up more energy making it move over a rough surface or over a smooth surface?* (The rougher the surface, the greater the friction force, so more energy is used up in moving the block.)

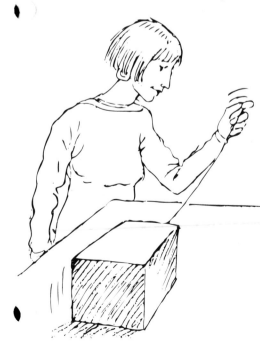

### GROUP ACTIVITY

*Do you think putting liquid on surfaces would make any difference to the friction?* Ask the children to explain their answers. Record their ideas on the board or flip chart. Encourage them to think of specific questions that they could test, such as: *Will it take less force to pull a block along a surface if there is oil on the surface?* or *Will a block slide down a slope faster if there is water on the slope?* Record these. Working in groups, the children should decide on a question to ask and decide what test they need to carry out. (Check that their ideas are workable and not too messy before they carry them out!) They need to think carefully about what observations or measurements they will make, and the best way to record their results.

### DIFFERENTIATION

Give less able children a choice of two or three of the questions about liquids and friction that the class thought of earlier. Help them to plan how they can find an answer to one of these questions. Make suggestions as to how they might record the results. Ask more able children to explain why using a slope might not be a good way of testing whether liquids affect friction. (The liquid will run down to the bottom, so the amount of friction will change as the object goes down the slope.)

**Vocabulary**

friction, energy, force, reduction, lubricant

UNIT 6 FORCES & MOTION

# LESSON 9

| Objectives | ● To know that when an object is pushed, an opposing push back can be felt.<br>● To decide what evidence to collect in an investigation.<br>● To explain results, using scientific knowledge and understanding. |
|---|---|
| Resources | Different types of string, drinking straws, adhesive tape, balloons, metre rulers, paper, pencils. |
| Main activity | Make a 'balloon racer'. To do this, tie a long string horizontally between two supports. Thread a straw onto the string. Blow up a balloon and, holding its neck tightly closed, fasten the side of the balloon to the straw with sticky tape. Release the neck of the balloon. Ask the children to investigate the factors that affect how far the balloon racer travels. |
| Differentiation | Less able children could find the connection between the size (diameter or circumference) of the balloon and how far it travels. More able children might investigate the effect of: the angle of the string (uphill or downhill); whether the string is tight or loose; what type of string is used (rough or smooth); or how big the straw is (in diameter and in length). Anything that increases friction between the straw and the string will reduce the distance that the balloon racer travels. |
| Assessment | During the Plenary session, ask children to explain why their balloon racer moved. *What forces made it go forwards? Were there any forces slowing it down?* |
| Plenary | Discuss the forces acting on the balloon racer. Make sure the children understand that it moves because stored energy in the stretched rubber skin pushes on the air in the balloon, forcing it out. The 'action' of the moving air pushing backwards causes a 'reaction' force pushing the balloon forwards. Discuss where the energy comes from to make the balloon move. (It comes from the stored energy in the stretched balloon skin: the more the balloon is blown up, the more the skin is stretched, so the more energy it stores and the further it can make the balloon move.) |
| Outcomes | ● Recognise action and reaction in a pair of forces.<br>● Recognise the change from stored energy in a balloon skin to movement energy in the air and the balloon.<br>● Can explain the results of an experiment in scientific terms. |

# LESSON 10

| Objectives | ● To use the force of moving air.<br>● To know that when an object is pushed, an opposing push back can be felt.<br>● To design a balloon-powered toy car.<br>● To evaluate the limitations of their own and other designs. |
|---|---|
| Resources | Balloons, string, adhesive tape, drinking straws, strong card or wood; axles and wheels from construction kits. |
| Main activity | Remind the children of Lesson 9. Ask them to use the principle of the balloon racer to design a toy car that can travel forward under its own power. A simple design might involve using a string threaded through a drinking straw attached to the car to determine the direction the car moves in. A more complex design might involve finding a way to hold the balloon so that the car travels in a predictable direction. Ask the children to predict and then test factors affecting how far the car travels. |
| Differentiation | Less able children could predict, then test, the connection between the size of the balloon and the distance the car travels. More able children could predict, then test, factors that will affect the level of friction acting on the car as it moves. |
| Assessment | Ask the children: *Where did friction act to slow your car down? How could you make friction less, or the forward force greater?* |
| Plenary | Discuss the forces acting on the car. Make sure the children understand that the car moves because energy stored in the stretched balloon skin forces the air out; as the moving air pushes one way, a reaction force in the opposite direction moves the car forward. Encourage the children to explain why some cars travelled further than others, using scientific language and their knowledge of forces, energy and friction. Discuss real machines that use the energy of moving air or gases to propel them along, such as hovercraft and jet aircraft. |
| Outcomes | ● Recognise action and reaction in a pair of forces.<br>● Recognise the change from stored energy in a balloon skin to movement energy in the air and a toy car.<br>● Can evaluate a design and make suggestions for improvement. |

# LESSON 11

| | |
|---|---|
| **Objectives** | ● To know that energy stored in an elastic band can be turned into movement energy.<br>● To ask scientific questions, plan an investigation to find the answers and decide what evidence to collect. |
| **Resources** | An elastic band crawler, a large diagram of an elastic band crawler, small cylindrical containers with flat ends (such as cardboard cocoa or 'Pringles' containers), used matches or small sticks, a wide selection of different-sized elastic bands, small masses with hooks (to fit in containers). |
| **Main activity** | Make an 'elastic band crawler' (see diagram) and a large copy of the diagram. Discuss how the crawler works, talking about where energy is stored and what happens when it is released. Discuss factors that may affect how well the crawler works, first defining what is meant by 'working well'. Ask the children to suggest scientific questions to investigate (or predictions to test) about what makes a crawler work well. They should work in small groups to design their own crawler, then test how well it works when a factor is varied. The emphasis should be on collecting appropriate evidence or measurements and recording in a clear and informative way. Ask the children to think carefully about how they will present their results. |
| **Differentiation** | Less able children could use a model to help them build their crawler. Discuss the evidence to be collected. Give help, where necessary, with the recording of measurements and other observations. More able children could look at diagrams of other machines powered by stretched elastic materials, such as a catapult, ballista or longbow. Can they use energy terms to explain how these machines work? |
| **Assessment** | Ask the children to describe the measurements and observations they made, and to explain and evaluate (according to their ability) how these helped them to answer the question they had asked. |
| **Plenary** | Discuss the limitations of elastic band power. The energy output is limited by the size of the elastic band. All the energy stored in the band came from us originally, so we are providing the energy to make the crawler go – this would be no good for powering something like a real car. It is useful for something like a bow and arrow, because we can put in energy gradually (as we stretch the bowstring) and give it all to the arrow at once. We cannot give as much energy to the arrow if we have to put it all in at once, as we do if we throw it. |
| **Outcomes** | ● Recognise the change from stored energy in a twisted elastic band to movement energy in the 'crawler'.<br>● Can decide what factors might affect how well the 'crawler' works.<br>● Can plan what to do and what evidence to collect in order to test an idea. |

Diagram within the Main activity cell, labelled: weight, matchstick, matchstick, hole, elastic band, cylinder.

## ASSESSMENT

# LESSON 12

### OBJECTIVES

● To assess the children's knowledge of the forces affecting moving water.
● To assess the children's knowledge of how stretched elastic bands provide a force and of the factors affecting the strength of the force.
● To assess the children's ability to describe physical processes in terms of energy changes.

### RESOURCES

Photocopiable pages 150 and 151, writing materials, red and blue coloured pencils.

### INTRODUCTION

You may decide to use the Assessment activities at the start of the lesson. Alternatively, you could begin with a short introductory session to remind the children of the main points they have learned in this unit. This could take the form of giving them a heading (such as 'Friction', 'Water power' or 'Strong and weak shapes') and asking them to suggest things they have learned about that topic.

Name

# Exploring forces and their effects

This picture shows three different nozzles that can go on the end of the hosepipe.

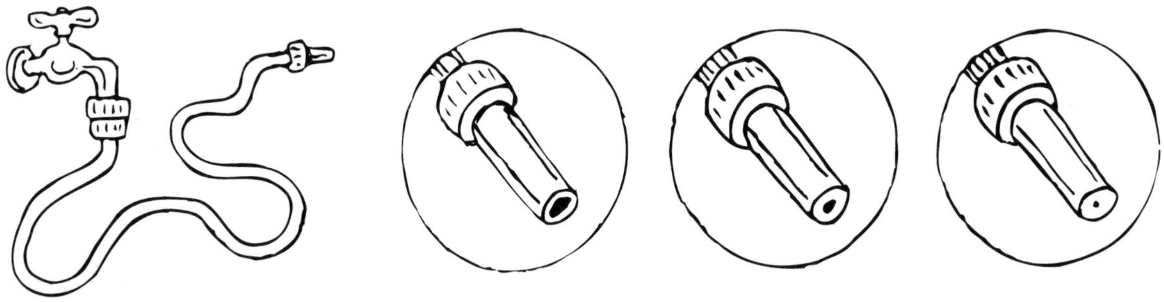

**1.** Tick the things that might change how far the water from the hosepipe goes.

☐ Turning the tap up.  ☐ Making the hosepipe longer.  ☐ Changing the nozzle.

**2.** Describe briefly how you could investigate whether changing the nozzle affects how far the water goes.

_____

_____

The jet of water hits a waterwheel.

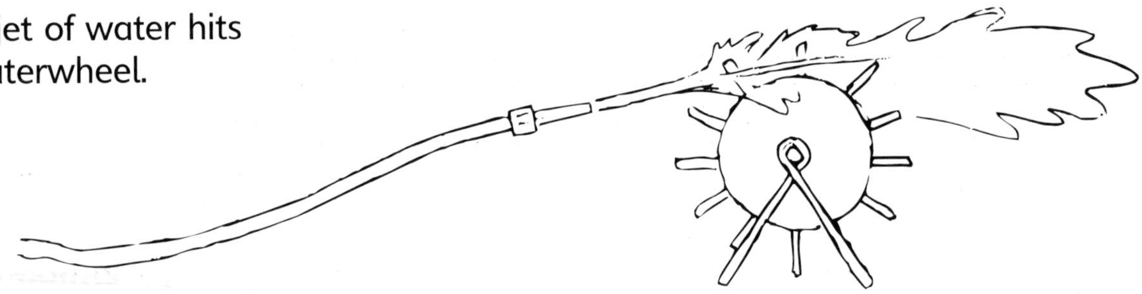

**3.** What will the waterwheel do? _____

**4.** Describe the energy changes that happen when the jet of water hits the waterwheel.

_____

_____

**5.** What would you expect to happen if the tap were turned up?

_____

_____

**6.** Why? _____

_____

# Exploring forces and their effects

These diagrams all show places where elastic things are being stretched.

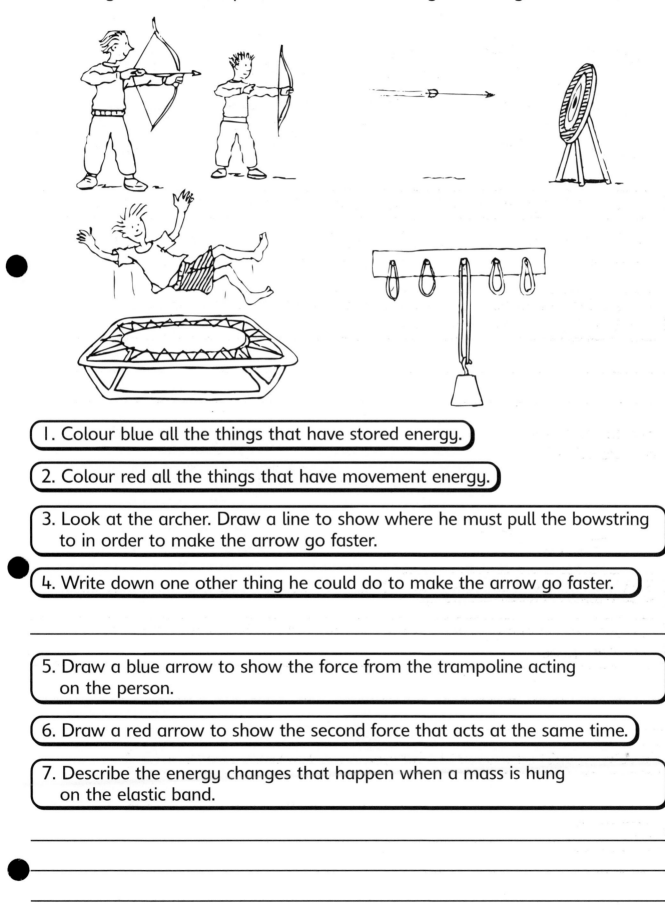

1. Colour blue all the things that have stored energy.

2. Colour red all the things that have movement energy.

3. Look at the archer. Draw a line to show where he must pull the bowstring to in order to make the arrow go faster.

4. Write down one other thing he could do to make the arrow go faster.

_____

5. Draw a blue arrow to show the force from the trampoline acting on the person.

6. Draw a red arrow to show the second force that acts at the same time.

7. Describe the energy changes that happen when a mass is hung on the elastic band.

_____

_____

_____

# Bending light and changing sound

## ORGANISATION (15 LESSONS)

| | OBJECTIVES | MAIN ACTIVITY | GROUP ACTIVITIES | PLENARY | OUTCOMES |
|---|---|---|---|---|---|
| **LESSON 1** | ● To know that when light rays pass through curved, transparent materials, the paths of the rays are changed. ● To make observations and draw conclusions. | Discuss the effect of looking through a curved transparent object. | Investigate the effect that looking through curved and flat transparent objects has on the appearance of a picture or writing. Draw examples of these effects. | Discuss where transparent materials are used and the advantages or disadvantages of using ones that change the path of light rays. | ● Understand that objects look different through a curved transparent material because the path of the light rays has changed. ● Can make observations and draw conclusions. |
| **LESSON 2** | ● To understand that lenses make light rays change direction. ● To decide what evidence to collect. ● To choose an appropriate way of presenting results. | Look at convex and concave lenses, and notice differences between them. | Investigate the effects of convex and concave lenses on a light beam. Use a convex lens to form an image on a screen. | Draw conclusions about the effects of convex and concave lenses on light. | ● Recognise the ways that light rays are changed by convex and concave lenses. ● Know that a convex lens can be used to make an image on a screen. ● Can decide an appropriate way to obtain and record investigation results. |
| **LESSON 3** | ● To know that we see things by light that enters the eye. | Look at pictures in a dark box with and without a torch. Identify the path light takes from the torch to our eye. | | Discuss light sources present at night, and the need for light to reflect off things so we can see them. | ● Know that in the absence of light, we cannot see. ● Know that light from a source is reflected off objects into the eye. |
| **LESSON 4** | ● To know that the eye contains a lens and a place where images form. | Examine changes in pupil size in different lighting conditions. Discuss how the eye forms images on the retina, and how spectacles can help with this. | Make a model eye. Use secondary sources to find out more about why spectacles are worn. | Recap on how the eye adjusts to different light levels and how it focuses. Discuss the importance of sight and use of eye protection. | ● Know that the eye can control the amount of light entering it. ● Can describe how the optic lens can focus on different objects. ● Can describe where an image forms in the eye. |
| **LESSON 5** | ● To know that lenses have a range of applications. | Study a range of optical instruments. Consider what they are for and where the lenses are. Use water drops to make observational drawings. | | Sum up how different optical instruments work. Discuss some unusual uses of lenses. | ● Can describe the uses of lenses in a range of optical instruments. |
| **LESSON 6** | ● To know that sunlight is made from a range of different-coloured light rays. | Use a prism to split a beam of light. Observe the colours present, and which colours deviated the most and least. | Make a spinner to show seven colours combining to make white. Make a model sky to show how it appears in different colours. | Discuss when and why rainbows are seen, why the sky looks blue and why sunrises and sunsets are red. | ● Recognise the colours of the spectrum. ● Can describe what happens to sunlight when it passes through a prism. |
| **LESSON 7** | ● To know that a range of vibrating objects produce different sounds. ● To make observations and draw conclusions. ● To make and test predictions. | Describe the sounds produced by a range of objects. | Use hearing, sight and touch to observe things that make sounds. Record observations and deduce what all sound-making objects have in common. | Discuss the fact that all sound is made by something vibrating. Predict the effect of making something unfamiliar vibrate, and ways to make vibrations louder or quieter. | ● Can make a generalisation that sound is made by something vibrating. |

## ORGANISATION (15 LESSONS)

| | OBJECTIVES | MAIN ACTIVITY | GROUP ACTIVITIES | PLENARY | OUTCOMES |
|---|---|---|---|---|---|
| **LESSON 8** | ● To know that sound travels in straight lines and can reflect off things, making echoes. ● To record data on a line graph. | Use the task of locating a sound source to demonstrate that sound travels in straight lines. | Plot graphs to show volume of sound recorded from different directions by a sound meter. Use secondary sources to study animals' ears. | Check all the children know that sounds travel in straight lines from source to hearer. Discuss advantages of large ears and ears that swivel. | ● Can describe the path of a sound from its source to the ear. ● Can draw a line graph using data from a table. |
| **LESSON 9** | ● To know that sound can travel through solids, water and air. | Demonstrate that sound travels through solids, water and air. Describe sound paths in different situations. | | Recap on how well sound travels through different materials. Discuss creatures that use underwater sounds. | ● Recognise that sound can travel through solids, water and air (a gas). |
| **LESSON 10** | ● To know that it is possible to change some solids so that sound travels better though them. ● To make a prediction and test it, choosing appropriate equipment for the test. | Discuss how sound travels from one end of a string telephone to the other. Consider what type of design would be best. | Build a string telephone. Test predictions about when it will work well. Write about how it was made and tested, including predictions and conclusions. | Children explain how the string telephone works, and when it works best. Discuss whether using wire instead of string would work better. | ● Can predict what factors make a solid able to transmit sound. ● Can test a prediction. |
| **LESSON 11** | ● To know that some materials can reduce sound. ● To plan and carry out a fair test. | Discuss what types of material would be suitable as sound reducers. | Assess the sound reduction properties of different materials. Design a poster to advertise a soundproofing material. | Discuss what materials reduce sound the most and why. Where might these materials be used? | ● Know that some materials can reduce sound. ● Can plan and carry out a fair test. |
| **LESSON 12** | ● To know that the pitch of some musical instruments can be altered by changing the size or tension of the vibrating part. ● To know how to make a test fair. | Listen to an elastic band sonometer. Discuss possible ways of producing higher or lower notes. Discuss and try ways of changing the note produced by a model drum. | Investigate the effect on an elastic band sonometer of changing one factor. | Identify similarities between the sonometer and a real instrument. | ● Can describe how the pitch of a drum or a stringed instrument is altered. ● Understand how to make a test fair. |
| **LESSON 13** | ● To know that the pitch of a wind instrument can be altered by changing the length of the vibrating air column. | Look at different wind instruments. What are the similarities and differences? | Make milk bottle instruments and drinking straw buzzers. Find out how to change the note produced. | Discuss how different notes are obtained on a real instrument. | ● Can relate the pitch of a sound made by a wind instrument to the length of the air column. |
| **LESSON 14** | ● To know that the loudness of musical instruments can be altered by changing how much they vibrate. | Build musical instruments using knowledge gained in Lessons 12 and 13. Create tunes. Vary the loudness of the notes. | | Groups describe what they have found out. Discuss the pitch of notes produced by various wind instruments. Groups play the tunes they have made. | ● Can make simple musical instruments and describe how to change the loudness of the note they produce. |

| | OBJECTIVES | ACTIVITY 1 | ACTIVITY 2 |
|---|---|---|---|
| **ASSESSMENT 15** | ● To assess the children's knowledge of the characteristics and uses of opaque materials and flat and curved transparent materials. ● To assess the children's knowledge of how sound travels from a source to a listener, and how well it travels through different materials. | Identify types of material by what things look like when viewed through them. Decide on appropriate materials for given optical uses. Draw what happens to white light passing through a prism. Explain this effect. | Draw sound paths from a sound source to different listeners. State which listener will hear the sound first, and why. Describe and explain the effects of echoes and of sound-reducing materials. |

# LESSON 1

## OBJECTIVES

● To know that when light rays pass through a curved transparent material, the paths of the rays are changed.
● To make observations and draw conclusions.

## RESOURCES

**Main teaching activity and Group activities:** A large selection of curved and flat transparent materials, such as glass or plastic optical lenses, sheets of clear plastic or perspex, drinking glasses, glass jars, the plastic stick-on lenses used when towing caravans, plastic rulers and so on; paper, writing and drawing materials.

## PREPARATION

Lenses and selections of transparent materials can often be borrowed from secondary schools.

*Vocabulary*

opaque, translucent, transparent, light rays

## BACKGROUND

Opaque materials (such as wood) do not let any light through. Translucent materials (such as thin paper) let light through, but we cannot see images through them. Transparent materials (such as glass) allow us to see images through them. Light is refracted ('bent') as it goes through any transparent material, which makes pools of water look shallower than they are and sticks going into water appear to bend. The degree of the bend (or refraction) depends on what the material is and how thick it is.

In this lesson, the flat sheets of transparent material will cause so little bending of the light due to refraction that it will not be noticeable. Any transparent object with a curved surface, so that some parts of the material are thicker than others, will act like a lens to bend rays of light. This makes a picture viewed through the material appear distorted. The amount of distortion depends on the curvature of the material.

A simple explanation of this effect is that the light is refracted when it enters the material and refracted back again when it leaves the material. If it enters and leaves the material in the same plane (as in a flat sheet of glass), its overall path will not be distorted. But if the plane of the material is different on the two sides (as in a curved piece of glass), the overall path of the light will be changed.

## INTRODUCTION

Ask the children to try and remember some things they know about light. Make a class list of important points they can remember.

## MAIN TEACHING ACTIVITY

Recap on the definitions of 'opaque', 'translucent' and 'transparent'. Ask the children to name examples of these different types of material. *Do we always see things clearly when we look at them though transparent materials? Why don't they always look 'quite right'?* Explain that sometimes looking at an object through a transparent material makes the light rays change direction and changes the appearance of the object we see. Use a few of the transparent objects to illustrate this, leading into the Group activities.

## GROUP ACTIVITIES

**1.** Warn the children of the dangers of breaking plastic and, especially, glass objects. Let them investigate a range of different-shaped transparent objects, some curved and some flat, and draw conclusions about which objects change the appearance of a picture or writing. They should find that objects with curved surfaces change the path of the light ray, while flat objects do not appear to. Encourage systematic investigation and recording.
**2.** Ask the children to select one object that they think changes the path of a light ray and one that does not, and to make accurate drawings of what some writing or a picture looks like with and without each transparent object in front of it.

## DIFFERENTIATION

**1.** Less able children could divide transparent objects into those that make something appear different and those that do not. More able children could relate these properties to the everyday uses of transparent materials (for example, we use flat glass in windows to have a clear view).
**2.** All the children should be able to participate in this activity.

## ASSESSMENT

While they are engaged in Group activity 1, ask the children to assess their own investigation for good and bad features. Can they suggest possible improvements?

## PLENARY

Ask a representative of each group to tell the class how they planned and carried out their investigation, and to show what they found. Discuss different places where transparent materials might be used, and the advantages and disadvantages of using transparent objects that change the path of light rays (including lenses).

## OUTCOMES

- Understand that objects look different through a curved transparent material because the path of the light rays has changed.
- Can make observations and draw conclusions.

## LINKS

Unit 7, Lesson 2: changing the direction of light rays.

# LESSON 2

## OBJECTIVES

- To understand that lenses make light rays change direction.
- To decide what evidence to collect.
- To choose an appropriate way of presenting results.

## RESOURCES

**Main teaching activity:** A selection of convex and concave lenses with varying curvatures; torches. Ray boxes can be used, but only if they can be adjusted to give a wide beam.
**Group activities: 1.** Photocopiable page 172, equipment as listed on page 172, writing and drawing materials. **2.** Convex lenses, torches or ray boxes, cardboard screens, paper clips, Blu-Tack, paper, writing and drawing materials.

## PREPARATION

Check that all torches or ray boxes work (and that you have enough sockets to plug in ray boxes if required). Test your arrangements for providing a dimmed work area. All light experiments give clearer results in darkened conditions. You do not need to black out your classroom; but if you can dim the lighting to the point where a torch beam shows up clearly, you will get better results. You can achieve this either by dimming the whole room or by allowing the children to conduct experiments inside large cardboard boxes turned on their side, with the open side pointing away from any windows.

You can attempt to make your own lenses using water-filled plastic containers, but these give poor results compared with plastic or glass lenses (because particles of dust or slight vibrations in the water distort the image). The easiest convex lenses to use are magnifying glasses, which can be obtained with a range of different powers. Alternatively, most secondary schools are willing to lend convex and concave lenses to primary schools, and many opticians are willing to supply a range of used lenses from spectacles.

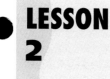

**Vocabulary**

convex, concave, lens, ray box, object, image, focused, unfocused, distorted, converge, diverge

## BACKGROUND

All curved transparent materials make light rays change direction. Lenses are transparent materials that have been shaped to alter the direction of light rays in a specific, designed way. Convex lenses make light rays converge to a point or focus; concave lenses make light rays diverge, making it possible to see a magnified image.

## INTRODUCTION

Remind the children what they found out about curved transparent materials in the last lesson. Show them some lenses and ask: *Does anyone know what these are?* Ask them to think of any places where they have seen lenses. Prompt them to think of spectacles, if necessary, but do not worry about any other uses of lenses at this stage. Explain that lenses are shaped so that they make light change direction in special ways. The children are going to find out what these special ways are.

## MAIN TEACHING ACTIVITY

Keep this section short, as the Group activities require plenty of time. Pass around some convex and concave lenses. Ask the children to look closely at them and describe any differences they notice. Emphasise the importance of handling breakable items carefully. Tell the children that lenses can be split into two types: **convex** (where the sides bulge outwards) and **concave** (where the sides squash inwards). Say that con**cave** lenses are easy to remember because they have sides like a **cave**: they cave in. Draw diagrams on the board or flip chart (see below).

Tell the children that they are going to investigate both types of lens to see what they do to light rays. Show them the torches or ray boxes they will be using and any arrangements for fastening screens inside the work area. Explain to them any arrangements you have for making the work area dimmer.

## GROUP ACTIVITIES

**1.** Give each child a copy of the instruction sheet (page 172). Allow them time to work in small groups to investigate the effect of putting convex and concave lenses between the torch and the screen on which it is shining. They should find that moving a convex lens towards the screen makes the image smaller, but moving a concave lens towards the screen makes the image larger.
**2.** Each group should now place a paper clip stuck upright in Blu-Tack just in front of the torch, and experiment with different positions of the convex lens to make the clearest possible image on the screen. Ask them to draw a diagram showing the positions of the torch, object, lens and image, and to draw or describe the image they get as accurately as possible. They should include details such as size, sharpness and which way up it is. (It will be upside-down.)

## DIFFERENTIATION

**1.** Less able children could draw the images they see with and without the lenses in place. More able children should try to relate the size of the image seen with the lens to the degree of curvature of the lens. They will find that the more curved a lens is, the more effect it has on the size of the image.
**2.** More able children could try to form a different clear image that is larger or smaller than the first one. They will have to change the distance between torch and screen to do this. Ask them to explain to a friend, with diagrams if these will help, what they could do to form a different-sized image. The groups who have clear images can be asked to make suggestions to help groups whose images are less clear.

## ASSESSMENT

Ask the groups to share their diagrams or descriptions in the Plenary session, so that other children can assess how clearly they show the results.

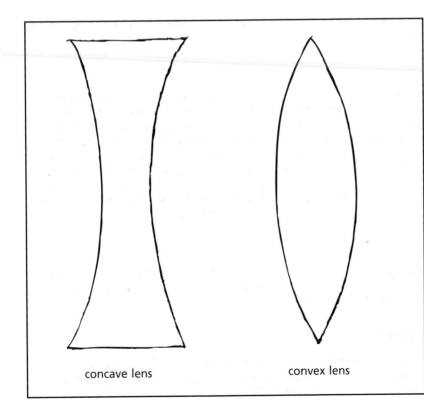

concave lens          convex lens

## PLENARY

Ask the children to draw conclusions about the effects that convex and concave lenses have on an image on a screen. (Convex lenses make the image smaller, concave lenses make it bigger.) *What does this tell us about the way the lenses affect the beam of light?* (Convex lenses make the beams of light converge or squash together, concave lenses make them diverge or spread out.)

## OUTCOMES

● Recognise the ways that light rays are changed by convex or concave lenses.
● Know that a convex lens can be used to make an image on a screen.
● Can decide an appropriate way to obtain and record investigation results.

## LINKS

Unit 7, Lesson 4: the human eye.

# LESSON 3

| Objective | ● To know that we see things by light that enters the eye. |
|---|---|
| Resources | A closed cardboard box, a heavy cloth (large enough to cover the box), a bright picture cut from a magazine, a torch. |
| Main activity | Either as a demonstration or as a group activity, make a 'picture box'. Cut a slit in the side of a closed cardboard box, near the top, long enough to allow a picture to be slid through the box. Make a small hole in the top to shine a torch through, and a small hole in the front to look through. Cover the whole box, except the front, with a heavy cloth to prevent light getting in. The children should look inside, when the torch is on and then when it is off. Discuss when they can see the picture, and what it is that makes the picture visible. Draw a diagram on the board of the path the light takes from the torch to our eyes, drawing arrows on the light rays; emphasise that the light goes **from** a light source **to** the object and then **into** our eyes. |
| Differentiation | Less able children could identify the light sources in various familiar and unfamiliar situations. More able children could identify the path of light rays in unfamiliar situations, involving reflection to reinforce knowledge gained in Year 4. |
| Assessment | At the beginning of the Plenary session, ask children to tell others in their group about looking into the box. They should explain how much they expected to be able to see, how much light was available, and where it was coming from. |
| Plenary | Discuss situations where it is easy to see and others where it is difficult, concentrating on the light sources present in different situations. Discuss the light sources available at night, and how much we would be able to see if it really was completely dark. Re-emphasise that we can only see things when light reflects off them. |
| Outcomes | ● Know that in the absence of light, we cannot see.<br>● Know that light from a source is reflected off objects into the eye. |

# LESSON 4

## OBJECTIVE

● To know that the eye contains a lens and a place where images form.

## RESOURCES

**Main teaching activity:** A model or large diagram showing the structure of the eye, mirrors.
**Group activities: 1.** Photocopiable page 173, scissors, adhesive, coloured pencils. **2.** Sources of information on eyes and spectacles. (Opticians can often provide these.)

## PREPARATION

If possible, arrange for an optician or a school nurse to talk to the children about how eyes work and how to look after them.

*Vocabulary*

cornea, pupil, iris, retina, long sight, short sight

## BACKGROUND

The structure of the human eye can be broken down into three main parts. The light enters the eye through the pupil, a hole that is surrounded by a circular muscle called the iris, before passing through the lens to the retina at the back of the eye. The iris responds automatically to changes in light level, opening or closing the pupil to let in more or less light. This control is needed because the light-sensitive cells of the retina can be damaged by too much light, and so have to be protected by the pupil closing when the light is too bright. Muscles holding the lens in place can contract or relax to make the lens thinner or fatter, changing how much the lens bends light rays passing through it. This is because rays of light from a nearby object have to be bent more to focus on the retina than rays from a more distant object of the same size.

## INTRODUCTION

Look at a model or large diagram showing the structure of the eye. Help the children to identify the major parts of the eye. Give them mirrors to help them identify some of the same parts in their own eyes: the iris, pupil, eyelid, eyelash and cornea.

## MAIN TEACHING ACTIVITY

Let the children use mirrors to examine their pupils when they have been looking towards a mildly bright light (such as a window), and when they have had their eyes shut. Ask them to describe the change. (The pupil is smaller in bright light.) Explain why this is so, using the model or diagram. Discuss why sunglasses are sometimes worn. Draw the children's attention to the area at the back of the eye. Explain that special light-sensitive cells here detect the light and send signals to the brain. If we have normal sight, light entering the eye forms a clear image here. If we are long- or short-sighted, the image will not be clear unless we wear spectacles: the lenses in the spectacles bend the light so that it forms a clear image at the back of the eye.

## GROUP ACTIVITIES

**1.** Give the children a copy each of page 173 and ask them to construct their own model eye.
**2.** The children can use secondary sources to find out about why spectacles are worn.

## DIFFERENTIATION

**1.** Give less able children a diagram of the eye to help them with labelling. More able children could write a few sentences to describe what happens when light enters the eye.
**2.** Less able children could find out what visual defects spectacles are worn to correct. *What is the difference between being long-sighted and being short-sighted?* More able children could find out what kind of lens is used to correct each type of defect, and how opticians test eyesight.

## ASSESSMENT

At the start of the Plenary, ask children to report what they have found out in their research.

## PLENARY

Recap on important features of the eye, how it adjusts to different light levels, and how it forms an image. Discuss the importance of sight, some ways in which eyes can be damaged, and situations in which eyes should be protected by dark glasses or protective goggles.

## OUTCOMES

- Know that the eye can control the amount of light entering it.
- Can describe where an image forms in the eye.
- Can describe how the optic lens can focus on different objects.

## LINKS

PSHE: looking after ourselves.

## LESSON 5

| | |
|---|---|
| **Objective** | ● To know that lenses have a range of applications. |
| **Resources** | Books about optical instruments, real optical instruments (as many as possible), microscope slides and eye-droppers, water. |
| **Main activity** | Study a range of optical instruments, using secondary sources and, if possible, real instruments. Possible instruments to consider are a magnifying glass, binoculars, a telescope, a camera, an overhead projector, a slide projector, a microscope, a periscope, an auriscope. Decide what each instrument is for – for example, enlarging very small or very distant objects, or making an image on a screen. Try to identify where the lenses in each instrument are, and whether it uses more than one lens. Each child can make a 'water drop microscope' by placing a small drop of water on a microscope slide, then looking through the drop at small objects held just underneath. They should draw what they see. |
| **Differentiation** | Less able children could identify the use of some of the instruments and make drawings of objects seen with and without each instrument. More able children could find out about an inventor of one optical instrument – for example, Zacharias Janssen (invented the compound microscope), Galileo (invented the refracting telescope), Kepler (improved Galileo's design) or Daguerre (invented the early camera). |
| **Assessment** | Start the Plenary session by asking some children to report to the class on what they have found out about one particular optical instrument. They should explain what it does and, if they can, how it works. |
| **Plenary** | Sum up some of the children's findings about optical instruments. Decide what type of image each instrument produces: *Is it larger, smaller, the right way up, upside-down?* Discuss some of the less familiar places where lenses can be found, such as endoscopes (for internal examinations), photocopiers, scanners and lighthouses (where a lens is used to produce a narrow beam of light). |
| **Outcome** | ● Can describe the uses of lenses in a range of optical instruments. |

# LESSON 6

## OBJECTIVE

● To know that sunlight is made from a range of different-coloured light rays.

### RESOURCES

**Main teaching activity:** A prism, a torch or ray box, a white cardboard screen.
**Group activities: 1.** For each child: card, string, scissors, coloured pencils. **2.** For each group: straight-sided glasses, water, milk, teaspoons, torches.

### PREPARATION

Practise using a prism to obtain a spectrum. If it gives you extra confidence, you could use a torch and mark out the positions you need for the torch and prism. This avoids the need to book a sunny day! It is possible to produce a spectrum using a light beam and a glass of water, but this is extremely difficult and unreliable. Make sure that the lighting can be dimmed for Group activity 2 (see Preparation in Lesson 1, page 154). You may wish to provide circles of card, marked into seven equal sections, to help the children make spinners.

*Vocabulary*

prism, spectrum, scatter, refracted, deviated

### BACKGROUND

White light is usually said to be made up of seven different colours: the bands visible in a rainbow. These colours correspond to different wavelengths of light. Sunlight actually forms a continuous spectrum of wavelengths, changing gradually from red through yellow and blue to violet; but we just give names to those colours we can recognise easily. Some scientists prefer to say that there are only six distinct colours (there is no true 'indigo' band). Because the colours have slightly different wavelengths, they are affected differently by passing through transparent materials such as glass and water. All light waves slow down when they travel through glass; but red light slows down less than blue light, so is deviated or bent less. Red light is also scattered less than blue light by particles in the atmosphere (see Plenary).

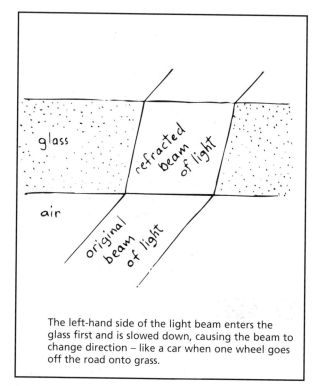

The left-hand side of the light beam enters the glass first and is slowed down, causing the beam to change direction – like a car when one wheel goes off the road onto grass.

### INTRODUCTION

*What colour is light?* Discuss situations where coloured lights are used, then ask: *What colour is sunlight?* The children will probably suggest that sunlight has no colour, but that the Sun itself looks yellow. Explain that when light does not seem to have any colour, we call it 'white light'. Tell the children that you are going to show them an experiment to find out whether there are really any colours in sunlight.

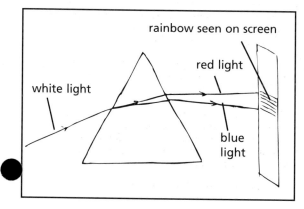

### MAIN TEACHING ACTIVITY

Demonstrate how to use a prism to split a beam of bright sunlight (or a torch beam) into the 'seven colours of the rainbow'. Use a large diagram on the board (see illustration) to help the children work out which colour has changed direction least – in other words, which colour is closest to the path the light ray would have taken if the prism had not been in the way. Red light changes direction (is deviated) the least; violet light is deviated the most. Ask the children to invent a mnemonic to help them remember the order of the colours in the spectrum. ('Richard Of York Gave Battle In Vain' is a traditional one that may not be very memorable to modern children.)

## GROUP ACTIVITIES

**1.** Ask the children to make card spinners divided into seven equal sections (they need to be approximately 51° per section). Ask them to colour each section in a different colour from the rainbow, then put a pencil or loop of string through the centre and spin it. *What colour do you see?* The spinner should look a whitish grey while spinning – thus demonstrating that white light can be made up from a mixture of seven different colours.

**2.** The children can make a model sky. In the sky, particles of dust and moisture act as minute prisms to scatter the light. This can be modelled using a glass of water and a torch in a darkened room. They should add half a teaspoon of milk to the water. A torch shone at the front of the glass reflects back with a bluish-grey colour, because the blue light is scattered back to us while the red light passes through. A torch viewed through the glass of milky water looks yellowish, like the Sun in the daytime. Adding one more teaspoon of milk means the light has to shine through more particles (like the Sun shining through a thicker layer of the atmosphere when it is low on the horizon at dawn or dusk). Now the torch looks pinkish when viewed through the glass, just as the Sun does at dawn or dusk. This is because only the red light reaches us: the blue light has been scattered so far that we cannot see it.

## DIFFERENTIATION

**1.** More able children could discuss what might happen if split light from the first prism were shone through a second prism. *Would it matter which way round the second prism was?* (If the second prism were the same way round as the first, it would spread the light further; if it were the opposite way round, the colours would recombine to make white light.)
**2.** All the children should be able to participate in this activity.

## ASSESSMENT

In the Plenary session, ask children to tell others what they have found out. Ask them to speculate on what they would see if they added more red or more blue to their spinners.

## PLENARY

Check that all the children understand that white light, such as sunlight, is made up from a mixture of other colours. Remind them of what happened when light was shone through a prism, and ask them to suggest why we sometimes see rainbows. Prompt them to suggest that rainbows happen when it is sunny and has been raining, so that bright sunlight is passing through water droplets in the air. Lead them to the idea that the droplets of water are acting like a prism to split the sunlight into its different colours. Link this to the action of lenses (see Lesson 4, page 157). Sometimes cheap lenses act like prisms, giving bands of different colours around the edge of the image.

Discuss why a clear sky looks blue. Red and yellow light comes straight to us from the Sun. The yellow light is brighter and stronger, so the Sun looks yellow. Blue light from the Sun is scattered so much by particles in the atmosphere that it comes to us from all directions, making all of the sky look blue. At sunrise and sunset, the Sun's light has to travel through so much atmosphere to reach us that only the red light, which is scattered less, comes through.

## OUTCOMES

- Recognise the colours of the spectrum.
- Can describe what happens to sunlight when it passes through a prism.

## LINKS

Art: sunrises, sunsets and colour mixing.

# LESSON 7

## OBJECTIVES
- To know that a range of vibrating objects produce different sounds.
- To make observations and draw conclusions.
- To make and test predictions.

### RESOURCES

**Main teaching activity and Group activity:** A flip chart and marker pen; a selection of sound-producing objects (for example: a drum, a stretched elastic band, a tuning fork, a ruler clamped to a table); a cassette recording of familiar sounds; paper, writing materials.
**Plenary:** A glass, a handbell.

### PREPARATION

Find out how long ago the children last studied sound, and what they covered. Check that all the sound sources you will use can either be seen or felt to be vibrating.

### BACKGROUND

Some children may not have studied sound since Year 1. This lesson should be aimed at finding out how much the class already knows about sound, and teaching that all sounds are made by objects vibrating. Asking children to describe sounds is a good way of checking both their understanding and their knowledge of the relevant vocabulary.

*Vocabulary*

loud/quiet, soft/loud, high/low, louder/quieter, vibrating/vibration

### INTRODUCTION

Tell the children that in the next few lessons, they are going to be finding out about sounds. *What do you know about sounds?* Brainstorm all the children's ideas about sounds; record their knowledge, including any misconceptions, on a flip chart. Keep this to be referred to at the end of the unit. Check that the children are aware that a 'sound' and a 'noise' are the same thing, but that we usually use 'noise' to refer to sounds that we don't like.

### MAIN TEACHING ACTIVITY

Study a selection of things that produce sound, and listen to a cassette recording of various familiar sounds. Ask the children to describe the sounds produced. Look for vocabulary such as 'high/low', 'loud/quiet' and 'getting louder/quieter'. Make sure the children understand words such as 'high', 'low' and 'soft' that have different meanings in other contexts. Discuss when particular sounds will seem louder or quieter. At this stage, you should be looking only for the knowledge that any sound seems louder when you are closer to what is making it.

### GROUP ACTIVITY

The children should examine various things that make sounds (see Resources). Using hearing, sight and touch, they should make very careful observations of the sound-producing objects. They should record their observations using writing or drawing, and try to deduce what all the things making sounds have in common. (They are vibrating.)

### DIFFERENTIATION

Less able children could use pictures to record which parts of some objects are vibrating to make sounds. More able children could think of things around the home that make sounds. Ask them: *What is vibrating to make the sound?*

### ASSESSMENT

Ask the children to choose one object and tell their friends what they observed about it. Can they describe what was moving and how they detected the movement?

## PLENARY

Make sure the children understand what vibration is. If they have used language such as 'All the things had bits that were moving', explain that when something keeps moving backwards and forwards (for example, a 'twanged' ruler) we use the word 'vibrating'.

Look at a less familiar situation, and ask the children to predict what will happen if you do something to cause vibration. Examples could be rubbing a damp finger around the top of a glass or tapping a handbell. For some familiar objects, ask the children to predict ways of making the sound produced louder or quieter. Test all their predictions.

## OUTCOME

● Can make a generalisation that sound is made by something vibrating.

## LINKS

PE and drama: fitting appropriate sounds to moods and actions.

# LESSON 8

## OBJECTIVES

● To know that sound travels in straight lines and can reflect off things, making echoes.
● To record data on a line graph.

## RESOURCES

**Main teaching activity:** A device that ticks, such as a metronome or timer; a long scarf, a cardboard ear tube.
**Group activities: 1.** Photocopiable page 174, graph paper, pencils, rulers. **2.** Secondary sources of information about animal ears.

## PREPARATION

Make an ear tube: a sheet of cardboard rolled and taped to make a tube about 7cm in diameter and about 30cm long.

## BACKGROUND

Sound waves travel outwards in all directions from a source of sound. A listener hears sound that has travelled in a straight line from the source to the ear, but he or she will also hear sound waves that have bounced off hard objects: these are echoes. The echo is always heard after the original sound, because the sound wave that has been reflected has always travelled further than the sound wave that has travelled directly from source to listener. Whenever sound waves hit a material, some of the sound energy is absorbed, so the sound that has travelled directly from source to listener is always louder than the echoes from surrounding materials. This means that the source of a sound can be located by identifying the direction in which it is loudest.

**Vocabulary**

sound, source, echo, volume

## INTRODUCTION

Remind the children that vibrating objects make sounds. Ask: *How does the sound get to us?* (It travels to us through the air.) *Do all sounds reach us?* (Obviously not, or we would be able to hear everything that was happening in Class 3 [choose your own suitable location]). Explain that we can work out things about how sound travels to us by finding out what sounds we hear best.

## MAIN TEACHING ACTIVITY

Show the children a source of sound. Something that ticks, such as a metronome or a timer, will be better for this than a variable source such as music. Adjust the volume by moving it until the children can still hear it, but it is quiet. Turn the sound source off. Ask for a volunteer to help work out how the sound travels from the source to our ears. Give him or her a scarf, or something soft and padded, to cover one ear (absorbing sound), and a cardboard tube to hold to the other ear. Ask the child to shut his or her eyes, then start the sound source again in a different part of the room from before. Keeping his or her eyes shut, the child has to turn around very slowly until the sound appears to be at its loudest, then stop with the tube pointing at the source of the sound. Repeat with other children, then discuss what this tells us about the way the sound travels. (It tells us that the sound is travelling directly to us from the source, not travelling around the room and approaching us from a different direction.)

## GROUP ACTIVITIES

**1.** Give the children a copy each of page 174 and some graph paper, and let them work through the task. Explain that the units of sound volume are relative.
**2.** The children can use secondary sources to study animals that have large ears or ears that can swivel around easily. Ask them to write a few sentences for each animal, describing the advantage these ears give it.

## DIFFERENTIATION

**1.** Less able children could plot a bar chart, using pre-labelled axes. More able children could label their own axes and draw a line graph. They could go on to discuss the effect it would have on the volume readings if the sound meter were placed close to a wall.
**2.** Less able children could find out about one animal that has large ears (not an elephant) and discuss what it uses its ears for.

## ASSESSMENT

In the Plenary session, ask some children to show the graphs they have drawn. Discuss the direction of the sound source, asking the children to explain why they chose the direction they did.

## PLENARY

Sum up the Main teaching activity, reminding the children that sounds appear louder when the ear is pointing directly at them because the sound can travel in a straight line from the source to the ear. Make sure all the children know what the line graph (or bar chart) of sound volume against direction should look like (see diagrams). Discuss what this tells us about the direction of the source of the sound, and why this is the case. Discuss the questions at the bottom of the sheet; make sure the children understand that the readings were repeated in order to make sure that the results were reliable. They should suggest checking the readings at 90°, since the large difference between the two readings indicates a probable error. The precise direction of the sound source cannot be given, but is close to 225°.

Ask some children to share what they have found out about various animals, drawing attention to why many animals have ears that can swivel. Relate this to what was discovered in the Main teaching activity: a source of sound can be located because the sound appears louder when the ear is pointing directly at the source.

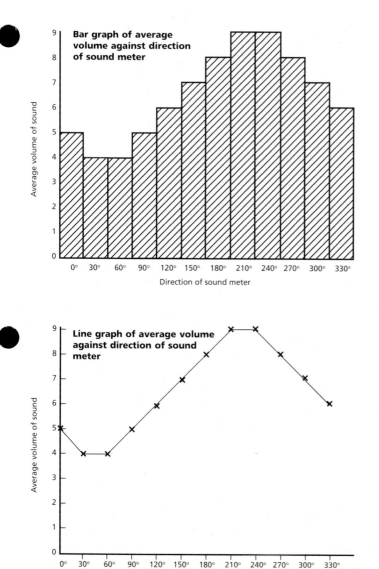

## OUTCOMES

● Can describe the path of a sound from its source to the ear.
● Can draw a line graph using data from a table.

## LINKS

Maths: calculating averages, plotting line graphs or bar charts.

# LESSON 9

| Objective | ● To know that sound can travel through solids, water and air. |
|---|---|
| Resources | A wooden or tin box with a lid, a bead or marble, a bowl of water, a source of underwater sound (eg two spoons to knock together), pictures of different situations showing a sound source and a listener. |
| Main activity | Talk about the evidence we have that sound travels through different types of material. *How do we know that sound can travel through air (a gas)?* (We wouldn't be able to hear each other talk if it didn't. Rattle a bead or marble in a closed wooden or tin box.) *What does that sound travel through to reach us?* If the sound could not travel through the solid box, we would not hear anything. Tap two spoons together in a bowl of water (or use any other method of making a sound underwater). *Can you hear anything?* This tells us that sound must be able to travel through water. Underwater swimmers cannot talk to each other because complicated sounds such as words get distorted by the movement of the water (like light through frosted glass).<br>    Ask the children to put an ear close to the desk and tap their fingers so lightly on the desk that they cannot hear it, then rest their ear on the desk and repeat the soft tap. The second time, they can hear the tapping clearly – so sound travels better through solids than through air. Discuss why echoes are fainter than the original sound: some of the sound bounces off to reach us, but the rest travels into the solid object.<br>    Give the children pictures of various situations showing a source of sound and a listener. Ask them to describe the possible paths that the sound can take to reach the listener and state what type of material the sound has to travel through on each path. |
| Differentiation | Less able children could draw the possible paths for the sound, using red where the sound travels through a solid, blue for a liquid and green for a gas. More able children could make up and describe different situations in which sound has to travel through solids, liquids and gases. |
| Assessment | Ask the children to talk about the sound paths they have found. Look for knowledge that sound can travel through solids, liquids and gases, and that it can reflect from some objects. Some children may be aware that sound travels better through solids than through air. |
| Plenary | Recap on how well sound can travel through different materials. Discuss creatures that use underwater sounds. All the creatures that communicate over any but very short distances use low-pitched sounds, which are distorted less. |
| Outcome | ● Recognise that sound can travel through solids, water and air (a gas). |

# LESSON 10

## OBJECTIVES
● To know that it is possible to change some solids so that sound travels better through them.
● To make a prediction and test it, choosing appropriate equipment for the test.

## RESOURCES

**Main teaching activity:** A ready-assembled string telephone.
**Group activity:** A selection of different plastic and cardboard cups or small containers (two of each type per pair), different types of string, scissors, paper, writing materials.

## PREPARATION

Make a string telephone (using cardboard cups). Prepare a suitable set of questions (perhaps for a classroom assistant) in order to help less able children describe how they built and used their string telephone.

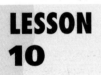

*Vocabulary*

stiff, floppy, solid, vibrate, transmit

## BACKGROUND

Sound travels well through solids because the particles in a solid are tightly bound together, giving a stiff structure which transmits vibrations well. If the structure of the solid is not stiff, it will not transmit vibrations well. If there are good connections between the cups and the string, and the string is tight, a string telephone will transmit sounds well: the vibrations of one cup will be transmitted along the string to the other end. A poor connection between the cup and the string stops the message being transmitted because the string does not vibrate. A floppy string will absorb the vibrations instead of transmitting them, so the message will not get through.

## INTRODUCTION

Ask the children to suggest ways in which they could get a sound message to someone else. Emphasise that it has to be a sound message: a telephone or a radio does not count, because these devices send electrical signals or radio signals. The children could shout, and they could use something like a megaphone to make the shout louder – but what if they wanted to send a whisper? Remind them what they have discovered sound travels well through (see Lesson 9).

## MAIN TEACHING ACTIVITY

Show the children a string telephone, already assembled. Ask who has seen or made one before. *How does it work?* Make sure the children know that the sound travels along the string from one mouthpiece/earpiece to the other. Tell them that they are going to work in pairs to make string telephones – but they have to think carefully about the design and how they will build it, so that it will work as well as possible. They need to consider, for example: *What is the best sort of cup to use? Does it matter how the string attaches to the cups? What sort of string is best?*

## GROUP ACTIVITY

Ask pairs of children to write down predictions about when the string telephone will work and when it won't, then choose their own materials to build a string telephone and test their predictions. They should find that the telephone will work when the string is tight and will not work if the string is loose. This is because sound travels easily through a stiff solid, but poorly through a soft or floppy solid.

Ask the children to write a few paragraphs about how they made their telephone, describing how it was built (probably using a diagram), their prediction about when it would work, what they found out and their conclusions (including whether their prediction was correct).

## DIFFERENTIATION

More able children could predict what would happen if someone held onto the centre of the string, then test whether they were right. (It will prevent the string vibrating, so the message will get through very faintly or not get through at all.) Less able children could be asked a set of questions, requiring only short answers, about how they built and used their telephone.

## ASSESSMENT

Look at the children's predictions and conclusions about their telephones. They should show awareness that the string has to be taut for the telephone to work, and that this is the case because sound travels better through hard or stiff solids than through soft or floppy solids.

## PLENARY

Ask children to explain how the string telephone works. (It works because vibrations caused by someone talking are transmitted along the string.) Ask them to report what they have found about when the telephone works. (It works when the string is tight, but not when the string is floppy.) *Do you think using wire in the telephone instead of string would make any difference?* (The telephone would work better with wire, because even when wire is bent it is still stiff enough to transmit sound vibrations.)

## OUTCOMES

● Can predict what factors make a solid able to transmit sound.
● Can test a prediction.

## LINKS

History: early methods of long-range communication.

## LESSON 11

### OBJECTIVES

● To know that some materials can reduce sound.
● To plan and carry out a fair test.

### RESOURCES

**Main teaching activity:** A sound source (such as a ticking clock or a buzzer), a selection of sound-reducing materials (see Preparation).
**Group activities: 1.** Photocopiable page 175, writing materials, sound sources, sound-reducing materials, measuring tapes, metre rulers. **2.** Art paper, coloured pencils, felt-tipped pens.

## PREPARATION

Collect many samples of three or four different materials that might be used around the home, such as foam plastic, carpet, vinyl and polystyrene. Make sure that there is enough for each group, and that the children can use equal thicknesses of each material if they wish. **Do not** use fibreglass loft insulation (which is sometimes used for soundproofing in walls), because handling it can leave very uncomfortable splinters in the fingers.

## BACKGROUND

*Vocabulary*

noise pollution, ear protection, soundproofing, sound reduction

There are many circumstances in which materials are used to reduce sound, from the ear defenders used by operators of noisy machinery to the soundproofing used in buildings to shut out the sounds of nearby roads or railway lines. Occasionally, scientists may use specially-shaped foam rubber padding to line a laboratory in order to make it 'anechoic' – that is, completely free from all echoes. The one feature that all materials used in these situations have is that they are soft and squashy, and so do not transmit vibrations. Most household furnishings, such as soft furniture, curtains and carpets, reduce sound transmission; this is why empty houses always sound more 'echoey' than furnished houses.

## INTRODUCTION

Ask the children to think of situations where they might not want to hear certain sounds, or where other people might be hearing sounds they do not want to listen to. Introduce the idea of 'noise pollution': disturbance of people's lives by sounds that are unpleasant or even dangerous to them. Talk about ear protection, soundproofing and situations where these would be used.

## MAIN TEACHING ACTIVITY

Set up a source of constant or regular sound. *What can we do to this buzzer to stop us hearing it?* If the children suggest turning the volume down, explain that there is no volume control and that there are some very loud sources of sound (such as factory machines) where the volume cannot be turned down either, yet people still don't want to hear them. When they suggest covering up the sound source, discuss what would be an appropriate material to cover it with. At this stage, they should be aware (see Lesson 10) that a soft material will be better than a hard one. Show them a selection of different soft materials. Say: *You have to plan and carry out a test to find out which of these materials is best at blocking the sound of the buzzer. Remember to make your test fair.*

## GROUP ACTIVITIES

**1.** The children assess the sound reduction properties of different materials. They can use copies of page 175 to help them plan the test and record the results.
**2.** The children design a poster to advertise a soundproofing material. They should include information on what the material is like, what it is made from and where it might be useful.

## DIFFERENTIATION

**1.** Less able children could focus on questions 1, 2, 4 and 6 on the sheet, only attempting the other questions if they are able and time allows. More able children could discuss whether various materials have advantages and disadvantages other than their soundproofing properties.
**2.** All the children should be able to participate in this activity.

## ASSESSMENT

Ask one or two groups to present their investigations and findings to the class. The other children can review the work presented and decide on good features and limitations. Look for the ability to tell whether a test is fair, and whether there are questions that the test could not answer.

## PLENARY

Look at the children's results and decide which material is best for reducing sound. Discuss the features that this material has that make it good at preventing sounds getting through. For example, it may contain pockets of air. Discuss situations where this material might be useful – and situations where (for other reasons) it would not be so good. For example, a flammable material would not be suitable near a blast furnace. Display the children's posters, picking out good points.

## OUTCOMES

● Know that some materials can reduce sound.
● Can plan and carry out a fair test.

## LINKS

PSHE: noise pollution and consideration for others.

# LESSON 12

## OBJECTIVES

● To know that the pitch of some musical instruments can be altered by changing the size or tension of the vibrating part.
● To know how to make a test fair.

## RESOURCES

**Main teaching activity: 1.** An elastic band sonometer. **2.** A model drum (see Preparation), balloon rubber, various jars or basins, strong elastic bands.
**Group activity:** Strong cardboard or plastic boxes, a large selection of elastic bands of different sizes and thicknesses, photocopiable page 176.

## PREPARATION

If possible, invite a musician (or ask a talented child) to attend the Plenary session, to play a stringed instrument to the children and demonstrate how the instrument works.

Make an elastic band sonometer from a strong cardboard box with a variety of elastic bands stretched across it (see page 176). Make a model drum by stretching a circle of rubber from a balloon across the top of a jar or basin (with a lip) and holding it in place with a strong elastic band.

*Vocabulary*

elastic band sonometer, stringed instrument, tension, pitch, volume

## BACKGROUND

There are many different types of stringed instruments around the world, but they all produce a range of notes in very similar ways. There are only three ways to change the pitch of the note produced by a vibrating string: changing the length, thickness or tension of the string. The pitch can be increased by reducing the length, reducing the thickness or increasing the tension. Drums and other stretched-skin instruments work in a similar way to stringed instruments: they just have a 'two-dimensional string'. The pitch of the note produced can be increased by reducing the area of the vibrating skin, reducing the thickness or increasing the tension. The volume of the notes produced can be increased by making the vibrations bigger – that is, by plucking the string harder or hitting the drum harder.

## INTRODUCTION

Tell the children that they are going to spend the next couple of lessons looking at musical instruments and finding out some of the ways that these instruments are used to make different notes. Ask the children to name some musical instruments. List them on the board and help the children to group them according to the way the sound is produced. All instruments can be grouped broadly into those you blow, those you hit or shake, and those that have strings. This lesson looks at instruments with strings and instruments that you hit.

## MAIN TEACHING ACTIVITY 1

Show the children an elastic band sonometer (sound maker). *How many of you have ever made one of these? What will happen when I pluck one of the elastic bands? Will all these bands make the same sound when I pluck them?* Test the bands and listen to the notes produced. Ask the children to suggest things that could be changed to make higher or lower notes. Write their suggestions on the board. The things that will affect the note produced by the elastic band are: the length of band plucked, the thickness of the band used and the tension in the band (how stretched it is).

## GROUP ACTIVITY

Each group should look at the effect on an elastic band's sound of changing one factor only. They should use copies of page 176 to help them carry out and record their investigation. Each group should then explain to a different group what they have found out. Talk to all the groups to produce a summary of their findings on the board.

## MAIN TEACHING ACTIVITY 2

Show the children a model drum (see Preparation). Have jars or basins with different-sized mouths and more balloon rubber visible. Tap the drum lightly, listening to the sound it produces. Ask the children to suggest possible ways of making drums that produce different notes. Try out their ideas and record the results on the board or flip chart. Discuss which factors can be changed, and which factors you need to keep the same. You will find that using a container with a larger mouth produces a note with a lower pitch, provided that you stretch the balloon rubber by the same amount. Using a container with the same-size mouth, but stretching the balloon rubber more, produces a note with a higher pitch.

## DIFFERENTIATION

Less able children could investigate the effect of changing how much the elastic bands are stretched by using small and large elastic bands of the same thickness. Make sure they understand that the small band is more stretched because they had to stretch it further to get it over the box. More able children could look at pictures of real stringed instruments and discuss why the strings give different notes, and how the strings can be 'tuned' to adjust the note they produce.

## ASSESSMENT

At the start of the Plenary session, ask the groups to explain to each other the results of their investigations. Ask the children to write down two ways of making the note higher for each instrument, and two ways of making it lower.

## PLENARY

Show the children a guitar or other stringed instrument. Ask them to pick out things that the real stringed instrument has in common with the elastic band sonometer. If necessary, help them to identify that both have several strings and a hollow box that the strings stretch across. Discuss how different notes are obtained on a real instrument, again stressing the similarities. Show them how different notes can be obtained by changing the thickness of the string, changing the length of the string (putting your finger on the frets) and changing the tension of the string (adjusting the tuning screws). Make sure that all the children know the factors that change the note, though they will not all remember the specific effect that each change has.

## OUTCOMES

● Can describe how the pitch of a drum or a stringed instrument is altered.
● Understand how to make a test fair.

## LINKS

Music: how musical instruments make sounds.

## LESSON 13

### OBJECTIVE

● To know that the pitch of a wind instrument can be altered by changing the length of the vibrating air column.

### RESOURCES

**Main teaching activity:** A selection of real wind instruments, pictures (perhaps of an orchestra) showing a range of different wind instruments.
**Group activities: 1.** A large number of clean, washed, empty glass milk bottles (plastic bottles do not work as well, but it is important to warn the children of the dangers of using glass bottles); some tall glass jars with larger mouths than the bottles; jugs for pouring water.
**2.** Photocopiable page 177, many plastic drinking straws, scissors.

## PREPARATION

If possible, ask a musician (or a talented child) to attend the Plenary session, to play a wind instrument to the children and demonstrate how the instrument works. Arrange for any children with wind instruments to bring them to school for this lesson.

## BACKGROUND

Wind instruments all work because patterns of resonating air are set up inside the tubes of the instrument. These patterns develop because a sound wave travelling down the tube bounces off the other end and travels back up the tube, interfering with the wave travelling down. At a certain pitch for each pipe, the sound going down and the sound coming back reinforce each other to produce a loud, resonant note that we can hear. The note heard depends on the length of the air column that vibrates – that is why the note can be changed by changing the length of the tube, or by using valves or holes that alter the proportion of the air column that vibrates. In real musical instruments, several different patterns of vibration (called 'harmonics') are set up at once. These harmonics give real instruments a much fuller, more musical tone than simple buzzers or milk bottles.

*Vocabulary*

wind instrument,
air column

## INTRODUCTION

Remind the children of the three main types of musical instrument: those that you hit or shake, those that have vibrating strings, and those that you blow. Make a list of as many instruments as you can that work by blowing, including whistles and squeakers. *Could we call the human voice a musical instrument? How does it work?* The voice works by air vibrating in the larynx (let the children feel this); we use muscles to change the shape of the mouth and throat, and so make different sounds.

## MAIN TEACHING ACTIVITY

Look at a range of pictures showing different wind instruments, and at some real instruments if possible. *What do all these instruments have in common?* (They all have a column of air inside them that vibrates.) *What are the differences between them?* Some instruments are bigger, with longer air columns than others. Some instruments (such as organ pipes and bagpipes) have air blown across them mechanically, while others (such as recorders and clarinets) have a person blowing them. Tell the children that they are going to find out how these instruments make different notes by making their own instruments and using them to find out what will change the note produced.

## GROUP ACTIVITIES

**1.** The children should try blowing across the tops of bottles that are part-filled with water, then investigate how they can adjust the note produced by the bottle. Warn them of the need to be extremely careful when using glass bottles.
**2.** The children should make drinking straw buzzers, using copies of page 177, then find out the effect of **(a)** changing the length of the straw and **(b)** making holes in the drinking straw (as in a recorder). *Does it matter what size the holes are?*

## DIFFERENTIATION

**1.** Less able children could investigate whether the size of the bottle mouth affects the sound made. More able children could work together to decide on a way of finding out whether it is the length of the air column or the amount of water that affects the sound.
**2.** More able children could try to find out whether the note produced by a drinking straw is the same as the note produced by a bottle with an air column of the same length. (It won't be the same, because the pattern of air vibrations set up inside an open-ended pipe is different from the pattern set up inside a column of air closed by water at one end).

## ASSESSMENT

Ask some children to demonstrate how they can use their home-made instruments to make high or low notes. Can they relate what they have found out to the notes they would expect real instruments to make?

Name

# Recording sound levels

Some children set up a sound meter to measure how loud a sound was:

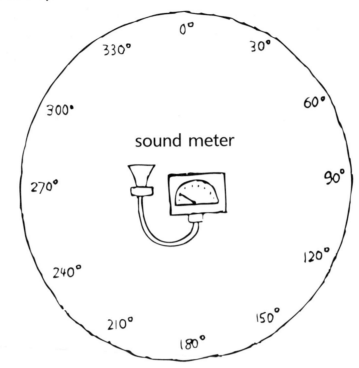

sound meter

They took two readings for each direction the sound meter pointed in.
They recorded the following results:

| Direction | Volume 1 | Volume 2 | Average volume | Direction | Volume 1 | Volume 2 | Average volume |
|-----------|----------|----------|----------------|-----------|----------|----------|----------------|
| 0° | 4 | 6 | | 180° | 9 | 7 | |
| 30° | 3 | 5 | | 210° | 9 | 9 | |
| 60° | 5 | 3 | | 240° | 8 | 10 | |
| 90° | 8 | 2 | | 270° | 8 | 8 | |
| 120° | 7 | 5 | | 300° | 6 | 8 | |
| 150° | 8 | 6 | | 330° | 7 | 5 | |

Then the children plotted a graph of the average sound volume (on the y-axis) against the direction the sound meter pointed in (on the x-axis).

Fill in the average values, then plot the graph on a separate sheet of graph paper.

Discuss these questions:

● Why is it a good idea to take more than one reading?

● Are there any readings you would want to check again?

● Which direction do you think the sound source is in?

# Materials for reducing sound

You need to test the materials you have been given to find out which is the best at reducing sound. You must decide whether you are going to wrap the sound source up in the material, or put a layer of the material between the sound source and you, or do something else.

1. Draw a diagram to show how you are going to do your assessment. Write a few sentences to say what you will do and why you have chosen this way.

2. What are you going to record?

3. Write down any things you did to help you get reliable results. For example, what did you keep the same?

4. Use the space below to record your results.

5. Which material reduced the sound the most?

6. Why do you think this material was the best?

# Elastic band sonometers

This diagram shows you how to make an elastic band sonometer.

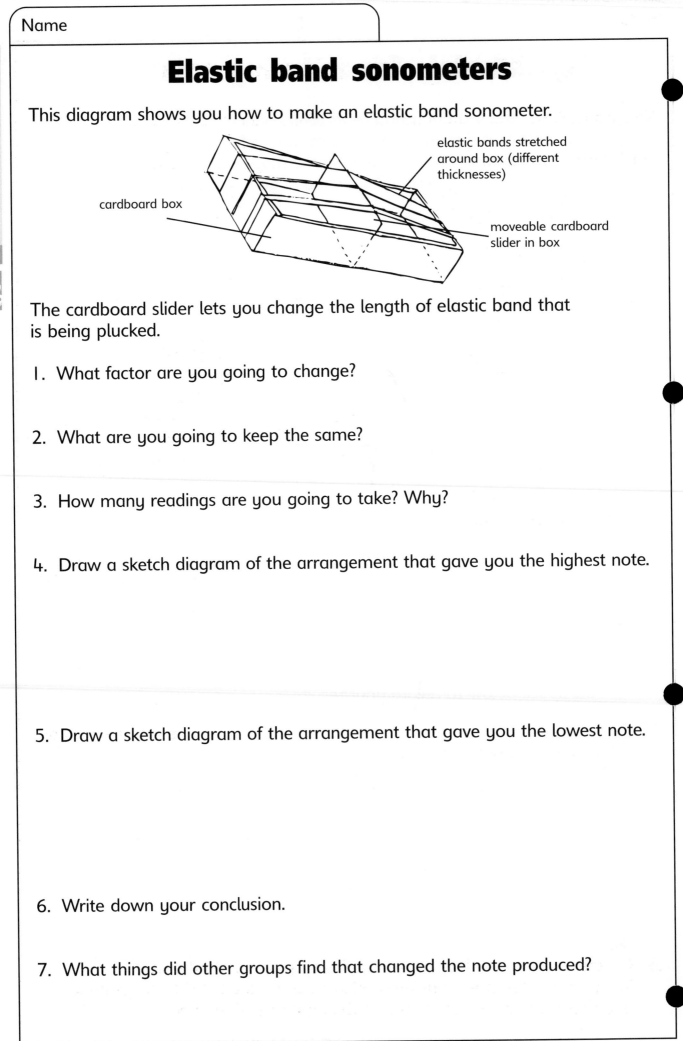

elastic bands stretched around box (different thicknesses)

cardboard box

moveable cardboard slider in box

The cardboard slider lets you change the length of elastic band that is being plucked.

1. What factor are you going to change?

2. What are you going to keep the same?

3. How many readings are you going to take? Why?

4. Draw a sketch diagram of the arrangement that gave you the highest note.

5. Draw a sketch diagram of the arrangement that gave you the lowest note.

6. Write down your conclusion.

7. What things did other groups find that changed the note produced?

# Making wind instruments

The instructions below show you how to make drinking straw buzzers:

(a) Cut straw to length.

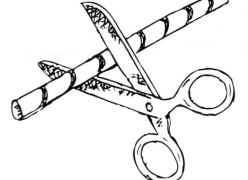

(b) Cut one end to a point.

(c) Put cut end in mouth
and blow hard.

1.  Draw what you could add to the drinking straw buzzer to make it play more than one note.

2.  Draw an example of a buzzer that will make a high note and a buzzer that will make a low note. Label them.

3.  On the back of this sheet, draw or stick on pictures of other wind instruments. Put those that make high notes on the left side of the page, and those that make low notes on the right side of the page.

Vocabulary

spherical,
eclipse

## BACKGROUND

Since the 1950s and 1960s, we have been able to see photographs of the Earth taken from space by rockets and satellites, showing that it is almost spherical. However, ancient Greek philosophers first deduced this in about 450BC from the indirect evidence of stars, ships, eclipses and shadows:

● They suggested that the Earth curved in a north-south direction because a traveller moving north sees some star constellations 'disappear' behind the southern horizon, while new ones appear over the northern horizon. (The rotation of the Earth hides this effect from a traveller travelling in an east-west direction.)

● Ships sailing away from all known ports 'disappear' hull-first, just as if they are sailing over a hill. This is indirect evidence that the Earth curves in all directions.

● During lunar eclipses, the Earth's shadow on the Moon always appears circular. The only shape that always casts a circular shadow is a sphere.

Understanding that the Earth is spherical is crucial to understanding how night and day occur, how seasons happen and how some places on Earth are always hot while others are always cold.

## INTRODUCTION

Ask the children: *What shape does the land around us appear to have? Early people thought the Earth was flat, apart from the hills and valleys.* Discuss ancient Greek ideas about the Earth and sky (see Background). Some children may be familiar with Terry Pratchett's 'Discworld', based on an ancient Indian model. (If you wish to read this description to the children, it can be found in *The Colour of Magic*, published by Corgi.)

## MAIN TEACHING ACTIVITY

Show the children the 'flat Earth' model. Place two model people near one edge of the 'land', then move one away. *What will the person left behind see?* Repeat with the 'round Earth' model. *What will the person left behind see now?* Establish that when a person disappears over a hill, the figure disappears feet-first instead of just looking smaller and smaller. Compare this with ships sailing away from land. *What does this tell us about the shape of the Earth?* Explain the difference between direct evidence (things we can actually see or measure) and indirect evidence (where we draw conclusions about something by looking at the effect it has on something else). Discuss other early evidence for a round Earth. *Is our evidence for a round Earth direct or indirect?* (All the evidence for a round Earth was indirect until we had photographs taken from space.)

## GROUP ACTIVITIES

**1.** Give the children a copy each of photocopiable page 193 and let them work through it.
**2.** Ask the children to write a newspaper report about the discovery that the Earth is round. If they know enough about Greek history, they could try writing a Greek newspaper report.

## DIFFERENTIATION

**1.** Less able children could work in groups, using the model from the Main teaching activity to find the answers to the questions on the photocopiable sheet.
**2.** More able children could use secondary sources to find out about more discoveries that led to the knowledge that the Earth is round. They might refer to lunar eclipses, Philolaus or Ferdinand Magellan.

## ASSESSMENT

Show the children star charts of the constellations visible in the northern and southern hemispheres, and ask them to suggest why these are different.

## PLENARY

Review what the children have learned about the shape of the Earth. Look at photographs of the Earth taken from space. Use a globe to identify different places on the Earth. *Can you tell where the photographs were taken from?* Look at pictures of the Moon, taken from Earth and from space. *Do they show the same view of the Moon? What shape is the Moon? Can you guess what shape the Sun might be?* Show them photographs of solar eclipses to help them decide whether they were right. Remind them of the importance of **never** looking directly at the Sun, because its rays can damage the light-sensitive cells in the eye.

## OUTCOMES
● Know that the Sun, Earth and Moon are approximately spherical.
● Can use indirect evidence to draw scientific conclusions.

## LINKS

Geography: using globes and photographs of the Earth.
History: ancient Greek astronomy and cosmology.

# LESSON 2

| Objectives | ● To know the relative sizes of the Sun, Earth and Moon. ● To know the relative distances of the Moon and Sun from the Earth. |
|---|---|
| Resources | Photos showing a solar eclipse and solar flares; coloured clothing or hats to represent the Moon (grey), Sun (yellow) and Earth (green); various spherical objects (beach ball, football, tennis ball, golf ball, pea, mustard seed); coloured collage materials. |
| Main activity | Copy Table 1 onto the board or flip chart and talk through it. The children can look at their hands and distant trees or buildings to demonstrate that closer objects look larger. Let them select appropriate-sized spheres to represent the Sun, Earth and Moon and experiment to find out that the Sun has to be **very** distant to look the same size as the Moon. |

Table 1

|  | Moon | Earth | Sun |
|---|---|---|---|
| Relative diameter | 1 | 4 | 400 |
| Distance from Earth | 30 Earth diameters | – | 12 000 Earth diameters |

| Differentiation | More able children can select a scale model from Table 2, suggest appropriate objects for it and work out the approximate distances between them, then make the model. Less able children can make collages of the Sun, Earth and Moon, using a simple scale. |
|---|---|

Table 2

|  | Sun | Earth | Moon | Moon to Earth | Earth to Sun |
|---|---|---|---|---|---|
| Model A | Football |  |  |  |  |
| Model B |  |  | Marble |  |  |
| Model C |  | Marble |  |  |  |

| Assessment | Assess the groups' models or collages. Invite other children to assess the accuracy of these, giving reasons for their judgement. |
|---|---|
| Plenary | Show cardboard models of the Earth (1cm diameter), Moon (0.25cm) and Sun (1m). Decide where these must be hung from the classroom ceiling to make an accurate model. You may have to take the Sun outside the classroom! Hang them as accurately as possible. |
| Outcomes | ● Can describe the differences in size between the three bodies. ● Can compare the distances between the three bodies. |

# LESSON 3

## OBJECTIVES

● To use scientific knowledge to explain observations.
● To know that the Sun's apparent movement across the sky is caused by the Earth spinning on its own axis.
● To know that the Sun appears to rise in an easterly direction and set in a westerly direction.
● To identify patterns of change in the sunrise and sunset times through the year.

## RESOURCES

**Main teaching activity:** A compass; a yellow item of clothing, hat or ball; a large globe, a toy person, Blu-Tack, a bright torch with a narrow beam, simplified sunrise and sunset times, graph paper, rulers, chalk; a large open space, such as the school playground.
**Group activities: 1.** Graph paper, rulers, coloured pencils. **2.** Photocopiable page 194, pencils, squared paper (for more able children).

## PREPARATION

Obtain or record simplified sunrise and sunset times (these are found in most diaries). For each month, record the sunrise and sunset times closest to the 15th of the month. Record times to the nearest quarter- or half-hour. Draw a large chalk circle in the playground.

## BACKGROUND

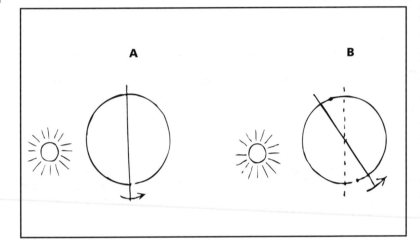

The Sun appears to rise in the east, travel across the sky and set in the west each day, giving shadows that change in shape and position. One conceivable explanation for this is that the Sun (and the other stars) move around the Earth. The second, and correct, explanation is that the Sun and stars stay still, but the Earth moves. The rotation of the Earth on its own axis makes the Sun appear to move across the sky.

If the Earth's axis of rotation were vertical (as in diagram A), day and night would always be the same length: 12 hours each. However, because the Earth's axis of rotation is tilted, day and night are different lengths in different places (see diagram B). Throughout the year, the Earth moves in its orbit around the Sun (see Lesson 7, page 187), so the northern hemisphere is sometimes tilted towards and sometimes tilted away from the Sun. This change of tilt causes there to be different day-lengths at different times of the year.

Lesson 6 (page 187) demonstrates how the temperature at any point on the Earth depends on the area over which the Sun's radiation is spread and therefore on the Sun's relative position in the sky. When the Sun is 'high', its radiation is spread over a relatively small area, so it feels hotter. Lesson 7 brings all this information together to show how the movement of the Earth around the Sun gives rise to the seasons, with their different characteristics of day-length and temperature.

**Vocabulary**

rotation, axis, spin, sunrise, sunset

## INTRODUCTION

Review earlier years' work on shadows. Check that the children know how shadows change throughout the day, and that this change is because the Sun appears to move across the sky. Shadows are shortest at midday, when the Sun is highest in the sky. *Why do you think the Sun appears to move?* Record the children's ideas. Discuss where the Sun rises and sets. If appropriate, encourage the children to use a compass to find out the direction of the Sun at the start and end of the school day, and at midday. Discuss the position of the Sun in the sky at different times of the year (see diagram).

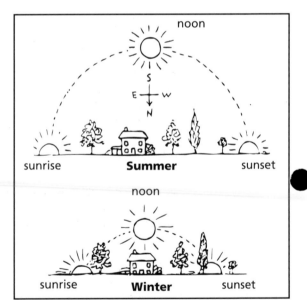

## MAIN TEACHING ACTIVITY

On the playground, help the children model how the Sun seems to move. Give one child something yellow. This child represents the Sun. Stand other children around a large chalk circle, facing straight outwards, toes touching the chalk line. They represent people standing in different places around the Earth. The 'Sun' stands outside the circle. *Put your hand up if you can see the 'Sun' without turning your head. What time of day is it when you can see the real Sun?* Encourage the children to suggest reasons why we can sometimes see the Sun and sometimes cannot. Lead them to the idea that they may stay in the same place on the Earth, but the Earth moves round. Ask the 'Earth' to move round in a ring, carefully.

Back in the classroom, demonstrate day and night using a large globe and a torch. Use Blu-Tack to attach a toy person to the globe in different places. Rotate the globe, encouraging the children to say when it is day for the person and when it is night. Discuss how the amount of daylight varies throughout the year. *What is it like when you get up in winter? What activities can you do on summer evenings?*

## GROUP ACTIVITIES

**1.** Ask the children to plot a graph of the sunrise times each month. They should then plot the sunset times on the same axes, but using a different colour. The finished graph should look something like this:

**2.** Give each child a copy of page 194 to complete. The answers are: 1. nighttime; 2. shadow; 3. longer; 4. morning; 5. rotate; 6. daytime; 7. facing; 8. noon; 9. dusk; 10. spherical. The shaded word is 'twenty-four', which is the answer to a question such as 'How many hours are there in a day?'

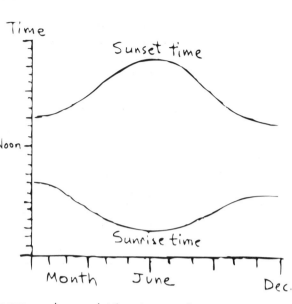

## DIFFERENTIATION

**1.** Less able children could plot separate bar charts of the sunrise and sunset times on prepared axes, plotting times to the nearest half-hour.

**2.** More able children could work together to plan their own small crossword on squared paper, then challenge another friend to solve it. For less able children, write in the first one or two letters of each answer on a master page before making individual copies.

## ASSESSMENT

Ask the children to compare their graphs within their groups. *Do they look similar?* Ask them questions such as: *Is it dark at 7o'clock in the morning in April?* Let them decide and then explain to you how they used their graphs to find the answer. Look for ability to use the axes to find particular points, and for an understanding that the area between the sunrise and sunset lines is 'day' and the rest is 'night'.

## PLENARY

Discuss how the day-length (the number of hours of daylight) changes through the year. Use the globe and torch to demonstrate how, if the Earth were 'upright', day-length would always stay the same (12 hours light, 12 hours dark). Show them the Earth tilting; use the torch to show how, when we are tilted towards the Sun, we spend more time in sunlight and so the day-length is increased. Practise this until the children are confident. *In winter, do you think we are tilted towards the Sun or away from the Sun? Why do you think that?*

## OUTCOMES

- Can describe how the Sun's path in the sky changes through the year.
- Can explain that the spin of the Earth makes the Sun appear to move across the sky.
- Can explain how day and night occur.
- Can draw line graphs and use them to identify patterns.

## LINKS

Literacy: poetry and descriptive writing about summer and winter.
Art: sunrise or sunset paintings.

## ASSESSMENT ACTIVITY 2

Give out copies of page 197 for the children to complete individually. As with Assessment activity 1, the answers can either be collected in for marking or marked in class.

**Answers** (see diagram below)
1. New Moon; 2. Half Moon; 3. See diagram; 4. The Earth has to turn a bit further before the Moon comes into view, so the Moon will rise later.

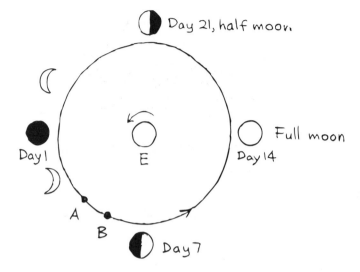

### Looking for levels

All the children should answer question 1 and place the full Moon correctly. Most of the children should answer questions 1, 2 and 3. More able children will answer question 4.

The answers to these assessments, together with any verbal testing at the beginning of the lesson, will demonstrate the children's understanding of this unit. It is expected that:
- Most children will know that the Earth, Sun and Moon are spherical and know some evidence supporting this; be able to explain how the motion of the Earth makes the Sun appear to move across the sky; understand how day and night occur; know that the Moon orbits the Earth; and identify patterns in sunrise and sunset times.
- Some children will know that the Earth, Sun and Moon are spherical, and be able to describe how shadows change as the Sun appears to move across the sky.
- Some children will be able to explain how the phases of the Moon arise and how they are evidence for a 28-day orbit of the Moon around the Earth; and be able to work independently to represent sunrise and sunset times in graphs.

## PLENARY

If you allow the children to mark each other's answers, the Plenary session can be used to go through the questions and discuss the correct answers. Encourage the children to ask questions about topics in the Assessment activities that they were unsure of, and any related topics that they would like to know more about. If you are going to mark the answers later, encourage the children to say which parts of the Assessment activities they found easy or difficult and why. Take time to clear up any obvious misconceptions, and encourage the children to ask any other questions they may have about the Earth, Sun or Moon, even if the answers are not covered by any of the lessons. If there are any questions that you cannot answer, help the children to decide how they can find out the answers.

# Round Earth or flat Earth?

Draw three pictures to show what the observer on land would see as the ship sails further and further away...

1. If the world is flat.

| | | |
|---|---|---|
| | | |

2. If the world is round.

| | | |
|---|---|---|
| | | |

As a ship approaches any land, anywhere in the world, the sails come into view first. What does this tell you about the shape of the Earth?

_____

Colour in blue the stars that observer A would be **unable** to see.
Colour in red the stars that observer B would be **unable** to see.
Explain to a friend what observer C notices about the stars she can see as she walks from A to B.

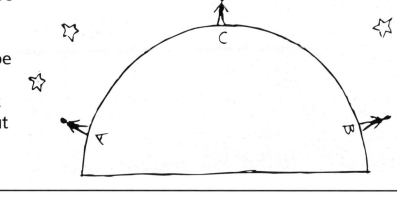

# Day and night crossword

Fill in the answers to the clues. Make up a question about the Earth with the answer that you find in the shaded squares.

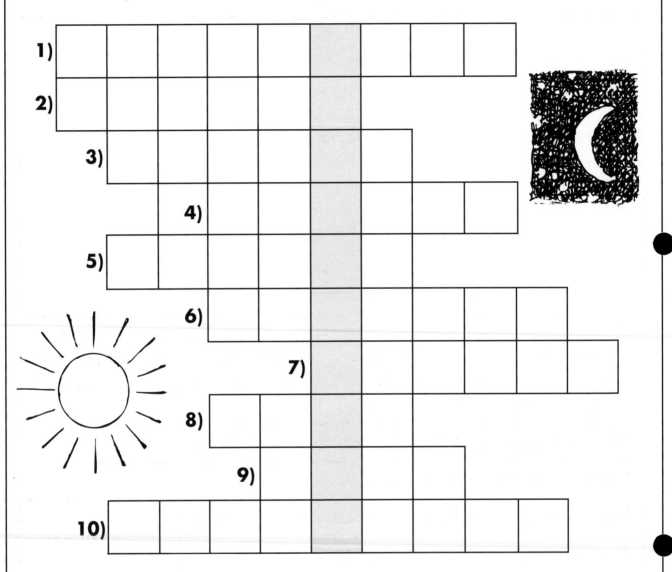

1. It is this time when you cannot see the Sun.
2. A stick in sunshine will have one of these.
3. As the afternoon passes, shadows will get _____ .
4. The time when shadows are gradually getting shorter.
5. The Earth does this once every day.
6. It is this time when you can see the Sun in the sky.
7. It is light in all places that are _____ the Sun.
8. This is the time when shadows are shortest.
9. This is the time when the Sun disappears below the horizon at the end of the day.
10. The Earth is approximately this shape.

# The seasons

1. Draw a diagram of the Earth and Sun to show the position that the Earth will be in when it is summer in Britain.

2. Some of the sentences below are correct when it is summer in Britain. Tick the ones that are correct. Remember: the Earth is rotating on its own axis.

| | |
|---|---|
| The South Pole is in constant darkness. | |
| The sunlight reaching Britain is spread over a large area. | |
| The North Pole is in constant daylight. | |
| The sunlight reaching Britain is spread over a small area. | |
| The South Pole is in constant daylight. | |
| The North Pole is in constant darkness. | |

3. Describe what happens to the seasons as the Earth orbits the Sun. Explain why the changes happen, and say how long the changes take.

_____

_____

_____

_____

_____

Name

# Sun, Moon and Earth

The graph below shows the time that the Sun rises on the first day of each month throughout the year.

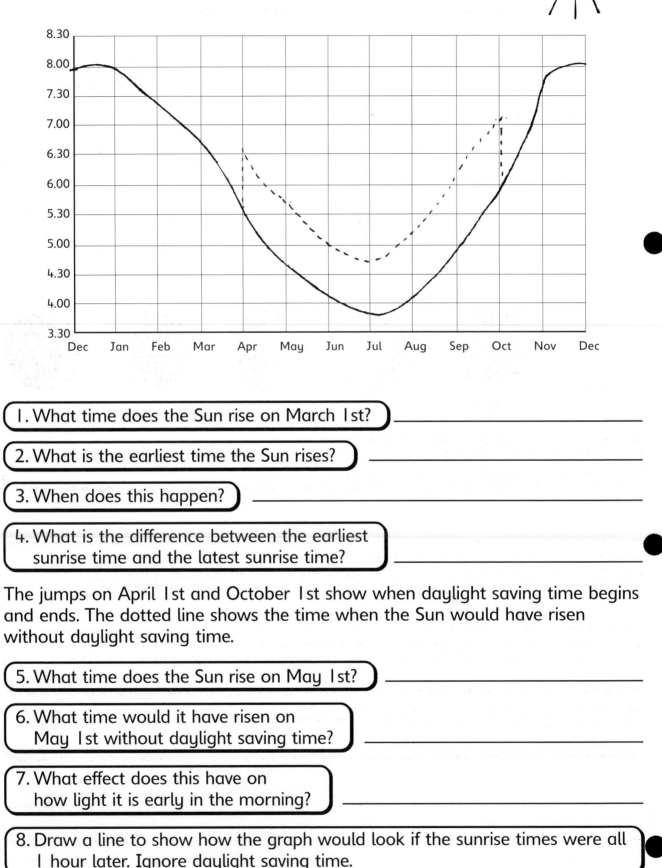

1. What time does the Sun rise on March 1st? _____

2. What is the earliest time the Sun rises? _____

3. When does this happen? _____

4. What is the difference between the earliest sunrise time and the latest sunrise time? _____

The jumps on April 1st and October 1st show when daylight saving time begins and ends. The dotted line shows the time when the Sun would have risen without daylight saving time.

5. What time does the Sun rise on May 1st? _____

6. What time would it have risen on May 1st without daylight saving time? _____

7. What effect does this have on how light it is early in the morning? _____

8. Draw a line to show how the graph would look if the sunrise times were all 1 hour later. Ignore daylight saving time.

Name

# Sun, Moon and Earth

The first diagram shows the Moon's orbit around the Earth. The arrows show the direction the Moon moves in and the direction the Earth is spinning in. The second diagram shows the phases of the Moon that we see.

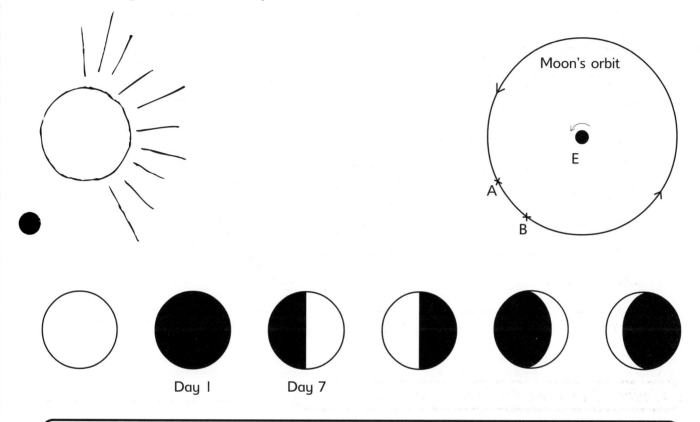

Day 1          Day 7

1. Put a 1 on the Moon's orbit where you would see Day 1 of the phases of the Moon. What is this phase called?

2. Put a 7 where you would see Day 7. What is this phase called?

3. Draw the other four phases of the Moon in the correct places on the Moon's orbit.

4. When the Moon is at A on its orbit, it 'rises' (is first visible) at 7pm. When it has moved to B, will it 'rise' earlier, later or at the same time? Why?

# National Curriculum in England

**LINKS TO QCA SCIENCE SCHEME OF WORK**

**1 Ideas and evidence in science**

**a** that science is about thinking creatively to try to explain how living and non-living things work, and to establish links between causes and effects

**b** that it is important to test ideas using evidence from observation and measurement

**2 Investigative skills – Planning**

**a** ask questions that can be investigated scientifically and decide how to find answers

**b** consider what sources of information, including first-hand experience and a range of other sources, they will use to answer questions

**c** think about what might happen or try things out when deciding what to do, what kind of evidence to collect, and what equipment and materials to use

**d** make a fair test or comparison by changing one factor and observing or measuring the effect while keeping other factors the same

**Investigative skills – Obtaining and presenting evidence**

**e** use simple equipment and materials appropriately and take action to control risks

**f** make systematic observations and measurements, including the use of ICT for data-logging

**g** check observations and measurements by repeating them where appropriate

**h** use a wide range of methods, including diagrams, drawings, tables, bar charts, line graphs and ICT, to communicate data in an appropriate and systematic manner

**Investigative skills – Considering evidence and evaluating**

**i** make comparisons and identify simple patterns or associations in their own observations and measurements or other data

**j** use observations, measurements or other data to draw conclusions

**k** decide whether these conclusions agree with any prediction made and/or whether they enable further predictions to be made

**l** use their scientific knowledge and understanding to explain observations, measurements or other data or conclusions

**m** review their work and the work of others and describe its significance and limitations

**1 Life processes**

**a** that the life processes common to humans and other animals include nutrition, movement, growth and reproduction

**b** that the life processes common to plants include growth, nutrition and reproduction

**c** to make links between life processes in familiar animals and plants and the environments in which they are found

**2 Humans and other animals – Nutrition**

**a** about the functions and care of teeth

**b** about the need for food for activity and growth, and about the importance of an adequate and varied diet for health

**Humans and other animals – Circulation**

**c** that the heart acts as a pump to circulate the blood through vessels around the body, including through the lungs

**d** about the effect of exercise and rest on pulse rate

**Humans and other animals – Movement**

**e** that humans and some other animals have skeletons and muscles to support and protect their bodies and to help them to move

**Humans and other animals – Growth and reproduction**

**f** about the main stages of the human life cycle

**Humans and other animals – Health**

**g** about the effects on the human body of tobacco, alcohol and other drugs, and how these relate to their personal health

**h** about the importance of exercise for good health

**3 Green plants – Growth and nutrition**

**a** the effect of light, air, water and temperature on plant growth

**b** the role of the leaf in producing new material for growth

**c** that the root anchors the plant, and that water and minerals are taken in through the root and transported through the stem to other parts of the plant

**Green plants – Reproduction**

**d** about the parts of the flower and their role in the life cycle of flowering plants, including pollination, seed formation, seed dispersal and germination

**4 Variation and classification**

**a** to make and use keys

**b** how locally occurring animals and plants can be identified and assigned to groups

**c** that the variety of plants and animals makes it important to identify them and assign them to groups

**5 Living things in their environment**

**a** about ways in which living things and the environment need protection

**Living things in their environment – Adaptation**

**b** about the different plants and animals found in different habitats

**c** how animals and plants in two different habitats are suited to their environment

**Living things in their environment – Feeding relationships**

**d** to use food chains to show feeding relationships in a habitat

**e** about how nearly all food chains start with a green plant

**Living things in their environment – Micro-organisms**

**f** that micro-organisms are living organisms that are often too small to be seen, and that they may be beneficial or harmful

**1 Grouping and classifying**

**a** to compare everyday materials and objects on the basis of their material properties, including hardness, strength, flexibility and magnetic behaviour, and to relate these properties to everyday uses of the materials

**b** that some materials are better thermal insulators than others

**c** that some materials are better electrical conductors than others

**d** to describe and group rocks and soils on the basis of their characteristics, including appearance, texture and permeability

**e** to recognise differences between solids, liquids and gases, in terms of ease of flow and maintenance of shape and volume

**2 Changing materials**

**a** to describe changes that occur when materials are mixed

**b** to describe changes that occur when materials are heated or cooled

**c** that temperature is a measure of how hot or cold things are

**d** about reversible changes, including dissolving, melting, boiling, condensing, freezing and evaporating

**e** the part played by evaporation and condensation in the water cycle

**f** that non-reversible changes result in the formation of new materials that may be useful

**g** that burning materials results in the formation of new materials and that this change is not usually reversible

**3 Separating mixtures of materials**

**a** how to separate solid particles of different sizes

**b** that some solids dissolve in water to give solutions but some do not

**c** how to separate insoluble solids from liquids by filtering

**d** how to recover dissolved solids by evaporating the liquid from the solution

**e** to use knowledge of solids, liquids and gases to decide how mixtures might be separated

Lessons where curriculum content is the main objective are listed below. Lessons where content is included but is not the main focus are shown below in brackets.

| Unit 1: Ourselves<br><br>Growing up healthy | Unit 2: Animals & Plants<br>Life cycles | Unit 3: The environment<br>Water and the environment | Unit 4: Materials<br><br>Gases, solids and liquids | Unit 5: Electricity<br><br>Making and using electricity | Unit 6: Forces & motion<br>Exploring forces and their effects | Unit 7: Light & sound<br>Bending light and changing sound | Unit 8: Earth & beyond<br>Sun, Moon and Earth |
|---|---|---|---|---|---|---|---|
| UNIT 5A | UNIT 5B | UNIT 5B, 5/6H | UNIT 5C, 5D | – | UNIT 5/6H | UNIT 5F | UNIT 5E |
| 5, 7 | 4 | 3 | 7 | | 3, 9 | 12 | 5 |
| 5, 7 | 4 | 3, 8 | 7 | | 1, 9 | 3 | |
| 7 | 4 | 3, 8 | 7 | 2 | 1 | 8 | |
| 7 | 4 | | 7 | | 9 | 13 | 1 |
| 7 | 4 | 3 | 3 | 2 | 2, 6 | | |
| 7, 15 | 4 | 3 | 4, 7 | 2 | 9 | 11, 12 | |
| | 5 | 3, 8 | 3, 4 | 2, 3 | 1, 2, 6, 10, 11 | 6, 10 | 2 |
| 8 | 5 | 8 | | | 2 | 8 | |
| 5 | | (3) | 3, 4 | 3 | 11 | 7, 14 | |
| 8 | 4 | 8 | 10, 11 | | 11 | 1, 2, 8 | 3 |
| 5, 8 | 5, 6 | 3, 8 | 3 | 2 | 3, 5 | 3, 6, 14 | 2, 6, 7, 8, 9 |
| 5 | (8), 6 | 3 | 3 | 2, 3 | 5, 8 | 6, 7 | |
| 7 | (6) | 3 | 7 | 2 | 11 | 10 | |
| 7 | 6 | 3, 8 | 7 | | 8 | 3, 7 | |
| 7 | 6 | 8 | 7 | | 11 | 11 | |
| 1, 2, (3), 4, 8, 9 | 10, (12), 13, 14, 16 | 10 | | | | | |
| | 1, 2, 3, 4, 7, 8, 9, 11, 16 | | | | | | |
| | (7) | | | | | | |
| 1, 2, (3), 15 | | | | | | | |
| 6, 15 | | | | | | | |
| (5), 7 | | | | | | | |
| 8, 9, 10 | | 10 | | | | | |
| 11, 12, 13, 14 | | | | | | | |
| (5), (6), (7) | | | | | | | |
| | 1, 2, 3, 4, 7, 8, 9, 11, 13, 16 | | | | | | |
| | | (8) | | | | | |
| | | (8) | | | | | |
| | | 4, 5, 6, 9, 11 | | | | | |
| | | (8) | | | | | |
| | | (8) | | | | | |
| | | | 1, 2, (6), 8, 14 | | | | |
| | | | 1, 6, 9, 10, 11, 12 | | | | |
| | | | 1, 6, 9, 10, 11, 12, 14 | | | | |
| | | 1, 2, 3, 4, 11 | 13 | | | | |

*SC4 Physical processes overleaf*

# National Curriculum in England (cont)

**LINKS TO QCA SCIENCE SCHEME OF WORK**

| | |
|---|---|
| **SC4 PHYSICAL PROCESSES** | **1 Electricity – Simple circuits** |
| | **a** to construct circuits, incorporating a battery or power supply and a range of switches, to make electrical devices work |
| | **b** how changing the number or type of components in a series circuit can make bulbs brighter or dimmer |
| | **c** how to represent series circuits by drawings and conventional symbols; how to construct series circuits on the basis of drawings and diagrams using conventional symbols |
| | **2 Forces and motion – Types of force** |
| | **a** about the forces of attraction and repulsion between magnets, and about the forces of attraction between magnets and magnetic materials |
| | **b** that objects are pulled downwards because of the gravitational attraction between them and the Earth |
| | **c** about friction, including air resistance, as a force that slows moving objects and may prevent objects from starting to move are pushed or pulled |
| | **d** that when objects are pushed or pulled an opposing pull or push can be felt |
| | **e** how to measure forces and identify the direction in which they act |
| | **3 Light and sound – Everyday effects of light** |
| | **a** that light travels from a source |
| | **b** that light cannot pass through some materials, and how this leads to the formation of shadows |
| | **c** that light is reflected from surfaces |
| | **Light and sound – Seeing** |
| | **d** that we see things only when light from them enters our eyes |
| | **Light and sound – Vibration and sound** |
| | **e** that sounds are made when objects vibrate but that vibrations are not always directly visible |
| | **f** how to change the pitch and loudness of sounds produced by some vibrating objects |
| | **g** that vibrations from sound sources require a medium through which to travel to the ear |
| | **4 The Earth and beyond – The Sun, Earth and Moon** |
| | **a** that the Sun, Earth and Moon are approximately spherical |
| | **The Earth and beyond – Periodic changes** |
| | **b** how the position of the Sun appears to change during the day, and how shadows change as this happens |
| | **c** how day and night are related to the spin of the Earth on its own axis |
| | **d** that the Earth orbits the Sun once each year, and that the Moon takes approximately 28 days to orbit the Earth |

# National Curriculum in Wales

| | |
|---|---|
| **SCIENTIFIC ENQUIRY** | **1 The nature of science** |
| | **the link between ideas and information in science** |
| | 1 to apply their ideas and knowledge and understanding of science when thinking about and investigating phenomena in the world around them |
| | 2 to consider information obtained from their own work and also, on some occasions, from other sources |
| | 3 that scientific ideas can be tested by means of information gathered from observation and measurement |
| | **2 Communication in science** |
| | **presenting scientific information** |
| | 1 to report their work clearly in speech and writing using relevant scientific vocabulary |
| | 2 to use a range of methods, including diagrams, drawings, graphs, tables and charts, to record and present information in an appropriate and systematic manner |
| | 3 to use ICT to select and present a range of relevant information, when this is appropriate |
| | 4 to use standard measures and units handling scientific information |
| | 5 to search for and access relevant scientific information, using ICT to do so on some occasions |
| | 6 to recognise that it is useful to present and consider scientific information in an appropriate form, making use of ICT to do so when appropriate |
| | **planning an investigation** |
| | 1 to turn ideas suggested to them, and their own ideas, into a form that can be investigated |
| | 2 that asking questions, and using their knowledge and understanding of the context to anticipate what may happen, can be useful when planning what to do |
| | 3 to decide what information should be collected |
| | 4 that in situations where the factors can be identified and controlled, a fair test may be carried out |
| | 5 to consider what equipment or other resources to use |
| | 6 to recognise the hazards and risks to themselves and others obtaining information |
| | 7 to use equipment or other resources correctly, taking action to control risks |
| | 8 to make careful observations and measurements and record them appropriately |
| | 9 to check observations and measurements by repeating them, when this is appropriate |
| | 10 to use ICT equipment and software to monitor changes |
| | **considering information** |
| | 11 to make comparisons and to identify and describe trends or patterns in data |
| | 12 to use the results of their investigations to draw conclusions |
| | 13 to try to relate the outcomes of their investigation or their conclusions to their scientific knowledge and understanding |
| | 14 to review their work and suggest how their data could be improved |
| **LIFE PROCESSES AND LIVING THINGS** | **1 Life processes** |
| | 1 that there are life processes, including nutrition, movement, growth and reproduction, common to animals, including humans |
| | 2 that there are life processes, including growth, nutrition and reproduction, common to plants |
| | **2 Humans and other animals** |
| | **nutrition** |
| | 1 how the teeth break up food into smaller pieces and the importance of dental care |
| | 2 that the body needs different foods for activity and for growth |
| | 3 that an adequate and varied diet is needed to keep healthy |
| | **circulation** |
| | 4 that the heart acts as a pump |
| | 5 how blood circulates in the body through arteries and veins |
| | 6 that the pulse gives a measure of the heart beat rate |
| | 7 the effect of exercise and rest on pulse rate |
| | **movement** |
| | 8 that humans and some other animals have skeletons and muscles to support and protect their bodies and to help them to move |
| | **growth and reproduction** |
| | 9 the main stages of the human life cycle |

Lessons where curriculum content is the main objective are listed below. Lessons where content is included but is not the main focus are shown below in brackets.

| Unit 1: Ourselves | Unit 2: Animals & Plants | Unit 3: The environment | Unit 4: Materials | Unit 5: Electricity | Unit 6: Forces & motion | Unit 7: Light & sound | Unit 8: Earth & beyond |
|---|---|---|---|---|---|---|---|
| Growing up healthy | Life cycles | Water and the environment | Gases, solids and liquids | Making and using electricity | Exploring forces and their effects | Bending light and changing sound | Sun, Moon and Earth |
| UNIT 5A | UNIT 5B | UNIT 5B, 5/6H | UNIT 5C, 5D | – | UNIT 5/6H | UNIT 5F | UNIT 5E |
| | | | | (1), (2), (3), (4), 6, (7), (8) | | | |
| | | | | (5) | | | |
| | | | | (2), (3), (4), (6) | | | |
| | | | | | (1), (2), 5, 6 | | |
| | | | | | 3, 4 | | |
| | | | | | (1), (7) | | |
| | | | | | 1, 2, 8, 9, 10, (11), 12 | | |
| | | | | | 3, 8 | | |
| | | | | | | 3, (15) | |
| | | | | | | (1), (2) | |
| | | | | | | 3, 4, (5), (6) | |
| | | | | | | 7, 14 | |
| | | | | | | 12, 13 | |
| | | | | | | 9, 10, 11, (15) | |
| | | | | | | | 1 |
| | | | | | | | (3), (6), 10 |
| | | | | | | | 3, (4) |
| | | | | | | | (3), 7, 8, 9, 10 |

| Unit 1: Ourselves | Unit 2: Animals & Plants | Unit 3: The environment | Unit 4: Materials | Unit 5: Electricity | Unit 6: Forces & motion | Unit 7: Light & sound | Unit 8: Earth & beyond |
|---|---|---|---|---|---|---|---|
| Growing up healthy | Life cycles | Water and the environment | Gases, solids and liquids | Making and using electricity | Exploring forces and their effects | Bending light and changing sound | Sun, Moon and Earth |
| 7 | 4 | 3, 8 | 7 | | 1 | 12 | 6 |
| | 4 | 8 | 7 | 3 | 1, 3 | | 1, 2 |
| 5 | 4 | 3 | 3 | | 8 | 3, 6, 7 | |
| 6 | 4 | 3, 8 | | 3 | 3 | 8 | 1, 2 |
| 7 | 4, 5, 6 | 3 | 7 | | 1 | | |
| 8 | | 8 | 10 | | | | |
| 7, 8 | 4, 5 | 3 | 7, 4 | | 1 | | |
| 8 | 6 | 8 | 11 | | | | 3 |
| 8 | 5 | 3 | 10 | | 3 | 8 | 3 |
| 5 | 4 | | 3, 7 | 2, 3 | | 10, 11 | |
| | | 3 | 3 | 2, 3 | 10 | 10, 11 | |
| 5 | | | | | | | |
| 15 | 4, 6 | | 7 | 2 | 10 | 12 | |
| | | | | | 1 | 10, 12 | |
| | | 8 | | | 2 | | |
| | | | | | 2, 10 | 12 | |
| 5, 8 | 5, 8 | 8 | 3 | | 2, 8 | 10, 11 | |
| 7 | | | 3 | 2 | | 3 | |
| | | 3 | | 2 | 3 | | |
| | 4, 5, 8 | | 7, 11 | 2, 3 | 2, 5, 6, 11 | 6, 12 | 1, 7, 8, 9 |
| 5, 7 | 4 | | 3 | 3 | 11 | 6 | |
| 8 | 5, 8 | 8 | 3 | 2 | 10, 11 | 10, 11 | |
| | 4 | 3 | 7 | | 1 | | |
| 1, 2, 3, 4, 8, 9, 10 | 10, (12), 13, 14, 15 | (7), (8), (10) | | | | | |
| | 13, 15 | | | | | | |
| (4) | | | | | | | |
| 1, (2), (3), 15 | | | | | | | |
| 2, 3, 15 | | | | | | | |
| 6 | | | | | | | |
| (6) | | | | | | | |
| 7 | | | | | | | |
| (7) | | | | | | | |
| (8) | | | | | | | |
| (8), 9, 10 | | | | | | | |

*Life processes and living things continued overleaf*

# National Curriculum in Wales (cont)

**LIFE PROCESSES AND LIVING THINGS (cont)**

**health**

10 that tobacco, alcohol and other drugs can have harmful effects

**3 Green plants as organisms**

**growth and nutrition**

1 to investigate the effect on the growth of plants of changing their conditions

2 that plants need light to produce food for growth, and the importance of the leaf in this process

3 that the root anchors the plant, and that water and nutrients are taken in through the root and transported through the stem to other parts of the plant

**reproduction**

4 the main stages in the life cycle of flowering plants including pollination, seed production, seed dispersal and germination

5 about the process of pollination in flowering plants

6 how pollen and seeds can be transported

**4 Living things in their environment**

**adaptation**

1 to find out about the variety of plants and animals found in different habitats including the local area

2 how animals and plants in two different habitats are suited to their environment

**feeding relationships**

3 that food chains show feeding relationships in an ecosystem

4 that nearly all food chains start with a green plant variation

5 how locally occurring animals and plants can be identified and assigned to groups, by making and using keys

**MATERIALS & THEIR PROPERTIES**

**1 Grouping and classifying materials**

1 to compare everyday materials, on the basis of their properties, including hardness, strength, flexibility and magnetic behaviour, and to relate these properties to everyday uses of the materials

2 that some materials are better thermal insulators/conductors than others

3 that some materials are better electrical conductors/insulators than others

4 to describe and group rocks on the basis of appearance and texture, and soils on the basis of particle size and permeability

5 to recognise differences between solids, liquids and gases, in terms of their properties.

**2 Changing materials**

1 to explore changes in materials and recognise those that can be reversed and those that cannot

2 that dissolving, melting, condensing, freezing and evaporating are changes that can be reversed

3 that irreversible changes result in a new material being produced, which may be useful

4 that the changes that occur when most materials are burned are not reversible, and result in a new material being produced

5 that mixing materials can cause them to change

6 that heating or cooling materials can cause them to change

7 that temperature is a measure of how hot or cold things are

8 the part played by evaporation and condensation in the water cycle

**3 Separating mixtures of materials**

1 that solid particles of different sizes can be separated by sieving

2 that some solids are soluble in water and will dissolve to give solutions but some will not, and that this provides a means of separating different solids

3 that insoluble solids can be separated from liquids by filtering

4 that solids that have dissolved can be recovered by evaporating the liquid from the solution

**PHYSICAL PROCESSES**

**1 Electricity**

**simple circuits**

1 that a complete conducting circuit, including a battery or power supply, is needed for a current to flow to make electrical devices work

2 to investigate how switches can be used to control electrical devices in simple series and parallel arrangements

3 that the brightness of bulbs and the rotation of motors can be controlled by altering the current

4 ways of varying the current in a circuit, including changing the power supply, and changing the length of conductor in a circuit

5 how to represent simple circuits by drawings and diagrams, and how to construct such circuits on the basis of drawings and diagrams

**2 Forces and motion**

**behaviour of forces**

1 to measure forces between objects and find out how the forces change in size

2 that forces act in particular directions

3 that forces con make things speed up, slow down, or change direction

**types of force**

4 that there are forces of attraction and repulsion between magnets, and forces of attraction between magnets and some materials

5 that the weight of an object is the force of the Earth on the object and is measured in newtons

6 about friction, including air resistance, as a force between surfaces which slows moving objects and may prevent them from starting to move

7 that objects that are stretched or compressed exert a force on whatever is changing their shape

8 that the change in shape of a spring is used in force meters for measuring forces

**3 Light and sound**

**everyday effects of light**

1 that light travels from a source

2 that we see light sources because light from them travels to and enters our eyes

3 we see objects because light falling on them is reflected

4 that most of the light falling on shiny surfaces and mirrors is reflected

5 that light cannot pass through some materials, and that this leads to the formation of shadows

**vibration and sound**

6 that sounds are made when objects vibrate but that vibrations are not always directly visible

7 that the pitch and loudness of sounds produced by some vibrating objects can be changed

8 that vibrations from sound sources can travel through a variety of materials

**4 The Earth and beyond**

**the Sun, Moon and planets**

1 that the Sun, Earth and Moon are approximately spherical

2 the relative positions of the Sun, Earth and other planets in the solar system

**periodic changes**

3 how the position of the Sun appears to change during the day, and how shadows change as this happens

4 that the Earth spins around its own axis, and how day and night are related to this spin

5 that the Earth orbits the Sun once each year, and that the Moon takes approximately 28 days to orbit the Earth

Lessons where curriculum content is the main objective are listed below. Lessons where content is included but is not the main focus are shown below in brackets.

| Unit 1: Ourselves Growing up healthy | Unit 2: Animals & Plants Life cycles | Unit 3: The environment Water and the environment | Unit 4: Materials Gases, solids and liquids | Unit 5: Electricity Making and using electricity | Unit 6: Forces & motion Exploring forces and their effects | Unit 7: Light & sound Bending light and changing sound | Unit 8: Earth & beyond Sun, Moon and Earth |
|---|---|---|---|---|---|---|---|
| (5), 11, 12, 13, 14 | | | | | | | |
| | 5 | | | | | | |
| | 1, 2, 3, 4, 6, 8, 15 | | | | | | |
| | 7, 8, 11, 15 | | | | | | |
| | 7, 8, 11, 15 | | | | | | |
| | | 4 | | | | | |
| | | | 1, 3 | | | | |
| | | | (4) | | | | |
| | | | 1, 2, 5, 8, 14 | | | | |
| | | 3 | 1, 6, 7, 9, 12, 14 | | | | |
| | | (9), (11) | | | | | |
| | | | 1, 10, 11, 12 | | | | |
| | | | 10, 15 | | | | |
| | | 1, 2, 3, (5), (6), (11) | 13 | | | | |
| | | | | 1, (7) | | | |
| | | | | (4), (5) | | | |
| | | | | | 1, 2, 8 | | |
| | | | | | 3, 5, 7, 12 | | |
| | | | | | (5), (6) | | |
| | | | | 2, 3, 6 | | | |
| | | | | | (1), (2), 5, (6) | | |
| | | | | | 3, 4 | | |
| | | | | | 9, 10, 11, 12 | | |
| | | | | | (4) | | |
| | | | | | | (1), (2), (6), (15) | |
| | | | | | | 3, (4), (5) | |
| | | | | | | 7, (14) | |
| | | | | | | 12, 13 | |
| | | | | | | (8), 9, (10), 11, 15 | |
| | | | | | | | 1, (9), (10) |
| | | | | | | | 2 |
| | | | | | | | (3), (4), (5), (6), (7) |
| | | | | | | | (8), 10 |
| | | | | | | | 3, (4), 5, (8), (9) |
| | | | | | | | 9 |

# National Guidelines for Scotland
## (Consultation draft)

**ENVIRONMENTAL STUDIES 5–14 SCIENCE**

| | | |
|---|---|---|
| SKILLS IN SCIENCE: INVESTIGATING | | **Preparing for the task** |
| | | **Planning:** understanding the task; planning a practical activity; undertaking fair testing |
| | D | ● show increasing awareness of the significance of variables in practical investigations |
| | | ● provide reasons for planning decisions |
| | | **Carrying out the task** |
| | | **Collecting evidence:** observing; measuring; using measuring devices; using units **Recording:** recording findings in a variety of ways |
| | C | ● select appropriate measurement devices |
| | | ● record findings in a greater range of ways including diagram annotation, table and bar chart construction |
| | D | ● make an appropriate series of accurate measurements |
| | | ● record findings in tables, databases, bar charts and line graphs |
| | | ● construct some of the above using ICT skills |
| | | **Reviewing and reporting on the task** |
| | | **Interpreting and evaluating:** understanding the significance of the findings **Presenting and reporting:** describing a practical activity; presenting findings |
| | C | ● write a report of an investigation communicating key points clearly |
| | D | ● draw conclusions consistent with the findings |
| | | ● suggest ways of improving the reliability of the results |
| | | ● provide explanations related to scientific knowledge |
| | | ● write a more formal report of an investigation using appropriate scientific vocabulary |

**EARTH AND SPACE**

| | | |
|---|---|---|
| | | **Earth in space** |
| | C | ● describe the Solar System in terms of movement of the nine named planets and make links between their positions relative to the Sun and their temperatures |
| | | ● explain the measurement of time in terms of the Earth's rotation |
| | D | ● identify the major components of the universe |
| | | ● give examples of the approaches taken to space exploration and of the benefits of our increasing knowledge in this area |
| | | **On planet Earth** |
| | C | ● give some examples of the effects of the Earth's atmosphere |
| | | ● explain a simple diagram of the water cycle |
| | D | ● make links between the observed structure of soil and its origins and properties |
| | | **Materials from Earth** |
| | C | ● list the main uses of water |
| | | ● explain why water conservation is important |
| | D | ● use common examples of solvents and solutions to explain the meaning of these terms and to distinguish between soluble and insoluble materials |
| | | ● give examples of the common causes of water pollution and describe the major techniques used in water purification |

**ENERGY AND FORCES**

| | | |
|---|---|---|
| | | **Forms and sources of energy** |
| | C | ● identify electricity as a form of energy |
| | | ● give examples of sources of electricity |
| | D | ● describe the range of available energy sources |
| | | ● explain the significant difference between renewable and non-renewable sources of energy giving examples of both types |
| | | **Properties and uses of energy** |
| | C | ● construct and identify the main components of simple battery-operated electrical circuits |
| | | ● classify materials as electrical conductors or insulators and describe how these are related to safe use of electricity |
| | D | ● identify some applications of different forms of energy |
| | | ● describe in simple terms how lenses work |
| | | ● give examples of simple applications of lenses |
| | | ● explain that a prism can split white light into a range of colours known as the visible spectrum |
| | | ● distinguish between heat and temperature |
| | | ● use the terms 'pitch' and 'volume' correctly in describing sound |
| | | **Conversion and transfer of energy** |
| | C | ● give examples of energy being converted from one form to another |
| | | ● describe electrical circuits in terms of energy conversion |
| | D | ● give some examples of energy conversions involved in the generation of electricity |
| | | ● describe how electrical energy is transmitted to our homes |
| | | **Forces and their effects** |
| | C | ● classify materials as magnetic or non-magnetic |
| | | ● describe the interaction of magnets in terms of attraction and repulsion |
| | | ● give examples of magnets in everyday use |
| | D | ● give examples of streamlining and offer some explanation of the way in which this lowers air resistance |
| | | ● use the term 'air resistance' to describe how a parachute works |
| | | ● describe the relationship between the Earth and gravity |

**LIVING THINGS AND THE PROCESSES OF LIFE**

| | | |
|---|---|---|
| | | **Variety and characteristic features** |
| | C | ● name some common animals using simple keys |
| | | ● recognise similarities and differences between plants and animals of the same species |
| | D | ● give the main distinguishing features of the major groups of flowering and non-flowering plants |
| | | ● give examples of continuous and discontinuous variation |
| | | **The processes of life** |
| | C | ● identify the main organs of the human digestive system |
| | | ● explain the main purpose of digestion |
| | | ● give broad functions of the skeleton, bones, and muscles |
| | D | ● identify, name and give the functions of the main organs of human reproductive systems |
| | | ● describe the main changes that occur during puberty |
| | | ● describe the main stages in human reproduction |
| | | ● describe the main stages in flowering plant reproduction |
| | | **Interaction of living things with their environment** |
| | C | ● give examples of living things that are very rare or which have become extinct |
| | | ● explain the importance of conservation |
| | D | ● describe examples of human impact on the local environment that have brought about beneficial change, and examples that have detrimental effects |
| | | ● give examples of how plants and animals are affected by environmental conditions |
| | | ● indicate how responses to changes in the environment might increase the chances of survival |

| | |
|---|---|
| **Developing informed attitudes:** pupils should be encouraged to | |
| ● appreciate the need to develop informed and reasoned opinions on the impact of science in relation to social, environmental, moral and ethical issues | |
| ● appreciate the need to take responsibility for their own health and safety | |
| ● be committed to participating in the safe and responsible care of living things and the environment | |
| ● think through the various consequences for living things and the environment of different choices, decisions and courses of action | |
| ● participate responsibly in the conservation of natural resources and the sustainable use of the Earth's resources | |
| ● appreciate the need for conservation of scarce energy resources and endangered species at local and global level | |
| ● appreciate the need to develop responsible attitudes that take account of different beliefs and values | |

Lessons where curriculum content is the main objective are listed below. Lessons where content is included but is not the main focus are shown below in brackets.

| Unit 1: Ourselves<br>Growing up healthy | Unit 2: Animals & Plants<br>Life cycles | Unit 3: The environment<br>Water and the environment | Unit 4: Materials<br>Gases, solids and liquids | Unit 5: Electricity<br>Making and using electricity | Unit 6: Forces & motion<br>Exploring forces and their effects | Unit 7: Light & sound<br>Bending light and changing sound | Unit 8: Earth & beyond<br>Sun, Moon and Earth |
|---|---|---|---|---|---|---|---|
| 5, 7 | 4 | 3 | 7 | 2 | 1, 2, 3, 10, 11 | 10, 11, 12 | 6 |
| 5, 7, (15) | 4 | 3 | 7 | 2 | 1, 2, 3 | 10, 11, 12 | 6 |
|  |  |  |  |  |  |  |  |
| 5, 7 | 5, 6 | (8) | 4, 10, 11 |  | 1, 2 | 8 |  |
| 5, 7 | 4, 5 | 3 | 7 | 2 | 1, 2 | 8 | (3) |
| 5, 7, 8 | 4, 5 | 3 | 7 |  | 3, 10, 11 | 8 |  |
| 5, 7, 8 |  | 8 | 7, 10, 11 | 2 | 3 | 8 | (3) |
| 5, 7, 8 | 4, 5 | 3, 8 | 7, 10, 11 | 2 | 3 | 8 | (3) |
|  |  |  |  |  |  |  |  |
| 5, 7 | 4 | 3, 8 | 7 | 2 | 1, 2, 3, 8, 9 | 8, 12 | (1), (2) |
| 5, 7 | 4, 5 | 3, 8 | 3, 4, 7 | 2, 3 | 3 | 3, 6, 7, 8 | 6 |
|  | 4 | 3, 8 | 7 | 2 | 1, 2 |  |  |
| 5, 7 | 4, 5, 6 | 3, 8 | 7 | 2 | 1, 2, 3, 8 | 10, 11, 12 | 6 |
| 5, 7 |  | 3, 8 | 7 | 2 | 8, 10, 11 | 10, 11, 12 | 6 |
|  |  |  |  |  |  |  |  |
|  |  |  |  |  |  |  | (1), (2), 3, 5, (6), 7, 8, (9), (10) |
|  |  |  |  |  |  |  | 3, 4, (10) |
|  |  | 1, 2, 3 | (2), (3), (5), (8) |  | (7), (8), (9), (10) | (8) |  |
|  |  | 1, 2, 3, 11 | (6), (7), 9, 10, 11, 12, (13), 14 |  |  |  |  |
|  |  |  | 4 |  |  |  |  |
|  |  | 6 |  |  |  |  |  |
|  |  | 6 |  |  |  |  |  |
|  |  |  | (1) |  |  |  |  |
|  |  | 7 |  |  |  |  |  |
|  |  |  |  | 1 |  |  |  |
|  |  |  |  | (1) |  |  |  |
|  |  |  |  | 7 |  |  |  |
|  |  |  |  | 1, 2 |  |  |  |
|  |  |  |  |  |  | 1, 2, (3), 4 |  |
|  |  |  |  |  |  | 5, (15) |  |
|  |  |  |  |  |  | 5 |  |
|  |  |  |  |  |  | 7, (12), (13), (14) |  |
|  |  |  |  | 3, 4, 5, 8 | 5, 6, 7, 8, 9, 10, 11, 12 | (7), (9), (10), (15) |  |
|  |  |  |  | 3, 4, 5, 8 |  |  |  |
|  |  |  |  | 7 |  |  |  |
|  |  |  |  | (7) |  |  |  |
|  |  |  |  | 2, (3) |  |  |  |
|  |  |  |  | 2, 3, 4, 5, 6 |  |  |  |
|  |  |  |  | 2, 3, 4, 5, 6 |  |  |  |
|  |  |  |  | (1), (2), 5, (6) |  |  |  |
|  | (7), (10) |  |  |  |  |  |  |
| 9, 10 |  |  |  |  |  |  |  |
|  | (8) |  |  |  |  |  |  |
| 9 |  |  |  |  |  |  |  |
| 4 |  |  |  |  |  |  |  |
| (1), (2), (3), (15) |  |  |  |  |  |  |  |
| (6) |  |  |  |  |  |  |  |
| (9), 10, (11), (12), (13), (14) |  |  |  |  |  |  |  |
|  | 1, 2, 3, 4, 5, 6, 7, 8, 9, 11, 13, 15 |  |  |  |  |  |  |
|  | 12 | 10 |  |  |  |  |  |
|  | 12 | 10 |  |  |  |  |  |
|  |  | 5, 8, 9, 10, 11 |  |  |  |  |  |
|  | (14) | 8, 10 |  |  |  |  |  |
|  | (14) | (4) |  |  |  |  |  |
|  | 12 | 6, 7, 8 |  |  |  |  |  |
| 1, 2, 3 |  | 8, 9, 11 |  |  | 4 | (11) |  |
|  | 1, 2 | 6, 7, 8, 11 |  |  |  |  |  |
|  | 1, (2) | 6, 7, 8 |  |  |  |  |  |
|  |  | 6 |  |  |  |  |  |
|  | 1, 2 |  |  |  |  |  |  |

# Series topic map

| Year/Primary | YR/P1 | Y1/P2 | Y2/P3 | Y3/P4 | Y4/P5 | Y5/P6 | Y6/P7 |
|---|---|---|---|---|---|---|---|
| Unit 1: Ourselves | This is me! | Me and my body | Keeping healthy | Teeth and food | How I move | Growing up healthy | New beginnings |
| Unit 2: Animals & plants | Looking at animals and plants | Growing and caring | Growing up | The needs of plants and animals | Different sorts of skeletons | Life cycles | Variation |
| Unit 3: The environment | Out and about | Environments and living things | Life in habitats | How the environment affects living things | Habitats and food chains | Water and the environment | The living world |
| Unit 4: Materials | Exploring materials | Properties of materials | Materials and change | Natural & manufactured materials | Warm liquids, cool solids | Gases, solids and liquids | Reversible and non-reversible changes |
| Unit 5: Electricity | Making things work | Using and misusing electricity | Making circuits | Electricity and communication | Switches and conduction | Making and using electricity | Changing circuits |
| Unit 6: Forces & motion | Pushing and pulling | Introducing forces | Making things move | Magnets and springs | Friction | Exploring forces and their effects | Forces and action |
| Unit 7: Light & sound | Looking and listening | Sources of light and sound | Properties and uses | Sources and effects | Travelling and reflecting | Bending light and changing sound | Light and sound around us |
| Unit 8: Earth & beyond | Up in the sky | Stargazing | The Sun and the seasons | The Sun and shadows | The Sun and stars | Sun, Moon and Earth | The Solar System |